VI

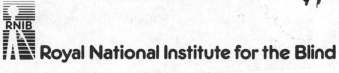

RNIB
Royal National Institute for the Blind

D1323167

Models of Mainstreaming for Visually Impaired Pupils

Studies of current practice with guidelines for service development

Jasmine Dawkins

London: HMSO

ISBN 0 11 701556 3

Royal National Institute for the Blind
224 Great Portland Street
London
W1N 6AA

HMSO publications are available from:

HMSO Publications Centre
(Mail and telephone orders only)
PO Box 276, London, SW8 5DT
Telephone orders 071-873 9090
General enquiries 071-873 0011
(queuing system in operation for both numbers)

HMSO Bookshops
49 High Holborn, London, WC1V 6HB 071-873 0011 (counter service only)
258 Broad Street, Birmingham, B1 2HE 021-643 3740
Southey House, 33 Wine Street, Bristol, BS1 2BQ (0272) 264306
9-21 Princess Street, Manchester, M60 8AS 061-834 7201
80 Chichester Street, Belfast, BT1 4JY (0232) 238451
71 Lothian Road, Edinburgh, EH3 9AZ 031-228 4181

HMSO's Accredited Agents
(see Yellow Pages)

and through good booksellers

Acknowledgements

I wish to express my gratitude and appreciation to everyone featured in these studies, including officers and advisers in local education authorities, the staff of visual impairment support services, headteachers, teachers, parents and the visually impaired young people themselves. They cannot, of course, be named since the studies are anonymous, but I am greatly indebted to the many people who have found the time and patience to respond to my enquiries, to discuss their work and concerns, and to comment on draft extracts of the book.

I should also like to express my thanks to colleagues at the Royal National Institute for the Blind (RNIB): Louise Clunies-Ross, Eamonn Fetton and Neil Anderson, who have offered their guidance and advice, and helped to shepherd the book through the various phases of its germination and growth. I am also most grateful to Ernest Butcher who read the manuscript and offered valuable comments.

The work of typing and repeatedly correcting and up-dating the manuscript was undertaken by Lola Little and Julia Matthews to whom I wish also to express my thanks.

Jasmine Dawkins
March 1991

Foreword

We have come a long way in the education of visually impaired children since the Vernon Report, and the appointment of the first peripatetic teachers in local education authorities in the 1970s. There are now many examples of blind and partially sighted children receiving a full, good quality education alongside their peers in mainstream schools. This is all most encouraging.

However, provision is still very uneven across the country, and there are many areas in which further progress is needed. It is particularly important that everyone concerned in visual impairment services should be fully informed about what can be achieved with skill, goodwill, imagination and the appropriate resources.

It is with that in mind that RNIB's Mainstream Education Sub-Committee commissioned the studies, commentary and guidelines which are presented in this book. The work provides useful information not previously available and perceptive suggestions for service developments. It should appeal to a wide readership, and we trust that it will make a major contribution to continuing improvements in the educational services available for visually impaired young people.

Colin Low
Chairman
RNIB Education and Leisure Committee

Contents

Introduction

The desirability of integrating visually impaired children into the mainsteam is now widely accepted. In many parts of the country, partially sighted and blind children are being successfully educated alongside their peers, and well structured, effective support services are provided for them. However, this is not yet the situation everywhere, and the quality of education which visually impaired children receive depends, in far too great a measure, on where they happen to live.

This book is designed to inform and assist those who are concerned in educating such children, and who are currently reviewing or developing services. It should be of value to local education authority officers and advisers in their management of the education of visually impaired pupils. Indeed it provides a compendium of reference material on which they may draw to inform committee members in their decision making. Specialist peripatetic and support teachers in the field of visual impairment and those who are delivering or studying for specialist qualifications in visual handicap will find that the book gives ready access to trends and developments around the country. Headteachers, staff and governors of mainstream schools where visually impaired pupils are being educated should also find much of value in the book, as will the parents of such children.

The book is the outcome of a study of visual impairment services in various parts of the country and their impact on the children for whom they are designed. The study was commissioned by RNIB. It is arranged in four sections, the first two of which present the analytical material of the study, whereas the other two sections provide a synthesis of the factual information collected and an interpretation of its significance.

Section I analyses the nature of provision which is currently made for visually impaired pupils in eight local education authorities. **Section II** provides individual studies of fourteen children or young people, ranging in age from five to twenty-four, and covering various types and degrees of visual impairment. All of them have had experience of the mainstream for all or part of their education. The two sections together seek to give as comprehensive a view as possible of the situation at national level at the start of the 1990s, the material being drawn from a range of areas in England, Scotland and Wales.

These sections may be read as a continuous sequence, or readers may choose to focus their attention on those studies which are directly relevant to their own situation. **Section III** provides the opportunity to have a consolidated overview of current practices and trends at national level. It draws together the facts collected relating to various aspects of service provision and offers a commentary on their strengths and weaknesses, and the strategies adopted in the light of the inevitable constraints within which the services function. This should enable many readers to see and to consider new approaches to tackling their problems.

On the basis of the studies and the wider experience of RNIB officers and organisations with which they are in contact, **Section IV**[1] sets out guidelines for those who are providing for the needs of visually impaired children, seeking to identify a range of suitable responses relevant to the very diverse circumstances in which the provision is made. This aims to provide a working structure within which the material of the studies may be used to good effect.

Following section IV a number of appendices provide additional information for reference. The first of these is a glossary of terms used in the field of visual impairment. Since some of this information is important to a full understanding of the text, a selected list of definitions is provided at the end of this introduction. Any readers who may not be familiar with the terms associated with visual impairment are invited to refer to that list.

LEA Studies

The first section of the book sets out to analyse the pattern of provision for visually impaired pupils in eight local education authorities all of which have developed a distinctive approach in the light of their circumstances. The authorities considered were selected in order to give as wide a span as possible of geographical and social environments, size, policy framework, nature of services and length of experience in the field of visual impairment. There is no suggestion that provision in these areas is necessarily better than that to be found in some other places and the order of

1. Section IV is an updated version of the text printed separately in 1989 under the title: *Bright Horizons*.

presentation in the study does not imply any rank order of preference. Obviously, a decision was made to select LEAs which show some strengths in this field, but the study inevitably also reveals features which some would consider to be weaknesses. It is to be hoped that other authorities may be able to learn lessons from both these aspects.

The salient features of the services selected for analysis are as follows:

Authority A
A large rural county with no major conurbations. For many families, special educational placements on a day basis are not a geographical possibility, and the authority believes that neighbourhood integration is almost always to be preferred to residential placements. Quite a large visual impairment service has now been built up which is deliberately structured to be able to support partially sighted and blind pupils in their local schools.

Authority B
A metropolitan district where there is a policy commitment to individual neighbourhood integration, even though it would be feasible for one school to be specially resourced and for pupils to travel to it. Support for partially sighted children in their local schools is well established, and there is an unusually high level of resourcing in technological aids. A recent decision has been made to integrate educationally blind children, and this also is being done in neighbourhood schools with a high level of teaching support.

Authority C
A large county containing major conurbations, but also having extensive rural areas. There are well established resource bases in mainstream schools in the urban area, but in more rural districts travelling distances mean that separate individual support has to be given in neighbourhood schools for some pupils. This authority has easy access to out-county special schools for day and residential placements, and is only just beginning to integrate blind pupils, of whom there are surprisingly few in the area.

Authority D
A small metropolitan district which has recently set up a new service, having previously relied on buying in services from a neighbouring larger authority. There is a policy of neighbourhood integration as a first option, but a school has also been designated as a resource base for more severely impaired children. An interesting aspect of this service is that, instead of following the

frequently encountered practice of appointing one teacher and allowing the service to grow, the authority has started from a longer term blue-print of a desirable service with pre-arranged stages of implementation.

Authority E

An urban borough which provides a service to nearby areas from a special school base. This authority has a well established day special school for visual impairment which receives pupils from a wide region and also runs a peripatetic service for its own area and for five other authorities which have no service of their own.

Authority F

A largely urban county which has recently extended its service directed chiefly towards resource-based provision. This authority established units for visually impaired pupils many years ago, but only recently appointed a qualified head of service. The realization at this stage that improvements were needed has led to rapid developments in both the level and nature of provision.

Authority G

A large metropolitan district with a well-developed system of resource-based provision. This authority has evolved its service over a decade and has a large visual impairment team. Partially sighted children are normally supported in their neighbourhood schools, and resource bases in mainstream schools provide for blind children.

Authority H

A county where a special school for visual impairment has recently been closed and replaced by resource bases in main-stream schools. The staff from the special school work in these bases which are therefore well resourced and able to cater for virtually any visually impaired pupil. There is also an experienced peripatetic team to support those children who are able to func-tion in their neighbourhood schools.

Background information

The authorities are not, of course, explicitly identified in the study. A brief description of the geographical environment of each is given, not as an aid to amateur detectives, but in order to particularise the local circumstances which are likely to have influenced the development of services. Statistical information on the numbers and types of visually impaired pupils is given in so far as this is available. The variations in these figures from one authority to another highlight the scale of the problem of forward-planning for a low-incidence handicap, but they also raise some disturbing questions about the extent to which some children with special needs may go unidentified. This matter is examined further in section III.

Details are also given of the numbers of pupils in the various categories of educational placement, including extra-district special schools. In fact, only one of the authorities under consideration has its own special school for visual impairment, and, because of the nature of this school's role in relation to neighbouring authorities, that study is presented in a somewhat different framework from the others. Generally, although the staff of a visual impairment service will be involved in decisions about extra-district special school placements, the main thrust of their work is towards supporting those pupils who remain within the authority, and this is why the special school provision may seem to receive less attention.

A history of each service from the time of its introduction is included, because the pattern of development has varied so much from one area to another. In the country as a whole, a high proportion of authorities began to introduce local provision for the visually impaired in the late 1970's and early 1980's. However, some authorities had their own special schools or units long before that, whilst others are seemingly entering the 1990's with no service whatever. This disparity of approach carries with it a vast fund of experience into which relative newcomers to the field may be able to tap through this study.

Provision for visually impaired school children
Substantial attention is given to the modus operandi of the peripatetic services. There is a fairly sharp distinction between those who see their principal role as the direct teaching of children, and those who aim to provide an indirect service by advising mainstream teachers. It is of interest also to see the extent to which it has been possible to introduce an element of subject or age-range specialism into their work. This is often difficult because numbers of staff are so small, but in what other area of the education service do we expect a teacher to cater for all age groups from birth to nineteen, for all ability levels, all areas of the curriculum and all levels of single or multiple disability? Yet this seems to be what is demanded of some peripatetic teachers. It is of interest also to consider how far the peripatetic staff support children in special schools catering for other areas of need.

5

Particular attention is given to the way in which pupils with a significant degree of impairment are supported in mainstream schools, whether this be schools which have been specially developed as resource bases or neighbourhood schools which may have no previous experience of visual impairment. This is described as "supported mainstream provision," and refers broadly to those pupils who are likely to have a Statement of special educational need. Obviously all children identified as being visually impaired should be "supported" in the broadest sense, but a distinction, albeit imprecise, can be made between those who need peripatetic oversight and those who require a more individualised service.

Apart from the actual nature of the day-to-day work of the support service, two major issues for consideration are the provision of technological and other material resources and the pattern of in-service training for members of the team and for other teachers. Here again, very wide discrepancies in the level and nature of provision are found. They are both matters where practices tend to be changing, on the one hand because of rapid developments in technology, and on the other hand as a result of national policies and trends in the structuring of in-service training. There is therefore food for thought both for those who are introducing new services and those who should perhaps be reassessing established practices.

Pre and post school education

All services are aware of the importance of early intervention when a baby is found to be visually impaired. Pre-school and family support tend to be major elements in the work of staff. This is a time-consuming role, and the efficiency with which the need is fulfilled will often depend on links with other services, as well as on the development of appropriate expertise. At the other end of the age spectrum, the further education sector is generally making rapid strides in providing for students with special needs, but colleges do not always have easy access to the support services which are available to schools. Some mention of this work is made in the study, but the relative brevity with which it is treated reflects the low level of service currently provided rather than any judgement of its level of importance.

A changing situation

The material presented in this study was collected in the course of 1989 and 1990. Services are of course constantly evolving and there have already been some changes in staffing levels, resources provided and even in operational arrangements. It is not considered that this need detract from the interest of the accounts which are samples of practice in a field where rates of development have been disturbingly uneven. They may be described as snapshots of specific stages in the evolution of a range of services from which other local authorities may select those most relevant to their own circumstances. In cases where definite plans have been drawn up for future developments or where staff have clearly articulated views on future needs, these have been outlined in the concluding section of each study.

Studies of individual children and young people

Selection of children

The second section of the book is made up of a series of fourteen case studies of visually impaired children and young people who have been integrated into the mainstream for part or all of their education. The subjects of the studies range in age from five to twenty-four years and have a variety of ocular conditions, eight of them being educationally blind and the other six partially sighted. The first paragraph of each study specifies the child's age, level of vision and educational placement, as a quick guide to readers who may wish to select the material most relevant to their own preoccupations.

The pupils were selected to give as wide a range of circumstances as possible within the confines of the exercise. They are of varying academic ability, and some have had to cope with personal or social difficulties in addition to their visual impairment. Three had experience of special school before moving into the mainstream, and the two oldest ones went to a specialist further education college after being fully integrated at school, then returned to mainstream higher and further education. Eight of the studies describe placements in neighbourhood schools as opposed to specially resourced schools, but all the children have received a substantial level of special educational support.

The studies contain many examples of good and successful practice which may serve as a source of ideas for others. They also reveal the difficulties and problems which may arise and indeed mistakes which have sometimes been made. In the case of the older children, it is easy to think that their early experiences date

7

from a time when services were less developed and that everyone has now moved on. That is not, unfortunately, always the case, and it would be rash to assume that history will never repeat itself.

Sources of information

The studies are based on discussions with the head teachers and staff of schools which the pupils attend, members of the visual impairment support team, parents and, where appropriate, the pupils themselves. Information collected includes factual details about the pupil's education, and individual perceptions of the provision and support which has been provided.

Enquiries have been restricted to people concerned with the child's education, because that is the focus of the book. Parents have often referred to their contacts with medical and social work personnel, and their comments are recorded even though it has not been possible to give consultants, doctors or social workers the opportunity to express their view of the situation. It is acknowledged that this may on the surface seem unfair, but it would have been neither feasible nor productive to seek to establish the exact truth about what was said in confidential meetings held, in some cases, many years ago. It is well known that, at a time of crisis in their lives, parents may fail to understand or indeed to hear what is said to them. What is important to those who are working with the family is that they should know what parents heard and what perceptions they have of a situation. That is what has been recorded in this study. The comments of many parents reveal that whoever is working closely with the family of a visually impaired child,and this will generally be the peripatetic teacher, has an important role to play in monitoring and guiding the parents' perceptions of their child's condition and needs.

A main concern of the studies has been to analyse the educational provision which has been, and is being made for the child or young person. Schools, whatever kind they are, are primarily in the business of providing a full education and this is the main criterion by which any scheme must be judged. On the other hand, a full education has to embrace both personal and social education; it has to deal with the child's development appropriately, not only as an individual and as a future worker, but also as a social being, in fact as a future citizen. In this respect, the social advantages of integration are an inherent part of the child's integration. The emphasis of the study is therefore on whether the children are experiencing a full and appropriate curriculum, and the extent to which they are judged to be achieving their full potential in all aspects of their educational development.

8

One of the studies is different from the others in nature. It records a young man's perceptions of his experiences as a child with deteriorating sight, of his education and of the personal lessons he has learnt as he has reached maturity. In this case, the views of other individuals or agencies concerned are not reported, and it is acknowledged that it is just one perspective on an individual situation. The difficulties which have arisen for this young man could occur anywhere at any time, and no criticism of others is implied or intended. The report is included because it is believed that lessons may be learnt from it which could benefit other visually impaired young people, and an attempt is made to direct the reader's attention to these lessons.

Lessons to be learnt
Few general conclusions can be drawn from child studies of which the principal interest lies in their individuality. However, the third section of the book provides an overall analysis of the implications of the studies relating both to local education authorities and to individual children. This seeks to highlight issues in the provision of local services which are illustrated by the material presented, and which may merit further examination in many parts of the country.

Guidelines for service development

After these extended studies of recent and current practice, the book addresses itself to the issue of suggesting a framework within which officers and advisers in local education authorities may reassess their service for visually impaired pupils.

There are no definitive right or wrong answers to the questions which must be asked. That which is appropriate for one child may be inappropriate for another; a scheme which is both feasible and relevant in one geographical area may be unattainable or mis-judged elsewhere. In the last resort, it is obviously only the officers and council of a local authority who can determine how their particular needs should be met, but it is hoped that these guide-lines will help to direct the thinking and will serve as a checklist as a detailed local scheme is evolved.

Services for visually impaired children are in a stage of rapid evolution, just as is the education service as a whole. The LEA and child studies portray a transient situation, and certain issues covered in the guidelines section may quite quickly become out of date. Nevertheless, services in different areas of the country have developed at very diverse rates, and that which seems past history in one area may be very immediately relevant in another. It is important to bear in mind that whatever may be the local circumstances, all LEAs have the same duty under the law to make appropriate provision for the special educational needs of their pupils. It is therefore hoped that the book will have something to offer to many people who are concerned to improve and develop educational opportunities for visually impaired children, whatever may be their own particular starting-point.

Selected Definitions

In order to avoid confusion, it may be useful to specify the usually accepted meaning of certain terms used in relation to visual impairment.

- **Visually impaired/visually handicapped** are used interchangeably to refer to a person with a significant degree of sight difficulty which is not fully corrected by the wearing of spectacles. Strictly speaking, "impairment" is a physical condition which gives rise to a disability, and "handicap" refers to the difficulties which the person faces as a result of the impairment.

- **Functionally blind** means that the person is not able to make any effective use of the visual senses. Such people may not be totally blind (very few people are), but they may have some light perception or a field of vision so restricted that their sight is of little real use of them, and they must rely entirely on other senses.

- **Educationally blind** means that a child cannot be taught by normal sighted means, and in particular needs to use braille or other means of communication not dependent on sight,and to be given access to most areas of the curriculum by non-visual teaching methods. Such a person may nevertheless have enough useful vision for mobility and other everyday activities.

- **Partially sighted** means that the person has a visual defect which is not fully corrected by spectacles, and which may affect near or distant vision. The term covers a diverse range of medical conditions. The person may be able to read and deal fairly satisfactorily with close work, but have little or no distant vision. On the other hand, some partially sighted people see quite clearly at a distance, but need enlarged print, low vision aids or special lighting in order to be able to read. Such people may also have a restricted field of vision, seeing only a small area immediately in front of the eye ("tunnel vision"), or perhaps having no central vision or seeing only on one side.

- **Visual acuity** is expressed in terms of the average vision of a normally sighted person. Thus, "6:6 vision" means that the person sees at a distance of 6 metres what an average person sees at that distance; "6:24 vision" means that the person sees at 6 metres what a normally sighted person sees at a distance of 24 metres. This provides a broad indication of the extent of the person's visual difficulty, but provides no information about the nature of the sight loss, as considered under "Partially-sighted" above.

- **Print sizes** on a scale known as "N prints" indicate the size of print that the person can read with reasonable comfort. Samples of this scale are given in appendix B.

- **Medical conditions.** Visual impairment may be associated with many different medical conditions. Teachers and other educationists do not need to have very detailed knowledge of medical factors, since relevant information concerning any particular child will be provided by doctors. However, brief notes about the most common causes of visual impairment in childhood are provided in appendix A.

- **Resource base/unit.** Where a mainstream school makes special provision for a group of children with a particular type of special need, the term "unit" has traditionally been used to describe this service. However, the word may seem to imply a separate area where children are educated apart from others. It is therefore considered more appropriate to use the term "resource base" or "facility" when the children experience a high level of integration, and any room allocated merely provides back-up support.

- **Neighbourhood integration.** However fully a child may be integrated in a school which has a resourse base, if the school is at some distance from home, the child may feel set apart from the immediate local community. The term 'neighbourhood integration' is used when a child with special needs attends the usual school nearest to home rather than one elsewhere which is specially resourced.

11

- **Locational/social/functional integration.** These terms were introduced in the Warnock Report. Locational integration refers to a situation in which provision is made for visually impaired children on the same site as a mainstream school, but they are educated separately. Social integration means that they mingle with mainstream children at lunch-time, breaks and for leisure activities, but are normally taught separately. Functional integration is the term used when the visually impaired pupils participate fully in both educational and social activities alongside their sighted peers.

Section I : LEA Studies

These studies analyse the current service for visually impaired pupils in eight local education authorities. They include background information about the areas concerned, and an account of the way in which each service has evolved and how future developments are envisaged.

1. Integration in a Large Rural County

Nature of the local authority

This authority is an almost entirely rural county and extends over 105 miles, with a width varying between 15 and 30 miles. There are no motorways and the roads are often very congested, with the result that a home-school travelling distance which would seem reasonable in some areas of the country would not be practicable here.

The concentration of population is very low, the total number of children in the 5-16 age-range being only approximately 64,000 in such a large geographical area. Consequently, children with any form of special need have tended to be widely scattered, and this has militated against concentrating them in day special schools or specially resourced mainstream schools. Certainly for a low incidence handicap, such as visual impairment, the only realistic options are neighbourhood integration or residential special school placement. There is a clear LEA policy to promote integration wherever this is feasible.

An interesting feature of the area is that in recent years there has been a noticeable migration into the authority of families with children who have special needs. In some cases the LEA agrees to continue to fund a residential placement in another authority if a move would unreasonably disrupt the child's education. In other cases the parents favour local provision, and this places unexpected demands on the special education service. In normal circumstances, the service would know of the existence of handicapped children at the pre-school stage, and be able to plan

13

the allocation of resources accordingly. When the number of newly arriving families is significant, a strain can be placed on the management of the service.

The LEA has a standard educational pattern of 5-11 primary schools, and 11-16 secondary schools, followed by a tertiary system of sixth form colleges and further education colleges.

Visually impaired pupils and their placement

A total of 124 pupils in the county are recorded as being visually impaired, which gives a figure of 1.9 visually impaired children per thousand of the child population. Of the registered children, 81 have a Statement of special educational need, whereas there are in all over 1800 children in the LEA who have Statements. Of the 124 visually impaired children in the authority, 32 are in other types of special school mainly on account of severe learning difficulties. This constitutes 26% of the total.

Between 1970 and 1975 the number of visually impaired children placed in out-county special schools ranged from 15 to 19. This figure then began to decline, so that only 9 or 10 children were so placed between 1980 and 1983. There are now just four visually impaired children in out-county schools, and three young people in specialist colleges, none of these having been placed within the past three years. There has therefore been a clear shift towards local provision, but the LEA would still place a child out-county if this were considered to be in the child's best interests, whatever the area of special need. Indeed a substantial number of physically handicapped and behaviourally disturbed children are in residential special schools.

As was explained above, the geographical nature of the authority precludes the development of resource bases in selected mainstream schools, since children would generally have to travel a prohibitive distance in order to reach such a base. It has therefore been found to be expedient, as well as philosophically desirable, to support visually impaired pupils in their neighbourhood school in the vast majority of cases. Currently eight educationally blind children and some twenty-five partially sighted children are being supported in this way. Details of the pattern of support provided are given later in this report. Many partially sighted children also normally attend their neighbourhood school, with advisory oversight from the peripatetic service and additional ancillary help if required.

The visual impairment service

There has never been a special school for visual impairment within the LEA's boundaries. A school in a neighbouring authority has traditionally been used for residential placements, but it is situated too far from the county boundary for day placements to be feasible in most cases. Special schools in other parts of the country have also been used in particular circumstances.

The first peripatetic teacher of the visually impaired was appointed in 1970. She had the daunting task of servicing the whole of this vast county, and continued to do so for many years.

In 1985 the county was organised administratively into three divisions, and by then there were two full-time members of staff for visual impairment. It became increasingly apparent that, with the progressive move towards integration, a higher staffing level was required. Additional teachers were therefore appointed between 1985 and 1990, creating a team of six.

The team's work is now distributed across the three administrative divisions, so that each division has an advisory teacher and a support teacher. All six members of this team hold a qualification in visual impairment, and they all undertake both classroom support and peripatetic advisory work with teachers. In each division the specific allocation of activities is the responsibility of the relevant advisory teacher, and there are therefore some variations in procedures in the three divisions. The balance of activities also varies considerably from time to time in the light of the extent to which the members of staff need to give concentrated support to educationally blind children.

The basic pattern of work is that children who require general monitoring of their progress receive a monthly or termly visit. Those with more severe impairments will be seen at least weekly. The teacher will then normally work with the child alongside the class teacher, but in certain cases the pupil will be withdrawn from class so that he or she may be given intensive teaching in a less distracting environment. The teachers support children in schools for severe learning difficulties as well as in all age-groups in the mainstream. Their wide geographical commitment makes any form of specialism within the team impracticable.

In each area, the advisory teacher is responsible for allocating duties, but she and the support teacher are engaged in similar activities. The advisory teachers are responsible to the County Adviser for special education and also work in liaison with the

Assistant Education Officer for special education. Now that the service has grown, it is not easy for the adviser to manage three area teams in a specialism which is not his own, and it is therefore proposed that they should be reconstituted as a single team with a co-ordinator, who would work to the adviser who is head of service. If the proposal is implemented it should facilitate a more co-ordinated approach to issues across the county.

The service has links with other support services through divisional teams and the county advisory team.

In this county there is exceptionally good provision for the teaching of mobility, since four members of staff have a mobility officer qualification and the intention is that the other two should be trained shortly. They are therefore able to provide training for children in their area as required. Typing tuition is bought in when needed.

Supported mainstream provision
It is now the established policy of the authority that, if a blind or otherwise severely visually impaired child is identified, a Statement is drawn up recommending how the child could be supported within the mainstream. This normally involves the appointment of an ancillary worker to work with the child in the classroom. Young blind children generally have full-time support, but this may later be reduced to part-time if appropriate.

There are currently 21 full-time and 11 part-time ancillaries working with individual visually impaired children. They work under the guidance of the advisory teacher or support teacher, and they generally learn braille if required and develop appropriate skills and experience. The child enters the school as a full member of a class group and may expect to be integrated for about 90% of lesson time. An advisory teacher or support teacher will be visiting the school regularly and, in the case of blind children, will use the remaining 10% of time for the teaching of pre-braille skills and braille, mobility and other basic skills. The ancillary helper works in partnership with her to reinforce new skills, either by withdrawing the pupil or by working alongside the class teacher. At primary level, the helper often works with a group of pupils providing general support which compensates in some measure for the extra demands being placed on the class teacher. The ancillary is also responsible for ensuring that the support teacher is kept informed about books and materials which are likely to be required in the near future.

When a young child enters school, additional playtime and lunch-time supervision may be provided, but this is phased out as soon as practicable so that the child may have the independence to mingle freely with his or her peers.

As the child grows older, the ancillary helper gives increasing time to the preparation of materials in braille or other tactile form. Until recently this work has been labour intensive, but the authority is now acknowledging the value of introducing more educational technology which will facilitate at least some of this work.

The authority has built up quite significant experience in the integration of primary aged blind children. Only rarely has a blind pupil remained in the mainstream at secondary level, but when this is possible, the approach is similar. In the initial stages, intensive teacher support is required not only for the pupil's sake, but in order to inspire confidence in the staff. Although the standard procedure for extra manpower is that only ancillary workers should be appointed, an additional teacher has some-times been allocated in special circumstances, such as when a child suddenly becomes blind.

The authority's approach to supported integration means that the visual impairment team spend more of their time in direct work with severely impaired pupils than is the case in some other authorities. This can create a conflict of interests, and they may well not be able to give as much time as might seem desirable to the support of the wider range of partially sighted children, though many receive weekly visits. On the other hand, the blind children are receiving qualified, experienced support, on an aver-age basis of three times a week. Certainly the children who are currently integrated appear to be making progress commensurate with their ability.

Equipment and resources

The visual impairment service receives a capitation allowance for the purchase of basic equipment and resources. Items remain the property of the service and are loaned out to schools, but resources have been built up in each of the three area bases and there is as yet no centralisation.

When larger items of technological equipment are needed for individual pupils, a special application is required, but this usu-ally receives a sympathetic response subject of course to the availability of funds. A recent special allocation has been made to boost the basic bank of technological equipment. A list of the major items currently in the possession of the authority is given in table 1.

TABLE 1

REPROGRAPHIC EQUIPMENT

Thermoform machines	-
Binders	-
Minolta copiers	-
Braille embossers	-

COMMUNICATION AIDS

Closed circuit televisions	7
Computers (specific to VI use)	9
Vincent Work Stations (or similar)	9
Perkins braillers	12
Electronic typewriters	-
Cassette recorders	5
Speech synthesizers	10
Talking calculators	8
Versabraille	-
Viewscan	-
Optacon	-
Braille writers	-
Microwriters and printers	13
Window displays	3
Braille'n'Print	3

Equipment is maintained by the LEA's own technology section, apart from certain specialised items for which there is a manufacturer's service contract. There is no established policy about providing children with equipment for home use, but individual arrangements have at times been made when required.

In-service training

As already mentioned, all members of the visual impairment team have qualifications in visual impairment, three of them having obtained the qualification by secondment from the authority. They are encouraged to attend appropriate out-county day courses and funds are available for this.

One of the roles of the team is to provide in-service training for mainstream teachers in the authority. Some courses are set up centrally within the county's overall INSET programme, whilst other more localised courses may relate more specifically to the needs of individual children. This includes awareness training before a child enters a school, and the training of individual class and subject teachers according to need. Great importance is attached to the training of ancillary helpers. The first essential is seen as being that the person is right for the job, and a member of the visual impairment team is therefore always present at the interviews for such appointments. Individual training then begins immediately. A scheme has recently been introduced whereby all ancillaries working with visually impaired pupils attend a one-day training session per term. These sessions, staffed by members of the team, cover general awareness, simulation exercises, the use of low vision aids, mobility and similar topics. The training is proving to be very beneficial and is much appreciated by the ancillaries.

Pre-school provision and parental links

The visual impairment service now has good links with the health authority and visually impaired children are referred early. This was not always the case when the service was much smaller, but the benefits of early contact with families are now being seen. Where appropriate, the teachers devise detailed developmental programmes, based on the Oregon project, and work alongside parents to implement these. The use of Oregon is often continued in nurseries and playgroups. The authority uses the Portage scheme with mentally handicapped children, and there is an input to this from the visual impairment team where required.

Moves are now being made to put parents of visually impaired children in contact with each other and to set up parent support groups of three or four families. The geography of the area makes this difficult to implement but it is considered to be a useful trend. There are also opportunities for parents to meet at County Parents' Days. Parents are fully consulted about Statements and about their child's educational placement, and their wishes are respected.

Post-sixteen provision

Where pupils are placed in sixth form colleges or further education colleges within county, they are supported by regular visits from members of the team in the same way as when they are at school, and whenever possible the ancillary helper transfers with the student. No one person has a particular brief for visual impairment in the further education sector.

In the case of severely impaired or blind students, it is sometimes considered that a residential placement is useful at this stage, both to give them a more specialised education and to encourage the development of independent living skills. For this reason, a number of students have been placed in out-county colleges specialising in visual impairment. The progress of such students is monitored by periodic visits from a member of the county's support team, despite the travel problems involved.

Current and future plans

The service has experienced a period of rapid growth, and its immediate need is for a period of consolidation. It is confidently believed that the approach to integration is the right one and that the children concerned are benefiting.

The problems associated with a wide geographical area are compounded by the fact that the service functions as three small area teams. It has therefore been agreed that the three groups should be amalgamated into one county team with its own head of service.

Provision for both sensory impairment services will remain centrally funded when the Local Management of Schools scheme comes into operation. The approach to the National Curriculum is that disapplication should not be used initially for any child. Full annual reviews are held on each pupil, and at that stage any difficulties will be considered and necessary action determined. The concern is not that any aspect of the curriculum may be inappropriate, but that training in extra skill areas required has to be fitted in somewhere, and that visually impaired children can become very tired and should not be over-stretched.

Comments

Many of the issues which have to be addressed by this LEA are atypical because of the geography of the area. Nevertheless, the approaches adopted here should be of interest to those LEAs which, whilst being largely urban in nature, still have substantial rural areas. Such authorities seem often to establish policies and structures to suit the circumstances in which most of their people live, and just make ad hoc arrangements for the outlying areas. They could perhaps learn some lessons from a region where population dispersion is the norm.

Notable features of this service are:

- A policy of neighbourhood integration for partially sighted and blind pupils.

- A team of qualified staff which has been built up quite rapidly.

- A strong dependence on ancillary workers to support individual pupils, but with a close working relationship between these workers and the support teachers.

- All specialist teachers undertake both peripatetic and support work.

- Four members of staff who are qualified mobility officers.

2. Integration in an Urban Area

Nature of the local authority

This LEA is a metropolitan district measuring approximately seventeen miles by thirteen miles. It is entirely urban, being composed of several towns where the traditional employment areas have been mining and small industry. There has been a substantial level of unemployment in recent years. Each town forms a closely-knit community, and there is relatively little social mobility. The authority is surrounded by a number of other metropolitan authorities which are equally urban in character.

The Council regards itself as a forward-looking authority, anxious to provide effective educational services, and is generally responsive to staff initiatives.

The school population is approximately 49,000. The basic educational pattern is 5-11 primary schools, some of which are divided into separate infant and junior schools, and 11-16 secondary schools followed by tertiary education in sixth form colleges. However, some secondary schools still have their own sixth form.

Visually impaired pupils and their placement

Some two hundred visually impaired pupils are known to the support service. However, only those who have binocular vision of 6/18 or less are considered to merit inclusion on the full-time caseload of the support service. There are rather less than one hundred children in this category, which amounts to approximately two per thousand of the child population. Currently, 77 visually impaired children have Statements of special educational need or are in the process of being assessed, and of these 32% have additional disabilities and are placed within a variety of special schools within the LEA.

The authority has easy access to two extra-district special schools for visual impairment. One of these has day and residential provision and has close historical links with the service in the authority under discussion. The other is a day special school which has effectively established its secondary department in a mainstream school where full integration is possible.

In 1980, seventeen visually impaired pupils from the authority under discussion were placed in these and other extra-district special schools. Four of these pupils have been transferred back to local provision, and others have reached school-leaving age, leaving six now in such placements. Only one of these has been placed recently. Nevertheless extra-district special schools do still remain an acceptable option if this is deemed to be the most appropriate provision for a particular child.

The LEA does not have a policy of resourcing specific mainstream schools to cater for the needs of the more severely visually impaired pupils. The aim is to integrate children wherever possible into their neighbourhood school with whatever special support is appropriate to their needs. This approach is considered to be socially preferable, even though there would not be any significant problem of travelling distances if the pupils were concentrated in one school.

Integrated provision for partially sighted pupils has been developing on this basis over a number of years. There are now approximately 20 children of primary age and 20 of secondary age with a substantial level of impairment who attend their local schools. In 1987 it was decided that educationally blind children should be given the opportunity of mainstream placement, and in particular two children who have only light perception have entered mainstream schools with special individual support.

Provision has also been introduced for partially sighted and blind students at further education level. This again is organised on the basis that support is taken to the student in whichever college he or she attends.

The visual impairment service

There has never been a special school for visual impairment in the authority, but the first peripatetic teacher was appointed as early as 1977. In 1981 this person was replaced by a head of service and a second peripatetic teacher. This level of staffing remained unchanged until 1988, since when a further 1.4 peripatetic teachers and two support teachers have been added to the establishment. The increase of course reflects the move to integrate blind children. This makes a total staff, including the head of service, of 5.4. Three further full-time staff are being appointed in 1990: one qualified peripatetic teacher to work with children having additional difficulties, and two support teachers who will offer specialist curriculum support at secondary level. The service has a physical base in one of the area offices.

The head of service is responsible to the Assistant Director for special education and the Senior Adviser for special education. She plans the individual timetables of the peripatetic teachers, most of whose work consists of intensive support for pupils with substantial needs arising from the visual impairment. These teachers work in the classroom on a "collaborative teaching" basis. Of the two full-time peripatetic teachers, one works principally with the two primary-age braillists and in a school for pupils with severe learning difficulties. The other specialises in the secondary level and spends half a day a week in each of six secondary schools, the actual days being changed in rotation so that he has oversight of all aspects of the curriculum. The part-time teacher works in a school for the physically handicapped and also has a small case load of primary and pre-school pupils. Each of the full-time peripatetic teachers also carries a small generic caseload ranging from pre-school to upper secondary, an arrangement which is designed to obviate the dangers of over-specialisation. The detailed allocation of the staff's time varies, of course, from term to term in the light of changing needs. For instance, it is not expected that, in the longer term, the recently integrated blind children will need the level of support which they at present receive.

The head of service, in addition to her administrative duties, undertakes the general peripatetic advisory work for less severely impaired pupils who are not on the full-time caseload and supports students in further education and three special schools, again chiefly on a "collaborative teaching" basis.

The service is a free-standing support service which relates to the authority's other support services as required at fieldwork level.

The head of service attends meetings with senior management and other advisory teachers as required. There are close links with the health authority. Three years ago, one educational psychologist was designated to take a particular interest in visual impairment across the administrative area boundaries, and this has proved to be increasingly useful as she has developed her expertise.

Typing tuition is bought in on an hourly basis as required. Some mobility training has in the past been provided by Social Services, but there is now a need for a teacher with a mobility qualification or the chance to buy in this provision. Some help is currently provided for two children by the Guide Dogs for the Blind Association.

Supported mainstream provision

It will be apparent from the account given above that a substantial element of the service's work is targeted on children with high levels of need, rather than the work being more thinly spread over a wider range. However, in addition to this, special arrangements have been made to support the two primary children who have only light perception.

One attends the second year infant class of her neighbourhood school, and walks to school. A full-time support teacher is allocated for her needs, but this teacher also gives some time to an educationally blind child who attends the nursery class of another school. The primary aged child, who is of above average ability, is integrated virtually full-time apart from one television lesson and occasional withdrawal for special tuition. She would not automatically be excluded from a television lesson, but the subject content of this particular programme is inaccessible to her. The support teacher prepares and adapts teaching materials and interprets classroom activities as appropriate. She works alongside the class teacher, often with a group of children rather than just with the blind one. The visiting peripatetic teacher provides braille tuition and oversees the progress of the scheme. The class teacher has the same concern for the blind child's overall educational progress as she does for all other members of the class. There is full social integration, with no special supervisory arrangements at playtime or lunchtime.

The other blind child, who is now nine years old and also of above average ability, attended a special school until a year before this study took place, when she returned to a local school at her parents' request. They had always wanted her to be integrated alongside her peers, but they accepted that the authority did not previously have the resources or experience necessary to ensure that she could be adequately supported. She now attends a junior school which is near her home, but not the nearest one. The school was chosen because it has a well-established unit for children with learning difficulties, and the staff therefore have some experience of teaching children with special needs. When it was initially proposed that the blind girl should be integrated, she first spent a day a week in the school for one term, so that a considered decision could be made as to whether the proposal was reasonable. She has a support teacher for three and a half days a week who works in a similar way to the one supporting the other blind child. This teacher also spends a day a week in the adjoining infants school where there is a partially sighted, braille-learning child and she gives some support to a child in another school. The pupil in the junior school travels by taxi, but she enjoys almost total integration, apart from one outdoor games lesson per week and occasional withdrawal for extra tuition in the additional skills she requires.

The two support teachers concerned have been appointed to the staff of the visual impairment service. The high level of help which the blind children currently receive may be modified as they progress through their education, and the services of the teachers would then be transferred to other pupils or schools as required. It is fortuitous that at present one school has another pupil who needs some extra help, and this of course leads to a more effective use of staff time.

The schools concerned and the families are satisfied with the pupils' progress, and the children themselves mingle confidently with their peers. The older one has also maintained contact with her former friends in the special school. The integration scheme is of course still in its early stages, but it seems to be progressing very satisfactorily, and has given the staff confidence to consider similar provision for other blind children. It should be noted that this authority does not appoint care assistants even for pupils who have a severe degree of impairment. It is considered that their need is for qualified teaching help.

Equipment and resources

The head of service believes firmly that visually impaired pupils should be given access to the best possible technological equipment. Items required are specified on the pupil's educational advice for a Statement and are then provided. When a new type of equipment is introduced, a well-argued case for its need has to be made, but once the principle has been established, similar items will generally be provided for other pupils without question. This includes for instance the provision of more than one closed circuit television in a school if the geography of the building makes it necessary, and the supply of duplicate equipment for home use, including closed circuit televisions, braillers, typewriters, computers and printers.

A list of the equipment currently owned by the LEA is given in table 2.

TABLE 2

REPROGRAPHIC EQUIPMENT

Thermoform machines	-*
Braille Binders	-*
Minolta copiers	-*
Braille embossers	2

COMMUNICATION AIDS

Closed circuit televisions	25
Computers (specific to VI use)	3
Vincent Work Station (or similar)	3
Perkins braillers	15
Electronic typewriters	12
Cassette recorders	10
Speech synthesizers	3
Talking calculators	3
Versabraille	-
Viewscan/Keynotes	5
Optacon	-
Braille writers	-
Toshiba speech/visual display	1
Manual typewriters	11

---

*The LEA does not have these items because reprographic services are bought in from the nearby special school.

All this equipment is on the inventory of the visual impairment service and can be withdrawn from particular schools and re-allocated as required. The Senior Adviser controls the budget for purchase of disposable materials and small items of equipment. The Assistant Director of Education is responsible for larger items as listed above for use with individual children. The visual impairment service is obviously very well equipped, and this is doubtless largely due to the determination of the head of service in bidding for funds. A particular point is made by the support service of training pupils to use effectively whatever equipment is supplied for them.

The authority does not have service contracts which are considered too expensive. Repairs are undertaken by one of the LEA's general technicians wherever possible. Apart from major items of equipment, smaller resources and disposable materials are funded from the service's annual capitation allowance which is controlled by the head of service.

In-Service training

All members of the peripatetic team already held a qualification in visual impairment at the time of their appointment. The support teachers have not had specialist training, but they are learning braille and it is intended that they should seek to qualify through a "distance-learning" course.

The full visual impairment team meets every Friday afternoon for briefing and internal training, and members of staff have the opportunity to attend regional meetings. The head of service provides "on the job" induction training for newly appointed colleagues.

Members of the team provide general awareness courses in mainstream schools as part of the formal INSET programme. This includes annual talks to the staff of schools which have visually impaired pupils. In preparation for the integration of the two blind pupils, the whole staff of the two schools attended a week-end course of training tailor-made for them by the RNIB and their own visual impairment team. This took place a few weeks after the children had been admitted to their schools, when the staff were able to identify what their own needs were. Funds for in-service training are allocated by the Adviser for Special Educational Needs.

Pre school provision and parental links

When babies are first referred to the service, the head of service establishes contact with the family and provides the first level of advice and support. Depending on the individual needs, she may then pass the case on to an appropriate colleague. Low vision children are normally recommended for statementing at the age of two years, but that does not preclude the provision of support at an earlier stage.

The health authority has a child development centre which provides an inter-disciplinary service for children with special needs from the age of six months. If visually impaired children are placed in Social Services' day nurseries or in the "special needs" nursery school set up by the education service they receive support in that setting from the visual impairment service. Placement depends on individual needs and on what happens to be available in the vicinity of the child's home. For example, if a local infants school has a nursery class, a handicapped child may be offered a place in it as a priority.

The peripatetic staff establish early links with families and undertake regular home-visiting of pre-school children. They seek to win the family's confidence and so be able to guide them to a suitable choice of placement. However, parents are in the last resort given a free choice, and could ask for an extra-district special school if they so wished.

The service does not have the time to organise a parents' group, although the possibility has been discussed. Braille tuition is provided for the parents of blind children if required.

Post-16 provision
Substantial support has been given for five years to visually impaired, including blind students in sixth form colleges and further education colleges. It is recognised that young people who have attended special schools up to the age of 18 may well be able to join the mainstream at this stage, and that further education is a serious option for more visually impaired pupils than may have been realized in the past. One young man who lost his sight after leaving school is now attending a local further education college.

Contact is made with a proposed college prior to a pupil leaving school, and a report is sent to the college and to the further education section of the LEA outlining the equipment and resources required.

The students are fully integrated, but receive additional support according to need. This may include specialist teaching on Wednesday afternoons when the colleges do not normally have time-tabled sessions. This avoids the stigma which some might feel about having a support teacher present in their classes. A braille embossing system and secretarial time is available within the college system, and staff training is provided within the college inset programme.

Current and future plans

Thought is now being given to the support which will be needed when the older blind child transfers to secondary school. The desirability of establishing one secondary school as a resource base for pupils with more substantial needs will be considered, although this would be a move away from the current policy of neighbourhood integration.

A request has been put forward that an additional 15 hours a week secretarial help should be provided for the peripatetic team in recognition of the substantial amount of reprographic work which the job entails. At present the specialist teachers only have access to some general secretarial support in the area office, and consequently have to spend time on the routine preparation of teaching materials which is not a cost-effective use of their time.

Under the Local Management of Schools scheme, the service seems likely to remain centrally funded. Funds will also be allocated to schools on the basis of recommendations in a pupil's Statement of special educational need. Although the use of such funds is at the discretion of the school, the visual impairment service will expect to work closely with the schools to achieve an appropriate balance of resources, and to ensure that staff are released for liaison time where appropriate.

The head of service has been involved in a regional exercise relating to the National Curriculum. A residential in-service course brought together representatives of some ten authorities to draw up guidelines on how the attainment targets for each subject area may be achieved by visually impaired pupils. A pack of guidelines is being drawn up and made available to all teachers in the region. It is not considered that any aspect of the National Curriculum targets will need to be disapplied or modified for partially sighted or blind pupils presently in a mainstream school. The only exception is that a newly blinded child may need to be withdrawn from the curriculum for a period of time in order to develop new communication and access skills.

A working party has recently been established to devise a sensory curriculum for use in schools for children with severe learning difficulties. It is hoped that it may be possible for one member of staff to be trained specifically to work in the Profound and Multiple Learning Difficulties (PMLD) and Severe Learning Difficulties (SLD) area of provision, where it is recognised that children could benefit from more specialized support.

Comments

This authority has a long-established service for partially sighted pupils, even though the team remained very small until quite recently, and there is a real commitment to ensuring that the children have access to the best possible education. The young people concerned have a notable degree of self-confidence which doubtless comes from the fact that they feel they are respected as individuals. The LEA's enlightened policy in the provision of technological equipment could certainly serve as a model for many others.

The integration of educationally blind pupils at school level is a new departure which is still in its early stages. There was a judicious reluctance to embark on this development until those concerned felt that they were in a position to make a success of it. The approach was carefully planned and is being closely monitored, but certainly seems to be working well at present.

Notable features of this service are:

- **A considered policy of neighbourhood integration, even though the development of resource bases would be geographically feasible.**

- **The extensive use of the most up-to-date technological equipment in the classroom, and the practice of training pupils to use it effectively.**

- **The regular use of teachers rather than ancillary workers to support pupils.**

- **Specialist teaching roles for each member of the team, in addition to generic caseloads.**

- **A member of the team of educational psychologists who has particular involvement with visually impaired pupils.**

3. A Large County with a Resourced Base Service

Nature of the local authority

This is a large elongated county, extending approximately thirty miles in one direction and ninety miles in the other. It has several major centres of population which together stretch along one side of the county forming a banana-shaped urban sprawl. Near its border with a metropolitan area, there is a substantial overspill population which, although geographically contained within the county, traditionally looks outwards towards the neighbouring city and would tend to favour special school placement there rather than facilities in-county which may actually be at a greater geographical distance. There is a significant ethnic minority population in the county town, chiefly of Asian origin, and some Eastern European groups elsewhere.

The other half of the county is very rural with a low density population. Vast areas in fact contain more sheep than people, and the nature of the terrain means that transport and communication problems are substantial, particularly in winter. Geographically the rural area covers over half the county but it contains less than 30 per cent of the population.

The county boundaries are not contiguous with those of the health districts, which means that some children receive medical support from a health service whose main educational links are with a different local authority.

The 5-16 population is approximately 123,000. There are also 11,500 full time students in the 16-19 age group. The authority has primary schools from 3-11, some of which are in separate infant and junior schools. At secondary level, there is a policy to move towards 11-16 schools with tertiary colleges providing the full range of community provision in the further and adult education sectors. Currently some schools still have sixth forms, and six or seven of these are likely to be retained in the longer term.

Shortly after the 1981 Education Act, the Council issued a public policy statement in support of the principle of integration, and of the broader issue of equal opportunities for all. Developments toward the integration of handicapped children have therefore had the advantage of declared political commitment and strong public support. Expectations have been raised and there has been a groundswell of positive feelings on the issue amongst teachers, school governors and parents.

Visually impaired pupils and their placement

There are some 330 children on the authority's visual impairment register, which is approximately 2.7 per thousand of the population. Only 19% of these are in schools for severe learning difficulties. This represents 0.5 per thousand of the population.

Over four thousand children in the authority have Statements of special educational need. Of these, approximately 60% are in mainstream schools and 40% are in special schools. These figures highlight the authority's belief in the benefits of giving a child with special needs the protection of a Statement, but aiming to provide for those special needs within the mainstream wherever possible. Forty-one of the statemented pupils are visually impaired, but only ten of them have a Statement solely on the grounds of visual impairment as opposed to other areas of need. The low proportion of visually impaired children who have a Statement may be explained by the fact that many will already have been receiving appropriate support before the procedures were introduced, and may not therefore have been put forward for Statements.

The authority has never had a special school for visually impaired children. In 1981, over sixty visually impaired children were in out-county placements. Currently nineteen children attend a range of eight out-county special schools for the visually impaired, but only seven of these have been placed since 1981. These figures include placements in a special school in a neighbouring authority which arranges part-time local integration at primary level where appropriate, and which has a secondary department based in a mainstream school where full, supported integration is provided. For some children, and certainly for those who live near to the authority's boundary, such provision is now, and is likely to remain as appropriate as anything which could be provided within the county.

Two mainstream schools in the LEA, one primary and the other secondary, are resourced to cater for the needs of visually impaired pupils. The term "special teaching facility" is used rather than "resource base". Both of these schools are near the county town in the south-east of the county, but they are easily accessible by road from most of the conurbations.

The primary school facility currently has only five visually impaired pupils placed in it. There has been a recent move towards catering for educationally blind children as well as the partially sighted in this school. The secondary school, which currently has eleven partially sighted pupils, is planning to take its first educationally blind pupil in 1992.

It is the authority's policy that no child should have to spend more than three-quarters of an hour travelling to school. This means that, if a child in a more remote area has a severe visual impairment, support is given in the local school by a peripatetic teacher or an extra staffing allocation if necessary, and the child is not transferred to the school with the special teaching facility. It is on the basis of travelling time that some children have been placed in out-county schools where this is geographically sensible.

Most of the pupils on the visual impairment register are in their neighbourhood school and they and their teachers receive support from peripatetic staff.

The visual impairment service

Plans were made in 1981 to establish in-county provision for visually impaired pupils. The first specialist teacher was appointed in April of that year to take on overall responsibility for this aspect of the education service. At the time of her appointment, arrangements had already been made to set up a special teaching facility at a primary school and this opened in September 1981.

The teacher appointed was faced with the daunting task of providing single-handed for the needs of this very large county right up until 1985 when an expansion of the service became possible. In April 1985, the secondary "special teaching facility" was set up and it received its first pupils in September 1985. At this point, two additional peripatetic teachers were appointed to the authority. A further peripatetic teacher was appointed in July 1986 and the secondary facility increased in size.

In 1988 two posts were established for peripatetic lecturers at further education level, but initially only one of these posts was filled because of a shortage of suitably qualified candidates.

The establishment of the service has therefore grown to a head of service, three peripatetic teachers and two peripatetic lecturers. This is in addition to four support teachers and two education care officers, a mobility officer and two resource technicians who are based in the schools which have special facilities.

The head of service is responsible to the Assistant Education Officer and the County Senior Adviser for special educational needs. All the support services have a similar line of responsibility, and there are regular meetings of heads of special schools and support services.

Administratively, the authority is divided into four geographical areas, and one peripatetic teacher works in each (the head of service being one of them). The intention is that the further education lecturers will also have area responsibilities, each catering for two of the four areas. Plans are currently under way in the authority to introduce fifteen "neighbourhood management groups" which will have the role of co-ordinating the local delivery of all council services. The peripatetic teachers will be required to serve on all the groups within their area.

The peripatetic teachers' caseload includes all children in the 0-16 age-range and of all abilities. It is a matter of agreed policy that their role is to advise teachers and not to undertake direct classroom teaching. They are each responsible for allocating their time as efficiently as possible, and the frequency of school visits depends on the pupil's needs and the inevitable time constraints. Thus the head of service herself has a full-time caseload, in addition to the overall management of the service.

Supported mainstream provision

The resourced primary school currently has two full-time support teachers and two full-time education care officers. Welfare assistance is allocated according to individual pupil needs, as it is to any child in the authority who has special needs, and may vary from year to year. There are at present only five visually impaired children in the school, but this is an exceptional trough in numbers. One child in the facility is educationally blind, and uses braille alongside print, and there are three blind children of pre-school age who are likely to go to the school. The service has a withdrawal classroom which is physically an integral part of the school. Children other than the visually impaired ones use it for some withdrawal activities, so it is not a socially divisive factor. On average, the visually impaired pupils are integrated into the mainstream curriculum for 75% of the time. The minimum level of integration is 60% and the maximum is 90%. The level depends on the precise needs of the children.

Major developments have begun in this service and should be fully effective by September 1990. A blind child with an additional physical disability has just been admitted to the school, and three other blind children will enter in the near future. The extra support for this provision is as follows:

- An additional support teacher, hopefully with a qualification in visual impairment.

- An "education care officer" with a nursery nurse qualification.

- An extra mainstream teacher on the staff of the school to take account of the additional demands to be placed on staff.

- A full-time mobility officer, who will be based in the primary school but will service the whole authority.

- A full-time technician, who will also provide a service for the whole authority.

- Ten hours a week clerical support.

- An increase to six hours a week of keyboard tuition.

The resourced secondary school has two support teachers and two part-time education care officers sharing a full-time post. One of the teachers is a qualified mobility officer. The school has a resource technician and part-time typing tuition is provided. There are currently eleven visually impaired pupils in the school. Two rooms within the main body of the school are made available for their use. The rooms are divided into individual study bays; space for equipment and work preparation; storage; staff work areas and visitor reception. The average level of integration into the mainstream curriculum is 84%, individual levels varying between 70% and 90%, and the pupils have full social integration. An interesting feature of the scheme is that pupils are able to play a full part in extra-curricular activities taking place after school because taxi times are changed as required for this purpose.

In both schools, the support teachers undertake some withdrawal teaching, but their main role is to work alongside class or subject teachers. They often work not just with the visually impaired children, but with a wider group of pupils, in a team-teaching situation.

These teachers are on the staff of the host school, being appointed by the head of the school who is their line manager. In recognition of the extra responsibility being placed on the school, an additional allowance is paid to the deputy head teacher.

In addition to the pupils placed in these facilities, some thirty primary and fifteen secondary children receive support in their neighbourhood school in the form of an agreed number of hours of education care officer time. This is generally because travelling distances make placement in the resourced schools inappropriate. The education care officers work under the guidance of the peripatetic teachers, who visit as regularly as their work schedule permits.

There is one pupil with both visual and hearing impairment who was attending a neighbourhood school with a full-time education care officer and some extra teaching with additional advice from the Sense organisation. She is now eight years old and has recently transferred to a school for severe learning difficulties. In this case, an exceptional type of provision was made in response to exceptional circumstances, and because the parents do not want a residential placement, which would have been the alternative.

Equipment and resources

The service is building up a stock of special resources. Equipment available is listed in table 3. Since the authority is only just beginning to integrate educationally blind pupils, they do not yet have much of the more specialised technology which will become necessary.

The visual impairment service has its own annual capitation allowance, and a special allowance is also allocated to the resourced primary and secondary facilities. All schools also receive enhanced individual capitation for severely impaired children who are placed in them. Where major items of equipment are required, a specific application is made to the Assistant Education Officer, and in certain extreme cases committee approval is required.

All equipment is the property of the visual impairment service and can be re-distributed as required. The problem of repairs and maintenance is under consideration. The authority has a good team of technicians, but they cannot deal with some specialist equipment for the sensory handicaps, and the need for appropriate technical help is acknowledged.

TABLE 3

Item	Special Teaching Facilities	Peripatetic Service	Total
REPROGRAPHIC EQUIPMENT			
Thermoforms	-	1	1
Binders (manual)	2	-	2
Minolta copiers	1	-	1
Braille embossers	1	3	4
COMMUNICATION AIDS			
Closed circuit televisions (black & white)	6	4	10
Closed circuit televisions (colour)	2	2	4
Computers (specific to VI use)	2	2	4
Vincent Work Stations (or similar)	1	-	1
Perkins braillers	5	3	8
Electronic typewriters	3	6	9
Cassette recorders	8	6	14
Speech synthesizers	1	4	5
Talking calculators	3	1	4
Versabraille	-	3	3
Viewscan	-	1	1
Optacon	-	2	2
Braille writers	-	-	-
Braille 'n' Print	1	1	2
Eureka	-	1	1
Vista	-	1	1
Navigator	-	1	1
Manual typewriters	3	5	8
Ordinary TV monitor	-	1	1
Photocopier/enlarger	2	-	2
Video camera	-	1	1
Small scientific equipment, eg.			
light probe (photo conductive)	-	3	3
digital thermometer	-	3	3
alcohol thermometer	1	1	2
personal printer	-	2	2
circuit boards	-	4	4
desk stands	6	20	26

Pupils are not at present provided with equipment for home use, although this has happened on occasions in the past. This is an issue which has been a matter of considerable debate, and it has not been satisfactorily resolved.

In-service training

The head of service had a qualification in visual impairment when appointed, but one reason for the slow development of the service in its early years was the difficulty encountered in finding suitably qualified staff. In more recent years, the authority has been unable to second staff for training because no funds were allocated to them by the DES for this purpose under the National Priority Area section of Grant related in-service training (GRIST) funding, which was then in operation. This was despite the regular applications which the authority made for such funding. All the peripatetic teachers now in post have a qualification, except the one working in the further education sector. One of them obtained the qualification by secondment. The second further education post is vacant because a suitably qualified person has not been found. When the secondary facility opened, a support teacher without a specialist qualification was selected as the best candidate, though in competition with a teacher who had a qualification. One of the support teachers in the primary facility obtained a qualification by secondment.

Under the LEATGS (LEA Training Grant Scheme) Local Priority Area heading, each support service receives an inset allocation in the same way as individual schools do. The head of service is therefore able to organise a staff development programme with these funds. This includes training provided locally, attendance at RNIB courses and participation in the regional meetings for peripatetic staff. Joint training sessions are also arranged for the various support services, and members of the team attend sessions in the authority's general inset programme as appropriate. This enables staff to keep abreast of general curricular developments of a local or national nature in the various educational sectors in which they are working.

The members of the team provide in-service training for mainstream teachers throughout the authority. The normal procedure is that individual schools or clusters invite them to contribute to "Baker Days" or other in-service programmes.

Attempts are made to involve classroom and education care officers in training where possible. However, this is often impeded by the lack of funding or national agreement about such provision. Resource technicians receive on-the-job training from peripatetic or support staff.

Pre-school provision and parental links

The peripatetic staff seek to establish early contact with the families of visually impaired babies. The young children may attend a diagnostic assessment centre or one of two paediatric assessment centres, where the visual impairment service contributes to the multi-disciplinary provision.

There is no designated nursery class for the visually impaired, but the level of nursery provision in the authority as a whole is good, and the admission criteria give priority to children with special needs. Consequently, visually impaired children normally attend a local nursery class where the staff receive peripatetic support as appropriate.

It is part of the ethos of the authority that parents should participate fully in discussions about school placements. They are counselled from an early stage, and if necessary, they have access to the Assistant Education Officer for further discussion. Advice is given, but in the last resort a decision would never be forced on them against their will.

There is at present no parents' group, but premises have been offered for such a group to meet, and the matter is under discussion with parents.

Post-16 provision

As mentioned above, the authority is introducing a policy of providing for further education students on the same basis as school children. The newly appointed staff will work as part of the overall visual impairment service. The County Senior Adviser for special educational needs currently has responsibility for post-school as well as pre-sixteen provision, but a bid has been submitted for an additional adviser under the TVEI scheme who would take on responsibility for post-16 special educational needs. The development in relation to visually impaired students is therefore part of a broader policy move. A technician is also being appointed for the further education sector and proposals have been put forward for a mobility officer. Currently the mobility officer attached to the social service department offers limited support.

Current and future plans

The introduction of in-county provision for educationally blind primary children is likely to lead to a demand for similar provision at secondary level in due course. It is acknowledged that this will necessitate a major injection of funds for technological equipment, and it is intended that this provision should be built into the budget in coming years.

Discussion is under way concerning some form of regional provision for deaf-blind children. It is considered that these children's very special needs should be able to be catered for by day placement where that is the wish of the family. The numbers involved are never likely to justify separate LEA provision, but it is hoped that a joint project with some neighbouring authorities may prove to be feasible.

The head of service sees a need for more intensive support generally for multi-handicapped children, and for a structured programme of training for education care officers and technicians.

Under the Local Management of Schools scheme, it is intended that the visual impairment service should continue to be centrally funded. The attitude to the National Curriculum is that only very rarely should a visually impaired pupil need to be excluded for an aspect of the work. It is recognised, however, that the time factor could be a problem and may effectively prevent some children from covering the full range of the curriculum to public examination level. The curriculum will be as broad as possible and will obviously have to include additional areas such as mobility and orientation, keyboard skills, self help and independence training.

Comments

This authority has a well-established service for the visually impaired, which is fully integrated into the overall framework of support services. There is a firm basis of council policy on integration and a willingness to accept extra expenditure when circumstances dictate that it is essential if avowed principles are to be respected. Administrative structures are clearly drawn and understood. The main difficulties which arise relate to the small size of the support service relative to the geographical scale of the authority.

There were internal reasons why the integration of educationally blind pupils was not a feasible option until recently. The new proposals have been thoroughly planned and will be well monitored, and they are being introduced at a time when there are several pre-school children who are likely to be able to benefit.

Notable features of this service are:

- **A well-established system of resource bases in mainstream schools, combined with a practice of neighbourhood integration for children living in rural areas.**

- **A service the development of which was delayed by difficulties in recruiting qualified staff, and which even now has a very small team relative to the LEA's size.**

- **A service with a clearly defined management structure and lines of communication.**

- **A declared policy that the visual impairment team work in an advisory, as opposed to a teaching role.**

- **The extensive use of education care officers to support pupils with special educational needs.**

- **The appointment of team members to take specific responsibility for the further education sector.**

4. A New Small Urban Service

Nature of the local authority
This is a small metropolitan district, measuring only some seven miles by eight miles in size, but nevertheless comprising nine towns. It is mainly an urban area and borders on a major city. Its compact nature means that all services are centralized and there are no significant travelling difficulties.

After local government reorganisation in 1974, the new authority initially preserved existing links beyond its borders, and continued to use outside services in various aspects of special education. As a result of this reliance on external support, the authority was not well resourced to make appropriate provision for children with special needs within its boundaries, and there was little scope for new developments. However, in recent years there has been a move towards greater autonomy, and a twelve-page Council policy for meeting special educational needs has been produced. The policy is based on the premise that all children and young people are likely to have both special and general educational needs in varying degrees and these should be catered for wherever the child is being educated. It is accepted that all children and young people are entitled to be educated with others of their own age in their own community wherever possible, but that special placements will sometimes be necessary. Within this overall framework, a service for the visually impaired was introduced in the authority in 1988.

The 5-16 population is approximately 30,000. Much store is set by pre-five education and there are 4 nursery schools and 41 nursery classes. The pattern of educational provision is 5-11 primary schools, a few of which are divided into separate infant and junior schools, and 11-16 secondary schools, with post-16 provision being in two sixth form colleges and a college of technology. There are three Roman Catholic secondary schools with a federated sixth form based on the site of one of the schools.

Visually-impaired pupils and their placement

Currently 72 pupils are on the visual impairment register, which is 2.4 per thousand of the population. However, in view of the recent introduction of the service it is possible that a larger number will be identified. Some six hundred pupils in the authority have Statements of special educational need, but at this early stage in the development of the service only twelve of these have visual impairment as their main disability. It is likely that, in the longer term, a higher proportion of the children on the register will have a Statement.

A facility for visually impaired pupils has been established in a resourced primary school, but as yet only two pupils have needed this type of support. This is in accordance with the authority's policy that pupils should remain in their neighbourhood school wherever possible, and where this is the wish of the parents. In fact two other braille users attend their neighbourhood schools. There are extra-district special schools within daily travelling distance. The six children currently attending these schools or residential schools elsewhere were placed before the authority's service was introduced, but there would still be a willingness to take up extra-district placement if this were considered to be the most appropriate option for a particular child.

Of the visually impaired children identified, 23 or approximately 30% are in schools for severe learning difficulties. These and children in mainstream schools are supported by peripatetic staff.

The visual impairment service

There has never been a school for the visually impaired within the boundaries of the present authority. The geographical area had previously been within the catchment area of two special schools, both of which became the base for peripatetic support services. The LEA under discussion bought in services from the authorities to which the special schools were allocated at the time of local government reorganisation and this remained the situation until the recent decision to establish its own independent provision.

Unlike many authorities which have started from the appoint-ment of one teacher and then increased the service as needs were identified, in this case a longer-term blue-print of the required service was determined, and then a phased introduction of it was planned. The LEA focused initially on the primary sector, with the intention of gradually developing the service throughout all phases of education. The service is being developed in line with an integrational policy for meeting special educational needs. A plan for in-service training was incorporated into the scheme, and a clear structure established for inter-service links and manage-ment responsibilities.

As a first step in the implementation of this scheme, a basic team was appointed, consisting of a team leader, another peripatetic teacher and a nursery nurse. A facility was set up in a primary school, and the whole staff of that school were provided with a day's awareness training.

A physical base for the visual impairment service was established in this school, using a large classroom area. This has been pleasantly fitted out with carpets and blinds, and has designated areas for teaching, for administration, for the preparation of materials and for informal meetings with parents or colleagues. There is an adjacent secure area, where expensive equipment belonging either to the service or to the main part of the school is stored.

The team leader is responsible to an Education Officer, working closely with the Special Educational Needs Adviser and the Head-teacher of the resourced primary school. The team leader attends the monthly meetings of heads of special schools and support services. Meetings are held as required with the medical officer and close contact is maintained with the health authority's child development unit. The smallness of the authority facilitates informal relationships, and indeed health service staff take part in joint training sessions with education staff.

The team leader and the other teacher in the team share the peripatetic work, which is seen as essentially a teaching role. The frequency of visits to individual children varies according to need, between two sessions a week and once a term. It is considered that if a child needs more than two visits a week, he or she will be better placed in the resourced school, unless there is parental objection to this. The team leader reserves approximately 0.1 of her time for administering the service, and the rest of her time is given to the peripatetic teaching.

This first phase of the service development has been set up to cater for primary aged children, but the staff also give some support to pre-school children and to special schools. Further resources will be required to cater for secondary needs.

The team leader teaches typing and has developed her own typing programme for use in schools, so mainstream class teachers are able to undertake much of the day-to-day skill training on the basis of this programme.

The second teacher is a qualified mobility teacher, which gives the authority a significant advantage over many others. Some help in mobility training has also been provided by the Guide Dogs for the Blind Association.

At present, brailling is undertaken by the team leader, and enlarging and the preparation of other materials by the nursery nurse. The service has one and a half hours clerical support per week.

The staff liaise with the eight educational psychologists as required. At present, none of them has special responsibility for visually impaired children, but the psychological service is considering developing individual specialisms.

Supported mainstream provision

As already explained, the visual impairment team has its base in the primary school which is specially resourced to support visually impaired pupils. This means that the staff are readily available to support the children placed in that facility as and when required. There are no separate support staff appointed to teach them.

The one visually impaired child currently placed in the school receives half-time support from the nursery nurse and teaching support for O.3 of the time. He has very little sight and is learning braille, but is fully integrated into the life of the school and into all aspects of the curriculum. He is withdrawn occasionally for special teaching and mobility training, but otherwise the special-ist staff work alongside the class teacher, sometimes teaching a group which includes the visually impaired boy.

Two other braille-using children are attending their neighbour-hood schools with special support. One, who is five years old, has a full-time nursery nurse, support for half a day a week from a peripatetic teacher and mobility training. The other, who is seven, has a half-time nursery nurse and peripatetic teaching for half a day a week. This arrangement is obviously more extravagant in staffing than placement in the special facility, but the authority decided that it was prepared to respect the wishes of parents for neighbourhood placement.

Equipment and resources

The authority acknowledged the difficulty which is involved in establishing an initial resource base for a service which depends so much on individual needs. Ideally what is required is a "demand led" model where equipment and materials are pro-cessed as they become necessary. However, advance financial provision obviously has to be made for this, so some form of contingency plan is required.

The solution chosen was that the sum of £25,000 was allocated to enable the service to function effectively from the time of its inception. This money has been spent partly on purchasing equip-ment immediately required for known children, and partly on beginning to build up a stock of items in quite general demand. The resource base thus established is shown in table 4.

It will be seen that priority has been given to communication aids rather than to reprographic equipment. This is because the ser-vice is initially directed towards primary education, and the

45

TABLE 4

REPROGRAPHIC EQUIPMENT

Thermoform machines	-
Binders	1
Minolta copiers	-
Braille embossers	1

COMMUNICATION AIDS

Closed circuit televisions	7
Computers (specific to v.i. use)	2
Vincent Work Stations (or similar)	-
Perkins braillers	8
Electronic typewriters	8
Cassette recorders	6
Speech synthesizers	2
Talking calculators	6
Versabraille	-
Viewscan	-
Optacon	-
Braille writers	-
Lamps	5

braille-using children do not yet need a substantial amount of braille or tactile material.

The service also receives an annual capitation allowance which should be sufficient to cover disposable materials and small items, and also to allow for certain additional major items as required for individual children. If needs arise beyond this, special consideration would need to be given to them.

Equipment is not purchased specifically for use by pupils at home, but items may be borrowed for home use from the resource base if they are available. All the equipment remains the property of the visual impairment service even when it is in use in particular schools.

Service contracts for maintenance are considered to be too expensive, and the arrangement at present is that any repairs which become necessary will have to be charged to the service's capitation.

In-service training

The team leader has a qualification in visual impairment. The support teacher is a qualified mobility instructor and is currently studying for a specialist teaching qualification by distance learning. The nursery nurse is a qualified NNEB and is learning braille and doing the Certificate of Post Qualifying Studies.

Each teacher in the service has an entitlement of 8 to 10 days' in-service training a year. Some joint sessions have been held with the staff of the school where the service is based.

The service receives £300 a year of LEATGS local priority area money, on the same basis as each school receives an allocation from these funds. A significant amount of available funds is also held centrally and allocated by the adviser as required.

The service has already provided several awareness sessions for mainstream teachers, in some cases in relation to the placement of a particular child. Twilight sessions cater for up to 40 teachers from different schools, and this is an economic way of providing training, since replacement teachers are not required. The visual impairment team also contribute to the training programmes which are provided for teachers nominated as co-ordinators of special educational needs in mainstream schools.

The peripatetic teachers at present provide on-the-job training for ancillary workers. The authority has a significant number of "special support assistants" for individual children for a range of reasons, and it is proposed that more specific training may be organised for them on the basis of a modular INSET programme in due course. The lack of national funding for the training of ancillary staff is a matter of considerable concern.

Pre-5 provision and parental links

Close links have been established with the health authority's Child Development Unit, which runs mother and child groups. Most families are introduced to the visual impairment service by the chief orthoptist, but parental referrals are also accepted. Generally young children are placed in mainstream or special school nursery placements, where they receive peripatetic support from the team, or else they are supported at home.

Parents are fully involved in all discussion concerning their child. It is part of the authority's declared policy that parents should be "equal partners in the education of their child" and their participation is conducted in a friendly, informal atmosphere with personal assistance being given when required, if necessary at home.

The local education authority does not make any arrangements for a parents' group, but the local voluntary blind association helps to establish links between families where appropriate.

Post-16 provision
There is as yet no support available at this level, but it will constitute a later phase in developments.

Current and future plans
Discussions are currently under way on reviewing provision beyond the primary sector with a feasibility study being conducted into the most effective way of making appropriate provision in the secondary and FE sectors. As a short-term contingency, an additional specialist teacher has been appointed to enable support to be given to secondary-aged pupils with visual impairments as they transfer to local high schools.

Consideration is also being given to adapting a similar structure of service provision for other areas of special need.

It is intended that, under the Local Management of Schools scheme, the visual impairment service will continue to be centrally funded and will cater for all statemented children through central funds. The approach to the National Curriculum is that it represents an entitlement from which visually impaired children should not be excluded. With few exceptions, the assessment targets should be attainable, and it is the responsibility of the support service to ensure that the children have access to them. A workshop is being held concerning the implications of the National Curriculum for all areas of special need. A general strategy will be agreed and detailed proposals will then be put forward concerning the approach required for each type of special need. The LEA has also participated in a regional, residential seminar designed to devise guidelines on giving visually impaired children access to the National Curriculum.

Comments
This is an example of a very young service which is being built on the sure foundations of a clearly defined structure and blue-print for further stages of development. The authority has an articulated policy for special needs provision, and detailed strategies for

the allocation of resources and approaches to training. Those involved are not, however, fettered by the theories, but are already modifying the detailed implementation of their scheme in response to identified needs.

Notable features of this service are:

- **A young service which has started its life with a team of staff, rather than an isolated teacher.**

- **An attempt to establish a balance between the advantages of a resource centre in a mainstream school and some parents' wishes for neighbourhood integration.**

- **A declared policy that the visual impairment team both teach and offer advice rather than operate purely in an advisory capacity.**

- **A clear management structure and a blue-print for future developments.**

- **A quickly established role for the team in providing in-service training for mainstream teachers.**

- **An LEA concern to tackle the problem of the training needs of ancillary workers and develop a well trained team of special support assistants to support pupils with a wide range of special educational needs.**

5. A Regional Service Based on a Special School

Nature of the local authority
This is an urban borough measuring approximately eight miles by four. It is in a particularly unusual situation in that it provides a visual impairment service, not only for its own population, but for five neighbouring boroughs.

This is of course fundamentally different from the practice in the other authorities which are being described here, and the structure of this account therefore differs in some ways from the others. Information is provided relating to the actual population of the home authority, but it is also thought appropriate to consider the impact of its external services on provision in the neighbouring authorities.

These boroughs together constitute a predominantly urban area. The local motorway network facilitates transport, with the result that a special school for visual impairment which is situated in the borough under discussion is able to offer convenient day placement to a highly populated catchment area.

The area boasts of a long local tradition of concern for children with special needs, a special school for handicapped children having been opened there as early as 1897 in response to the Mental Deficiency Act. Subsequently a range of services were developed for various types of handicap, and this sympathetic interest in special education was inherited by the present borough when it came into existence in 1969.

The 5-16 population is approximately 30,000 and there are some 4000 students in the 16-19 age range. The educational pattern is 5-11 primary schools, some of which are separate infant and junior schools, 11-16 secondary schools and a sixth form college.

Visually impaired pupils and their placement
In the authority, approximately 500 children have Statements of special educational need, and of these over 50 are visually impaired. This represents 1.7 children per thousand of the population, but it must be stressed that the figure refers only to those who have Statements.

Twenty children resident in the borough attend the authority's own day special school for the visually impaired, with some integration into the mainstream where appropriate. 33 children, that is 66% of those visually impaired children who have Statements, are placed in other local special schools, chiefly those for severe learning difficulties. Many others who have less severe impairments are supported by peripatetic staff in their neighbourhood schools.

The special school for the visually impaired
A special school for the blind was established in the area in 1918, with the title "The Blind Council School." In 1973, when new buildings were required, the decision was made that the new school should be on the same site as mainstream schools in order to facilitate integration. The buildings are therefore on the same

campus as a primary and a secondary school, so the pupils are able to benefit fully from the foresight shown in 1973. The buildings of one section of the special school have recently been redesigned to take account of changing educational needs and plans are under way to modernise the remainder of the building.

The school draws pupils, not only from the six boroughs with which it has a close association, but from a total of thirteen local education authorities. Ten years ago, there were 77 children in the school, but now there are over one hundred. The increase is partly attributable to the closure of some other special schools and also to a growing preference for day rather than residential placements. Most of the pupils live within easy travelling distance of the school, although some do come from further afield, the longest daily distance travelled being about 40 miles. The campus location has undoubtedly also favoured the growth in numbers, since placing authorities and parents know that the children need not be totally segregated from their sighted peers. The number of braille-using pupils in the school is currently 17, but it is increasing rapidly and is expected to reach 50% of the school population. This is partly because many partially sighted, print-using children are now able to attend mainstream schools, and it is the more severely impaired ones who are in special schools. The trend also reflects a growing recognition that braille may be a useful additional skill for pupils who can use print but only with great difficulty. Ten per cent of the pupils in the school have additional disabilities.

The school has a nursery class and primary and secondary departments. There is the opportunity for primary pupils to spend half a day a week or sometimes two half days in the on-site primary school, and up to eight pupils at a time have done so. They do however spend most of their time in the special school. When pupils are being integrated, a teacher from the special school works on a team teaching basis in the primary classroom, and the educational programme is prepared and monitored in conjunction with the head teacher and the relevant class teacher in the primary school.

A more significant move towards integration is seen at secondary level. 75% of the pupils are integrated for some lessons from the age of thirteen years, and this proportion goes up to 90% from the age of fourteen. They are integrated for between one and seven subjects on the curriculum, according to their individual abilities. The proximity of the schools gives ample opportunity for social integration with fully sighted children, but the extent to which this operates in practice is varied. There is some participation in extra-curricular activities.

The peripatetic service

It was decided in 1980 that the special school should serve as a base for an outreach peripatetic service for visually impaired pupils in the region. The first peripatetic teacher was appointed in that year and a team was gradually built up to reach the current level of six full-time equivalent teachers. The team has a physical base within the special school and the team leader is responsible to the Deputy Head Teacher of the school. The overall line management is through the Head Teacher, the Governors of the school and the Assistant Education Officer for special services.

The team of teachers provides peripatetic support for mainstream schools in the borough and in the five surrounding authorities. It should be noted that this is the only type of visual impairment service which some of the other authorities have, although at least one has now appointed a peripatetic teacher of its own. Undoubtedly, the existence of this external service has militated against most of the LEAs concerned developing their own service.

Each of the teachers has a caseload of approximately 100 pupils, who are divided into specific categories according to the level of support required. Some are visited once a week, some every two weeks, and for some there is just a "watching brief". One part-time teacher undertakes more concentrated classroom work with a small number of pupils, but the others advise teachers rather than working directly with children.

Although the peripatetic teachers all work with a wide age and ability range, each of them also has a particular specialism, be it an age-group or subject area. Consequently, at least two members of the team contribute to work in any one authority. There is a named liaison officer in each authority, who may be an Assistant Education Officer, an adviser or a psychologist. This liaison officer and sometimes other officers of each authority meet the teachers working there on a termly basis, with the head of service attending these meetings wherever possible. There is also an annual meeting in the providing authority for all users of the service. This is normally attended by the Assistant Education Officer for special educational needs and a finance officer from each authority. The service is financed by recoupment from the participating authorities for the level of service provided.

The borough in which the special school is situated has a junior special school for pupils with hearing difficulties, which is also the base for an all-age peripatetic service, and this functions in much the same way as the visual impairment service. The two services co-operate in providing for the needs of children with dual sensory impairment. The authority also has a special school for learning difficulties which has a deaf-blind department, and the peripatetic teachers give some support here.

One of the educational psychologists in the borough has a specialist brief to work with visually impaired pupils, and similarly educational psychologists are nominated for other specialisms. In issues concerning areas of the curriculum, the peripatetic teachers and the school are able to liaise with subject advisers, but they do not have access to similar support on matters concerning special educational needs, since the LEA has no adviser for special education.

The health districts are contiguous with the education authorities, and good links are maintained with them and with ophthalmological services.

There is a full-time post for mobility training made up of two part-time officers, who work in the special school and in mainstream schools throughout the six boroughs. The Social Services Department funds this service for the special school and within the home borough. They provide the service for other boroughs and recoup the cost according to the level of service provided. This represents a far clearer commitment to providing for the mobility needs of school children than is usual from Social Services Departments.

Equipment and resources

For the provision of equipment, an interesting agreement has been reached between the contributing authorities. Each funds the purchase of items of equipment required for pupils, but when an item is no longer needed by the pupil it goes into a common pool from which all the authorities are able to draw. It is considered that, over a long period of time, the benefits to the various authorities will even out.

There is a local authority contract for the maintenance of all equipment, and in the special school a part-time technician is provided.

If pupils need to have equipment for home use, this is funded by their own authority. In some cases, larger items such as computers are lent to children for use during school holidays.

In-service training

The authority has over a number of years encountered difficulty in recruiting teachers with a qualification in visual impairment. Only one of the peripatetic team currently has a qualification, but three others are undergoing training now that local part-time courses are available.

Whenever new members of staff are appointed to the peripatetic team, they are trained for this role by a one-term induction course, provided by the head of service and the head of the special school. The staff of the special school have an in-school training programme, and there is some attendance at outside courses.

The head of service and staff provide a range of in-service courses for mainstream teachers in all the boroughs concerned. This may be for the staff of an individual school, or for special needs teachers from a range of schools. Mainstream teachers who have visually impaired pupils also have the opportunity to visit the special school.

There are some thirty classroom assistants (full-time or part-time) in the special school, and they are provided with a training course in the form of five evening sessions. These are financed from the school's own funds.

Pre-five provision and parental links

Although some children attend the nursery class in the special school, many other visually impaired children are placed in their local nursery classes and supported by peripatetic staff. One of the peripatetic teachers specialises in pre-school work and she advises her colleagues on their cases in this age-group. A scheme is in operation to co-ordinate the home visits of the various agencies concerned with pupils who have special educational needs.

The school arranges meetings for the parents of nursery and infant aged children twice a term. These are structured meetings which also create the opportunity for social interaction between parents. This provision is to be expanded to form two groups covering the full primary range, and it may later be extended to the secondary sector.

The extent to which parents are involved in decisions about their child's school placement varies from one authority in the group to another. During the discussion stage, parents are normally given the opportunity to visit the special school in order to help them towards a full understanding of the various options available. Of the parents who visit the school, some 40% do not in the event send their child there. Very few referrals are made through the peripatetic service, whose role is to support children where they find them rather than to participate in discussions about placements. This means, of course, that although the peripatetic staff provide reports for Statements, no-one with expertise in visual impairment has a direct input into decisions about placements.

Post-16 provision

Pupils who attend mainstream schools are normally able to move into mainstream further education within their own authority. The usual practice is for the staff of the visual impairment service to accompany the young person on an initial visit and "present" him or her to the college, if such is the student's wish. The peripatetic staff do not usually continue to give sustained support at this stage of education.

Current and future plans

As far as is known at present, the LEAs concerned in this scheme will continue to buy in services from the special school on a centrally funded basis when the Local Management of Schools scheme comes into operation. Should they not in the event be able to do this, major problems would of course be created for the providing authority.

The school itself is involved in a research study concerning the National Curriculum. In partnership with a polytechnic, they are undertaking the trial use over a three month period of materials relating to the assessment targets in English. The aim is to analyse the appropriateness of the materials for visually impaired pupils and to produce a report which may be of help both to special schools and to mainstream schools which have visually impaired pupils.

A proposal has been put forward to set up short-term residential provision for visually impaired pupils within the borough, so that older pupils could receive periods of intense tuition in specialist skills and daily living skills. It has also been suggested that a further education residential hostel should be set up on a different site from the school. The students would attend mainstream colleges, but would have the opportunity for additional tuition and support in the evenings, and for structured independence training.

Comments

This authority is in the fortunate position of having a special school whose geographical position and ready access to mainstream schools hold out a very viable future. The provision of outreach services to neighbouring authorities is well-established and has an effective working structure with good co-operation in both financial and managerial terms. Within this well planned and co-ordinated framework, optimum use is being made of scarce expertise and resources, but it should be noted that the level of support in these LEAs is very low compared with all the other services studied. It also means that each LEA does not have direct professional control over the service which is provided for visually impaired pupils, and the provision of an internal service is unlikely to be seen as a priority when external support is available.

Notable features of this service are:

- **A joint support service for six LEAs, based in a special school located in one of them.**

- **Geographical circumstances which give viability to a day special school for visually impaired pupils.**

- **A special school on the same site as a primary and a secondary school, which provides scope for varied levels of integration.**

- **Well-structured inter-authority liaison which makes the joint service financially manageable.**

- **The benefits of team contacts and an element of specialisation within the team which would be difficult to achieve if each LEA concerned had an isolated peripatetic teacher.**

6. A Medium Sized County with Resource Bases

Nature of the local authority

This is a county authority which is made up of three densely populated towns and a thinly populated rural area. It has a declining industrial base, but new industries and tourism are beginning to bring in greater prosperity. The authority measures approximately forty miles by twenty-five miles. The geographical nature of the rural area means that travelling times tend to be long. A home-to-school journey the length of which would be quite feasible in some parts of the country may here be unacceptable because of the time involved, and also because local communities are close-knit and somewhat parochial.

The 5-16 population is approximately 64,000. The pattern of educational provision is 5-11 primary schools, 11-16 secondary schools and 16-19 tertiary provision.

Visually-impaired pupils and their placement

There are some three hundred children on the visual impairment register, which amounts to rather more than four per thousand of the population. Of these, 75 to 80 have a severe visual impairment requiring either unit or peripatetic support. At present, 2,200 children have Statements of special educational need and of these 32 are visually impaired. This is of course a very low percentage of the children on the register, but it may partly reflect the fact that the procedures have so far been used chiefly for new referrals rather than for children who are already receiving appropriate support.

A special school for the visually impaired provided by a neighbouring authority is within travelling distance and day placements are therefore possible. Only six children are placed there at present. Children may also be placed in residential schools if this should be appropriate to their needs.

The LEA has five resource bases in mainstream schools which are referred to as "units." There is one at nursery level with eight pupils, one in an infants school with nine pupils, two in junior schools with thirteen pupils and one at secondary level with ten pupils.

The normal practice is that children with significant educational needs arising from visual impairment are placed in these units.

There are a number of severely visually impaired children sup-ported in their local schools, usually at their parents' request. Four of the children in units are braille users, and some have additional needs such as a physical handicap, learning difficulties or hearing loss. The maximum distance travelled by pupils attending units is about ten miles.

There is a girl with impairment of both hearing and vision who was placed in the authority's unit for the hearing impaired but who is now placed out of county in a special school for visually impaired children which has a newly resourced deaf-blind facility. Thirteen pupils in schools for severe learning difficulties are supported on a weekly basis by peripatetic staff, whilst others in such schools are supported on an advisory basis.

The remaining visually impaired pupils in the authority are sup-ported in their neighbourhood schools by peripatetic teachers.

The visual impairment service
Before local government reorganisation in 1974, the area covered by this authority was part of a larger county council which had its own special school for the visually impaired. The new authority has continued to place children in that school, but the number of children concerned declined steadily as other forms of local pro-vision were introduced, until it has reached 6 of whom 4 are of secondary age.

In 1974, an "organising teacher" for the visually impaired was appointed, whose role included pre-school home visiting. She did not have a qualification in visual impairment, although she had extensive experience in the field. The development was in itself progressive at that time.

There was already a unit in a primary school which had been set up at the instigation of a consultant ophthalmologist some time in the 1960's, but the teacher in it was without specialist training. A secondary unit was established in 1974.

When the organising teacher retired, she was not immediately replaced, the work being covered by the Advisory Teacher for the physically handicapped. Consequently, despite the early start which had been made, visually impaired children in the authority were then left for a long time without specialist support other than one scale 1 peripatetic teacher and the help of the local RNIB Adviser. Eventually in 1984 a qualified advisory teacher for the visually impaired was appointed and she was replaced by the current post-holder in 1986. At this stage, the whole pace of developments changed, and the nature of provision for the visually impaired quickly took on a completely new complexion with the whole-hearted support of the local education authority.

Very soon an additional temporary appointment was made, and in 1987 a second temporary peripatetic teacher was appointed. A further permanent teacher was appointed to the junior unit, and a second unit was then also opened.

There were a number of respects in which the service, which had developed in a piecemeal way, was seen to be inadequate to identified needs. The head of service therefore put forward a strong case for a review which was taken up by the special needs adviser. This led to a Committee report and some significant changes in 1988.

The two temporary peripatetic teachers became permanent, and a teacher from the secondary unit was also transferred to the peripatetic team. The unit provision at secondary level was transferred to a different school, which had the advantage of being more centrally placed. A new permanent teacher was appointed to this unit. At the same time a nursery unit was established with a newly appointed permanent teacher for visually impaired children.

The peripatetic service, as distinct from the support staff in units, now consists of a head of service known as the County Advisory Teacher (Visual Impairment) and three peripatetic teachers. The advisory teacher is currently responsible to the senior advisory teacher for sensory services, but a new structure is being introduced for the Special Needs Suppport Team,and this is shown in table 5. It is relatively unusual to encounter such a clearly articulated structure for special needs support services.

The advisory teacher for visual impairment will therefore have a line of responsibility through the senior advisory teacher, whose own specialism is hearing impairment, to the principal advisory teacher. The Special Needs Support Team as a whole lies within the responsibility of the Adviser for special educational needs.

Educational psychologists play a prominent part in decisions about placements, and chair the placement panels. There are well-established links with the health authority staff.

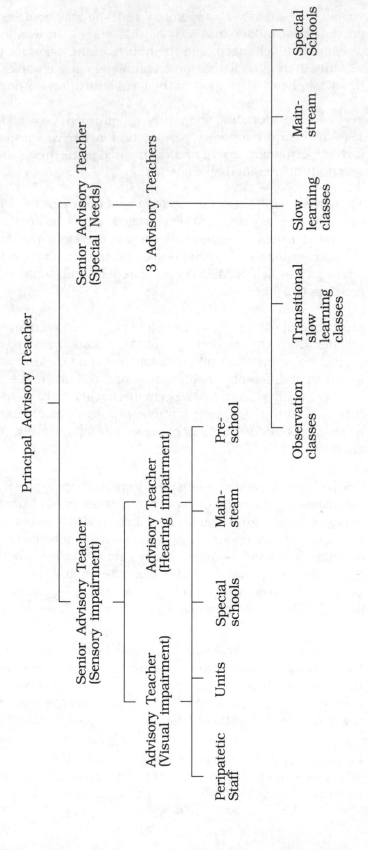

Special Needs Support Team

Principal Advisory Teacher

Senior Advisory Teacher (Sensory impairment)

Senior Advisory Teacher (Special Needs)

Advisory Teacher (Visual impairment)

Advisory Teacher (Hearing impairment)

3 Advisory Teachers

Peripatetic Staff

Units

Special schools

Special schools

Main-steam

Pre-school

Observation classes

Transitional slow learning classes

Slow learning classes

Main-stream

Special Schools

Each peripatetic teacher has a caseload covering all age-groups and all ability levels, although there is also an element of specialisation in their work. One has particular expertise in children with additional difficulties, special schools and diagnostic units. One specialises in the infant and lower junior level and also provides tuition in touch typing. The third works principally in secondary schools.

They work chiefly with children who have a substantial amount of special need arising from their visual impairment. Such children are visited once, twice or even three times a week and are either withdrawn from class if a less distractible environment is required, or supported in their class on a team-teaching basis. In a number of cases it is found that a period of individual teaching apart from the class is beneficial, because the child's visual difficulties are compounded by more general learning problems or problems over concentration. About thirty children are supported in this way. The teachers are normally expected to deal with three children in a morning and two in an afternoon, which means that, since the children are often in different schools, they work to a tight schedule.

The peripatetic staff spend Friday afternoons at the team base, dealing with administrative matters, contacts with parents and discussions with the advisory teacher.

The approach adopted means that many less severely impaired children on the register do not receive frequent visits. To compensate for this, the last two weeks of the Christmas and Summer Terms, when normal school time-tables are often disrupted, are devoted to an overall review of all children known to the service, including visits and a re-assessment of level of need where appropriate. This means that such children are kept in review, and general support is available to their teachers, even though the peripatetic staff are principally concerned with a more intensive teaching role.

This service as a whole receives regular technical support from the authority's computer centre which has two staff allocated for special educational needs. They maintain an up-to-date stock of software for visually impaired pupils, and provide training and advice for the visual impairment team and for mainstream teachers.

Mobility training is very occasionally provided by Social Services but there is no structure established for giving any form of regular service to children. However, a feasibility study on mobility provision for visually impaired children is currently under way.

Supported mainstream provision

Each of the five units in mainstream schools has a support teacher and an ancillary helper, apart from the secondary unit which now has 1.5 teachers. These staff are all appointed by central office to the visual impairment service, and are not on the staffing establishment of the host schools. The advisory teacher has management responsibility for them, although they of course work in close co-operation with the head teacher and staff of the school where they are placed.

In the nursery unit, the visually impaired children are fully integrated and the other children are not told that they are in any way different from themselves. A group of blind children attend the class in the mornings and a group of partially sighted children in the afternoons. This is a new development which seems to be working extremely well and recently a fully equipped light stimulation room was set up with joint funding from the local education authority and parent support group.

The infant unit and one junior unit were established many years ago, when the usual practice was for special units to function almost as separate entities from the schools in which they were placed. The situation now is that children are integrated for a varying proportion of the curriculum according to the level of their individual needs. However, it is of course difficult to change established working patterns in a school, and the children are still based in the unit and are not full members of mainstream classes, although social integration is encouraged.

In an attempt to provide more integration for the visually impaired pupils, an arrangement has been made in the junior units whereby some mainstream children attend the visually impaired class for some areas of the National Curriculum. With this arrangement, it is possible to concentrate the support given to the visually impaired pupils within a mainstream setting, and any possible disadvantage to the fully sighted pupils is offset by the benefits of being part of a relatively small class.

At secondary level, the intention in the newly designated unit is that pupils should have as high a level of integration as possible. They are full members of classes and support is given within mainstream classes. A small room serves as a base for the unit, and pupils are withdrawn there for special teaching when necessary. An additional room is shortly to be allocated to the service, chiefly to take account of the space required for equipment and materials and reprographic work. The head teacher and staff are very enthusiastic and positive about the unit. Though only in its second year, the staff and pupils are gaining confidence and becoming well-established.

Some of these units could cater for more pupils than they currently do, but there is sometimes considerable parental pressure for a child to remain in a neighbourhood school and he or she is then supported on a peripatetic basis, even though it might be more efficient for the child to be placed in the unit. This applies in particular to one boy in a secondary school, for whom a full-time ancillary helper has been allocated in addition to peripatetic visits. He is an able boy who is making very good progress despite severely impaired vision.

Equipment and resources
The visual impairment service has an annual capitation allowance, and in addition special application may be made for major items of equipment.

Details of equipment provided are given in table 6. This equipment is the property of the visual impairment service and remains under central control. Pupils are not provided with equipment specifically for home use, but they are allowed to take typewriters and portable computers home with them.

There is no technician with particular responsibility for visual impairment equipment, but all computer equipment is serviced by the Computer Centre, and some other items are repaired in county workshops. Otherwise manufacturers' repair services are used.

In-service training
The advisory teacher, one peripatetic teacher and the teacher in charge of one junior unit have qualifications in visual impairment. Three other members of the team are now studying for qualification by distance learning and part-time courses, and two of these will shortly have completed their training. A new initiative has been the establishment at a local university of a diploma course for teachers of visually impaired children. Two teachers from the

TABLE 6

REPROGRAPHIC EQUIPMENT

Thermoform machines	-
Binders	-
Minolta copiers	-
Braille embossers	-

COMMUNICATION AIDS

Closed circuit televisions	6
Computers (specific to VI use)	8
Vincent work station (or similar)	1
Perkins braillers	12
Electronic typewriters	19
Cassette recorders	14
Speech synthesizers	-
Talking calculators	2
Versabraille	-
Viewscan	-
Optacon	-
Braille writers	-
NEC portable computers	3
Microwriters	1

authority are currently studying at the university and are released for one day per week. The advisory teacher is involved as regional tutor on this course.

The advisory teacher provides a monthly in-service session for her staff, and there are occasionally opportunities for attendance at external day courses or the funding of a visiting speaker, funds being allocated by the adviser for special educational needs.

Termly awareness courses are available for mainstream teachers, provided by the advisory teacher with support from peripatetic staff. Attendance at outside courses is also a possibility for teachers in schools which have visually impaired pupils.

There is very little opportunity for classroom assistants to receive any training. Recently, however, a course has been initiated for nursery nurses in special needs but this was over subscribed and clearly demonstrates a need.

Pre-five provision and parental links

The Advisory Teacher makes regular home visits to the families of blind babies. She provides counselling and encourages them to use the Oregon developmental programme. The Reynell-Zinkin scales are used for assessment.

When parents are ready, they are encouraged to meet other parents, either at the team base or in the nursery unit. If appropriate the child is placed in this unit, but the authority has good nursery provision generally, and many visually impaired children attend their neighbourhood nursery school or class. In this case, the nursery staff are provided with an awareness programme on visual impairment. In addition, once a month an "opportunity group" meets at a local community centre for the nursery and pre-school children and parents. This has proved very successful.

Some parents have formed a group called VIP's (Visually Impaired Pupils Supporters). Others meet through parents' events at the mainstream schools where there are units. Parents are fully involved in all decisions about school placement and strongly expressed wishes are always respected by the LEA. The parents are invited to be present at assessments and at the termly panel meetings for statemented children.

Post-16 provision

One further education college has been designated for visually impaired students and provided with lap-top computers and closed-circuit television. No special lecturer has been appointed because of the low incidence of the need, but a peripatetic teacher visits weekly, advises staff and helps with the preparation of materials. Most visually impaired students touch type efficiently by the time they reach college.

A blind, physically handicapped girl is returning from the special school to attend a mainstream college, and will need ancillary support.

Current and future plans

A county policy decision has now been introduced that blind pupils should be educated in-county instead of attending special schools. There are currently several blind children in the pre-five age-range and this policy has come into operation and is now well established. A firm case has therefore been put forward for additional staffing and resources to meet these needs.

It has been agreed that, under the Local Management of Schools scheme, the whole visual impairment service will remain centrally funded including the staffing of the units and major items of equipment. Each school which has a unit will also receive a so-called "premises related allowance" which will provide for the additional overhead costs to the school arising from the physical presence of a unit. Furthermore, statemented children generate extra capitation for the school to cover the cost of materials and small equipment. The LMS plans are therefore well-advanced, but the implementation will obviously need to be monitored.

The team's approach to the National Curriculum is that in principle it is an entitlement for visually impaired pupils just as for others and disapplication would not be encouraged. It is, however, acknowledged that some assessment targets may not be appropriate for blind children. A booklet of guidelines on each core subject is being prepared for mainstream schools. These will suggest teaching approaches to be adopted, modifications required and materials and equipment which may be helpful. It is also being suggested that, where a child is not able to observe something directly, he or she should at least seek to understand the concept by working as a member of a group of sighted children.

In addition to this specific work undertaken by the visual impairment staff, the overall special needs team is using task analysis to tackle issues raised by the National Curriculum.

The nursery is to move into new accommodation on the site of a primary school which is a feeder school for the secondary school where the unit is placed. The authority are considering the feasibility of placing the infant and junior units on the same site as the nursery school so that the children concerned would have better social integration by being able to progress through the school system with the same peer group.

Improvements are needed in the links with the health authority, and it is hoped that this will be achieved by the recent nomination of one medical officer to take particular responsibility for visual impairment.

Comments

This is an example of an authority which has a long tradition of providing for visually impaired pupils, but the service had not evolved with changing needs because of the lack of a suitably qualified head of service. Developments since the arrival of the present advisory teacher and the support of the special needs adviser show how much can be achieved, despite the usual financial constraints, when an effective impetus is provided.

The service places considerable emphasis on giving functional integration with the help of specialist teaching where it is required, and takes the view that withdrawal from mainstream lessons is often necessary to do this. However, considerable store is also set by the importance of social integration. It is believed that, if the right level of support is given in a mainstream environment, special school placement should very rarely be required.

Notable features of this service are:

- **An LEA with a long tradition of providing units for visually impaired children.**

- **Recent significant developments in up-dating the approach to integration and increasing the size of the support service.**

- **A marked preference for integration into specially resourced schools, but tempered with an acknowledgement of the parents' right to choose neighbourhood integration.**

- **An emphasis on sustained support for the most severely impaired pupils, with peripatetic staff having a tightly structured teaching schedule.**

- **Well-developed support at the pre-five stage within the framework of the LEA's commitment to this age group.**

- **A recent policy decision that in-county provision should now be made for blind as well as partially sighted children.**

7. A Large Metropolitan District with Resource Bases

Nature of the authority
This is a large, metropolitan authority, measuring some 15 miles by 12 miles. At the time of local government reorganisation in 1974, it was constituted from a major city and a number of fairly

rural surrounding districts. These districts and also some suburbs of the city have very strong local identities and loyalties with the result that, although geographical distances are not great, parents often show a psychological resistance to children being placed in schools outside their own neighbourhood.

The city has a long cosmopolitan tradition with waves of immigrants arriving from many parts of the world at various times during the past century. There are currently a number of substantial ethnic minority communities for whom English is not the first home language.

The 5-16 population is at present slightly under 90,000 and there are some 8,000 students in the 16-19 age group. The authority has a mixture of educational patterns, some districts having a 9-13 middle school system, whilst others have 5-11 primary schools, followed by 11-18 secondary schools. Plans are under way to discontinue the middle school system and to introduce a tertiary education system. Many urban primary schools have nursery classes, but there is less nursery provision in the rural areas.

Visually impaired pupils and their placement

There are 280 pupils on the visual impairment register which represents approximately three per thousand of the school population. 77 of these, that is 27%, are in schools for severe learning difficulties.

In the authority as a whole, 2305 children have Statements of special educational need, and of these 146 are visually impaired.

The general policy in the authority is that children who are visually impaired should be integrated whenever possible, either in their neighbourhood school, or in a specially resourced mainstream school. It is, however, acknowledged that there will be some children who require special school placement, at least for part of their education.

A decade ago there were 18 children in extra-district special schools for the visually impaired. Now there are only six and all of these are of secondary age.

Resource bases have been developed in a first school, a middle school and a secondary school, all of which are within the same pyramid, with the result that, where appropriate, children may progress through these schools alongside the same peer group. It is intended that the first and middle schools will merge to form a 5-11 primary school. At present 5 primary aged and 3 secondary aged visually impaired children are placed in these schools, but numbers have at times been larger than this.

Fourteen pre-school children are being supported in their homes using the Oregon teaching materials and two other children are being educated at home because of the nature of their disabilities.

A further sixteen pupils receive substantial special support within local neighbourhood schools. In their cases, this option has been chosen for social or educational reasons or at parental request. On the whole, it is generally only educationally blind children who are considered to need placement in the specially resourced schools. The remaining children on the visual impairment register attend their neighbourhood schools and are supported by peripatetic staff.

The visual impairment service

The authority has never had a special school for visual impairment within its boundaries. Units for partially sighted pupils were introduced in the early 1970s but these did not have any teachers with specialist qualifications.

The first teacher of the visually impaired was appointed in September 1979. A base for the service was established in the primary school which had a special unit, and part-time clerical support was provided. The teacher's initial role was to investigate the level of need in mainstream schools and to begin to build up a resource base, in addition to providing advice and support to schools which had visually impaired pupils.

As is usual when a new service is introduced, an unexpectedly large number of visually impaired pupils was identified and a need for further staffing quickly became apparent. Furthermore, the families of two blind children were not prepared to agree to placement in a residential school, and it therefore became necessary to extend the concerns of the service to the educationally blind rather more quickly than might otherwise have happened.

The authority provided quite generous financial resources so that the necessary bank of equipment and materials could be built up. The room which served as the service's base rapidly became filled with equipment whilst also having to serve as an office base and a withdrawal teaching area. An early start was also made on building up a braille library.

69

The staffing establishment was increased year by year, but because of the national shortage of qualified staff it was found to be extremely difficult to fill the posts appropriately. As a result, the service functioned for a number of years with some temporary members of staff who had no specialist qualification, and with interrupted periods of service because teachers had to be granted secondment in order to obtain a qualification. Indeed, in some cases teachers who had been so seconded subsequently left the service to take up posts in other local authorities which were then introducing new services.

The position now is that the team consists of ten teachers, all of whom have both peripatetic duties and support roles in resourced schools. The service also has a nursery nurse, three ancillaries and two clerical assistants. In addition, the services of seventeen non teaching assistants and nursery nurses, on a part-time or full-time basis, are allocated to individual children via their Statement of special educational need.

All of the teachers in the team have an age range specialism. Their peripetatic role includes advice and support to teachers. The way this service is provided varies according to the level of support required by a particular child, and the frequency of visits is also very flexible. All staff also undertake some direct teaching of pupils within the mainstream classroom, and this is known as "companion teaching".

One of the members of the team is a qualified mobility officer and provides individual instruction as required. Typing instruction is provided for pupils of any age at a local college of further education.

The head of service is responsible to the Director of Special Education, and also has close links with other support services. One educational psychologist takes a specialist interest in visually impaired pupils. The authority is contiguous with two health districts and the service therefore liaises with medical officers in both of them. There are also well established links with local opthalmological services.

The service has now moved to a more spacious base in a disused school but it is likely that there will be a further move shortly.

Supported mainstream provision

The units for partially sighted children which previously existed have now altered fundamentally. With changing attitudes and now that adequate peripatetic staff are available, it is nearly always possible for partially sighted pupils to attend their neighbourhood school. By contrast, it is educationally blind children who are considered to need placement in a school that is specially resourced to cater for their needs. The three schools which housed the original units now have resource bases for those children.

The 5-9 first school currently has three special pupils who are all braille users. The base has one support teacher and two classroom assistants, but the pupils are members of mainstream classes with full social integration. The base, which is an adapted classroom, houses the extra equipment and provides for withdrawal teaching in specialist skills when required. On average the pupils are integrated for 90% of the mainstream curriculum, but the individual level of integration varies between 50% and 100%. The view is held that a relatively high level of withdrawal teaching in the early stages of a blind child's education may facilitate more successful integration as the child grows older.

The 9-13 middle school currently also has three pupils who are braille users. There is one full-time classroom assistant, and four teachers are involved in support work, but all of these also undertake peripetatic work with children in other schools, the amount of support which they give in the school varying from time to time according to need. Here again the base is housed in an adapted classroom, but the pupils are all class-based with full social integration and functional integration for an average of 90% of the time.

The 13-18 secondary school currently has only two visually impaired pupils neither of whom is a braille user. This is only because of a chance trough in the number of blind children in the authority, the school having had braille using pupils in the past. No additional teaching or ancillary support is currently provided for the two partially sighted pupils, other than peripetatic oversight.

All the teachers who work in the resource bases are on the staff of the visual impairment service, and are not appointed to individual schools. This facilitates the very flexible allocation of staffing which is a fundamental tenet of the service. When working in the resource bases, the teachers undertake some individual or small group withdrawal teaching and also "companion" teaching within mainstream classes. In addition, they help in the preparation and adaptation of teaching materials.

71

Alongside this specialist provision, one child who is a braillist attends a neighbourhood primary school at the parent's request. Two teachers each provide support for half of each morning, so the child has the equivalent of two and a half days each week of specialist teaching. A nursery nurse is present in the afternoons to help him. This is obviously a financially extravagant form of provision, and the authority is likely to review whether it can continue to respect the parent's wishes in view of the drain on resources. There is also a blind boy who attends his local secondary school, once again in accordance with his family's wishes. Since he is the only braille-using pupil of secondary age, the necessary support can be provided in that school as economically as it could have been in the resourced school.

Equipment and resources

The service has an annual capitation allowance from which it has to provide small equipment and materials and also larger equipment. All items purchased remain the property of the service and over the decade of its life it has been possible to build up a reasonable bank of equipment. Details are provided in table 7.

The service's central base and the primary school base each have a thermoform machine and binder, so that materials can be produced close to where they are needed. Servicing of technological equipment is undertaken when required by the local Teachers' Centre or the Computer Service Centre. There is no technician allocated to the service.

Pupils are provided with duplicate equipment for home use whenever this is considered appropriate to their needs. Items provided include braillers, cassette recorders and closed circuit televisions.

The service has steadily built up its own braille library, and now has almost 1,500 volumes on its shelves. The transcription work has been undertaken by a local voluntary group, two prison braille services and the RNIB. The books which are no longer needed for current use are now to be put in storage with the RNIB. The work which has been done in building up this collection means that blind pupils can readily be supplied with standard textbooks and other supporting materials in regular use, and attention can quickly be directed towards obtaining new books which come into use in schools. Copies of the books held are made available to other authorities on request.

TABLE 7

REPROGRAPHIC EQUIPMENT

Thermoform machines	2
Binders	2
Minolta copiers	1
Braille embossers	4

COMMUNICATION AIDS

Closed Circuit Televisions	9
Computers (specific to V.I. use)	4
Vincent Work Stations (or similar)	2
Perkins Braillers	24
Electronic typewriters	-
Cassette Recorders	30
Speech synthesizers	4
Talking calculators	6
Versabraille	-
Viewscan	-
Optacon	-
Braille writers	5
Braille'n'Speak	1
Concept keyboards	2
Characters reader	1

In-service training

Eight members of the team have a qualification in visual impairment and the other two teachers are studying for a qualification by distance learning. In the past five years, four members of the staff have been seconded by the authority for training. This is a measure of the importance which is attached to providing a high level of qualified teaching support to pupils.

No additional training is provided for the staff within the authority, but they are able to attend courses elsewhere as appropriate.

All members of the team contribute to inset courses for mainstream teachers in the authority. An information sheet is issued listing the areas of training which are available as follows:

> A whole school approach to the integration of visually impaired pupils.

Appropriate adaptations to the school environment.

Presentation and adaptation of curriculum materials.

Use of low vision aids from low magnification to CCTV systems. Linkage with GCSE and A-level Examination Boards for pupil concessions.

Access of visually impaired students to specific FE courses. Mobility training, with various canes, to allow access to public transport.

Teaching physical education to the visually impaired.

Educational implications of eye conditions and methods of assessing levels of visual functioning.

Communication aids for the visually impaired.

Mobility within an integrated setting.

Braille service for parents and others who would like to learn braille.

Working with children with profound and multiple learning difficulties.

Supporting visually impaired pupils in the classroom.

Tactile pictures - adapting work.

Resources for visually impaired children and how to make them (particularly for nursery nurses, school assistants, etc).

The role of the support teacher of the visually impaired.

Pre-braille skills.

Pre-school Oregon nursery work.

Working with pre-school visually impaired children using the Oregon checklist.

On the basis of this list, individual advisers, head teachers or groups of head teachers can plan, in discussion with the head of service, a training programme appropriate to their needs.

Pre-five provision and parental links
Children are referred to the service at as early an age as possible, and support is given to families in their homes, including the use of Oregon project materials.

Where possible by the age of three years the children are placed in local nursery classes where the staff are given advice on providing for their needs. In some cases additional staff time is allocated through the child's Statement of special educational need.

There is no nursery class with specialised resources at present but it is possible that when the first and middle schools merge to form a 5-11 primary school, space released in the school will enable a nursery class to be opened, and blind children would then be able to have early support in this environment.

Links with parents are well developed, staff being available at all times for face to face or telephone contacts. Families participate fully in discussions about educational placements. A parent and toddler group has been introduced to give parents the opportunity to meet each other.

Post-16 provision

Visually impaired students, including those who are educationally blind, can pursue further and higher education within the authority, and where appropriate they are supported by members of the peripetatic team. In some cases this has involved a major injection of specialised equipment and resources.

Current and future plans

Under the Local Management of Schools scheme, the visual impairment service will be centrally funded under the "Discretionary exceptions" heading. Statements of special educational need will now include an a - d classification on the basis of which a child's school will receive extra funds for an appropriate level of ancillary or nursery nurse support. The head of service is of the view that a team of nursery nurses and non-teaching assistants should be a full-time part of the service rather than being allocated to individual children on the basis of Statements from a central pool. This would give greater scope for such staff to develop specific skills relating to visual impairment, and the matter is under discussion.

A policy statement has been made that children with sensory handicaps are entitled to experience normally the full range of the National Curriculum, and the relevant support services will ensure that any necessary measures are taken so that they may have access to it.

It is proposed that an independence training centre should be introduced at post 16 level, which could make resources available for educational and general public use.

Comments

This is a large service with a relatively long history in the field of integration. It has the advantage that a large population is concentrated in a small geographical area, but even here the low incidence of the handicap means that the needs of various age

75

groups differ sharply from one year to another. This situation is handled by using available staff in a very flexible way, and inter-weaving the functions of "peripatetic teacher" and "support teacher" which in most authorities are kept quite distinct. At the same time the number of staff involved enables specialist teaching roles to be developed.

Notable features of the service are:

- **A large team of staff all of whom have or are obtaining a qualification in visual impairment.**

- **A marked change of philosophy, with traditional units for partially sighted pupils being transformed into resource bases for the educationally blind.**

- **The early introduction of the integration of blind children, and the building up of a substantial braille library.**

- **The practice of all staff having a dual role as peripatetic and support teachers, either concurrently or consecutively.**

- **A highly structured programme of inset on offer to mainstream schools.**

8. A County Service Evolved from a Special School

Nature of the local authority
This is a shire county which has several major conurbations, but also extensive rural areas. The road distance from one extremity to the other varies between approximately 40 and 45 miles, and the county town is centrally situated. The 5-16 population is in the region of 135,000 including a significant proportion of ethnic minority children.

The county has a range of different types of educational organisa-tion, including 5-11 primary schools feeding into 11-16 or 11-18 secondary schools, and a three-tier system with 10-14 middle schools, feeding into 14-16 or 14-18 secondary schools. Some of the secondary schools are designated as Community Colleges.

Visually impaired pupils and their placement

There are 243 pupils on the LEA's visual impairment register, which means that 1.8 children per thousand of the 5-16 population are recorded as being visually impaired. Of these, 42% are in special schools because of other special needs, the vast majority of these having severe learning difficulties.

Until recently, the LEA had its own day special school for the visually impaired. Some ten years ago, there were 45 pupils in this school and 16 in out-county special schools. In 1987 a decision was made to close the LEA's special school and to replace it by resource bases in mainstream schools. Of nine pupils currently in out-county special schools, five were placed there at parental request when the authority's special school closed. Out-county schools are still an option if this is the parents' wish or because of exceptionally complex special needs, but it is expected that such placement will rarely be necessary in the future.

The main provision for pupils with severely impaired vision is now in three resource bases, of which two are in primary schools and one in a secondary school. Currently 37 children are placed at these schools.

One blind pupil is being supported in her local school rather than in a resourced school because of the travelling distance which would be involved. She initially attended both her local primary school and the special school on a 50/50 split basis before being placed full-time in the primary school at the age of 9 years. She has now moved on to the middle school. The vast majority of less severely visually impaired pupils attend their neighbourhood school and are supported by peripatetic teachers according to their level of need.

At pre-school level, pupils may attend a nursery class if their neighbourhood primary school has one, and those with substantial special needs may attend the nursery classes in the resourced primary schools.

At further education level, peripatetic support is available, and a growing number of visually impaired students are now maintaining successful placement on college courses.

The visual impairment service

A peripatetic service was set up in 1983, one teacher being appointed to work from the special school of which the head teacher was designated head of service. The teacher had responsibility for visually impaired children over the full 2-19 age-range.

A second peripatetic teacher was appointed in 1985, and was also based in the special school. The two teachers then each covered the full age-range in half the county. In 1986 a third teacher joined the team with responsibility for secondary schools and further education colleges throughout the county. A fourth was appointed in 1987. Three teachers now cover the 3 LEA administrative areas, working mainly with children aged 0-12. The fourth continues to have responsibility for secondary schools and FE colleges throughout the county. Two support teachers from resource bases each also undertake half a day a week of peripatetic work. The head of service is responsible to an Assistant Education Officer and leads the full team which includes both peripatetic staff and all the support staff working in resource bases. He also carries a half-load of advisory and teaching responsibility.

The peripatetic staff are concerned principally with the identification and assessment of the needs of visually impaired children and the consequent design and implementation of individual learning programmes. In addition to providing general assistance in the supervision and general management of all visually impaired children within county and having an active involvement in an expanding in-service training programme to meet the needs of teaching and non-teaching staff working with visually impaired children in schools and colleges, the responsibilities of the peripatetic support staff are broadly divided into the following three main areas:

- Support for children of pre-school age in the home and in pre-school placements. This includes working with all professionals who may be concerned with the child.

- Support for children of school age placed in mainstream or special schools or units. The aim is to enhance the classroom skills of teachers involved with visually impaired children, to provide specific advice on resources, teaching styles, teaching methods and the implications of visual impairment. In certain circumstances, the actual teaching of a severely impaired pupil may be undertaken.

- Support for students attending county-based and national colleges of further education. This includes advisory and actual teaching support.

The service has well-established links with other support services for pupils with special educational needs. The Head of Service is a member of the Advisory and Inspection team. An educational psychologist is assigned to work on a part-time basis with children attending base schools and she visits regularly. Close links are maintained with medical officers working within the area health service and with ophthalmologists, and they provide a prompt service in response to referrals. Feedback from ophthalmic examinations is very good. In return medical personnel receive copies of all educational reports from the visual impairment team.

There is also good contact with heads of other support services. The adviser for special educational needs takes a close interest in the work of the peripatetic service, and has visited the resource base schools and the team base to meet staff and offer advice and support. The level of interest shown has been of considerable benefit to the developing service.

Supported mainstream provision

This service is characterised by a very well resourced support scheme in three mainstream schools. When the special school closed, its human and material resources were transferred to these three schools, together with most of the special school pupils. Each facility was originally resourced to make provision for up to twelve pupils. However, there has been an increased demand for places within the host mainstream schools which has necessitated an enhancement of the level of supportive provision.

One primary school has twelve visually impaired pupils supported by two teachers, a nursery nurse and three part-time ancillary workers who provide 85 hours a week between them. The school is open-plan with the year groups working on a team-teaching basis. Each member of the staff team is "class tutor" to a group of pupils, but they all work in the same year-group room. One of the support teachers for the visually impaired is a member of a year team and has a class group composed of visually impaired and fully sighted pupils. The pupils are fully integrated members of the school. A small, centrally placed room serves as a base for the storage of equipment and individualised teaching when required. When the resource base was set up, the school had opened only recently, and did not yet have its full complement of pupils. This undoubtedly helped the staff to adopt a forward-looking approach to their work with visually impaired pupils.

The other primary school also has twelve pupils who are supported by two teachers, a nursery nurse and a full-time ancillary. This is a more traditional school with separate infant and junior buildings, the resource base being in the junior building. In each primary school, the pupils are integrated for approximately 85% of the curriculum.

Ancillary help is provided where required for integrated pupils. The staff are funded by a central LEA scheme, but specific guidelines are issued relative to the needs of visually impaired pupils. These guidelines state that the aim of providing ancillary help is to enable the pupil to benefit from the mainstream curriculum, to ensure his/her safety, and to minimise the difficulties placed on pupil and teachers, but without creating an atmosphere of handicap or dependence. The range of classroom activities where help may be appropriate is specified, and suggestions are made about the preparation of materials and adaptations to the environment. The ancillary therefore has a clearly defined role set out in a written document.

At secondary level, fourteen pupils are placed in a Community College which has a firm philosophy of social integration, and had previously had experience of physically handicapped pupils. There are five specialist teachers, one of whom is designated teacher-in-charge, and some additional part-time teaching help. The service also has an ancillary and a resource technician who, though based in the secondary school, works on behalf of the whole service.

The teachers all support pupils over a range of subjects, but each is also linked to a particular faculty. Each one attends the appropriate faculty meetings and is the first point of contact for mainstream staff in planning and adapting work for the visually impaired pupils. In some cases the teachers are working in faculties which were previously their own teaching specialism, but in other instances they have had to learn about the subject area from contact with their new colleagues. There is no suggestion that they become fully competent to teach that subject but they quite readily acquire sufficient knowledge and experience to be able to support the pupils in the classroom and to know when to seek the intervention of the subject teacher who continues to have overall responsibility for the pupils' work in that area. This means that a specialist teacher has, or is developing skills and understanding in each of the main subject areas studied by pupils, and can therefore give informed help to both teachers and pupils both inside and outside the classroom. In practical subjects in particular these teachers work with the pupils on the basis of a good grasp of what the class teacher is seeking to achieve, and with the confidence of knowing that they can turn to that teacher for help if needed. They also often support pupils other than the visually impaired ones, which in some measure compensates for the extra demands which are being placed on the teachers.

The pupils have full social integration into the life of the school, including participation in extra-curricular activities. Where necessary, they are withdrawn from the mainstream curriculum for specialist teaching on an individual or small group basis, but individual pupils are integrated for between 75% and 100% of the curriculum, the average being 87%.

In the three resource bases taken together, seven pupils are braille users. Nine have additional special needs, including hearing, physical, speech and language impairments. The maximum distance travelled to attend a resourced school is 20 miles. The blind girl who attends her local school is supported by a full-time teacher, and is integrated for approximately 90% of the curriculum. Another educationally blind child is on the role of one of the bases but attends her local primary school for one day a week, for half of which she has peripatic teacher support. She enjoys 100% integration in both schools.

All the support staff involved are members of the Visual Impairment Service team, but administrative responsibility for the work is shared jointly by the Head of Service, the Head Teachers and the Governing Bodies of the schools.

Equipment and resources
This authority has a good stock of material resources, much of which was inherited from the special school. Details are given table 8.

All the equipment is the property of the visual impairment service. In addition to a central capitation for the service, each resource base receives special funding equivalent to two and a half times the standard capitation, and this is currently administered by the head teacher. With the coming of the Local Management of Schools, a new system is being introduced under which a lump sum will be allocated to the head of service for redistribution as appropriate. Pupils are being provided with equipment for use at home, including CCTV, typewriters, Viewscan and Perkins braillers. Insurance cover is provided by the LEA, but parents have to give a written assurance that the equipment will not be misused or abused.

81

TABLE 8

REPROGRAPHIC EQUIPMENT

Thermoform machines	3
Binders	2
Minolta copiers	-
Braille embosser	1

COMMUNICATION AIDS

Closed circuit televisions	29
Computers (specific to VI use)	9
Vincent Work Stations (or similar)	4
Perkins braillers	25
Electronic typewriters	17
Cassette recorders	20
Speech synthesizers	4
Talking calculators	6
Versabraille	1
Viewscan	1
Optacon	1
Lap-top computer	1
Braille writers	5
Braille labelling machine	1

In-service training

Only three of the peripatetic staff had a qualification in visual impairment at the time of their appointment, but there has been a regular programme of secondment for training, and now all the members of the peripatetic team and all but four of the support teachers are qualified. Since 1983, three qualified members of staff have left for posts in other authorities. Progress towards a fully qualified staff has therefore been impeded by the national shortage which means that staff, once they become qualified, tend to be in high demand.

Funding is made available which enables team members to undertake the equivalent of 1.5 days per term in-service training which may possibly be provided out-of-county, for instance on RNIB courses. The whole team also meet together for service-focussed training on the professional development/training days set aside for teaching staff.

The service team has a role in the provision of in-service training for mainstream teachers. Some of this is conducted informally by day-to-day contact. In addition, five INSET county days are provided annually. Two of these are for primary teachers, two for secondary and one for special schools. The attendance at each is generally about 35.

There is also financial provision for nursery nurses to receive in-service training through attendance at courses, but unfortunately these funds cannot be used for the training of ancillary workers. The head of service strives to overcome this problem by providing "mini-workshops" for such workers in the base schools during the working day.

It can thus be seen that there is an acknowledged commitment to in-service training and an established structure for its implementation.

Pre-five provision and parental links

Peripatetic staff work closely with parents at the pre-school stage aiming in particular to encourage them to participate in the developmental programme recommended for their child. The parents are consulted about school placement, and every effort is made to work in co-operation with them. Each month a meeting is held in a toy library for parents and pre-school children. Social events and outings are arranged by this group. Parents of newly referred visually impaired children are put in contact with others as appropriate.

Current and future plans

It is envisaged that support staff currently working in resourced schools will develop an outreach role so that they may support certain children placed in other schools who require more regular help than can be provided by the peripatetic staff. This will increase the flexibility in the use of staff time, and may lead to an increase in the number of staff based in the resourced schools.

Two of these schools have been pilot schools for the Local Management of Schools scheme. However, a longer term decision about how the visual impairment service should be funded has yet to be made. The three possibilities are that the whole service should be centrally funded; the peripatetic service should be central, but funds allocated to schools for the resource bases; or that all support should be bought in by individual schools. In the first case, Statements could allocate appropriate funds to each school, but the main concern would then be for children who did not have a Statement but still needed support. The head of service feels that central funding for the whole service would be most satisfactory, with the possible exceptions of in-service training and initial assessments.

A series of full-day and half-day courses on the National Curriculum have been held. These have brought together all members of the visual impairment service, in some cases in combination with mainstream staff. These groups have looked at possible modifications to the curriculum, but have held to the view that exclusion from any element would be inappropriate. Areas have been identified in the three core subjects of English, Maths and Science which may give rise to difficulties, and lists of hints, suggestions and guidelines have been drawn up. These are being presented as booklets which will in due course be made available to mainstream schools. In this work, the visual impairment staff are working closely with the designated educational psychologist.

Comments

This authority has a clear integrationist philosophy, with emphasis being placed on the need to provide visually impaired pupils with high quality specialist teaching appropriate to their needs whilst giving them access to mainstream education. The experience and resources of the special school are being put to good effect, and provide a firm foundation for the future growth of the service. Attitudes among the former special school staff and mainstream staff are supportive,and the teething problems of the change of structure seem to have been tackled sensitively and without conflict.

Notable features of the service are:

- **A high level of resourcing of bases in mainstream schools, made possible by the closure of the special school.**

- **The concept of secondary school support teachers developing subject specialisms.**

- **The high level of technological equipment provided.**

- **The significant role allocated to in-service training.**

- **The provision of specific guidelines on the role to be undertaken by ancillary workers.**

- **A clearly articulated role for peripatetic staff, with the emphasis on assessment and the design of learning programmes.**

Section II : Studies of individual children and young people

Individual Studies

These studies describe the educational experience of a range of children and young people who are visually impaired. The first few concern young children who are still in the early stages of their development, and we then move on to older children who, of course, began their schooling when services were, in many places, less developed than they are to-day.

1. Robert S. aged 5

Robert is a five year old blind boy with only some light perception in one eye. He attends a primary school which is experienced in providing for nursery aged children with special needs, and he will shortly transfer to his neighbourhood primary school. He experienced some developmental delays in his early years, but appears now to be of average ability.

At birth, Robert's left eye was unformed and he had a malformation of the right eye. He was first seen by an ophthalmologist at six weeks and he has attended Moorfield hospital since the age of three months. An operation was performed on his right eye, but it is thought that he has never had more than limited light perception. He has a prosthesis in the left eye.

The Early Years

Mrs S. does not recall receiving any advice in the early stages about how to help her child in his development. He is the elder of two boys and she therefore had no previous experience of a baby to provide a point of comparison. Robert was a happy baby and became toilet-trained quickly.

When he was two years old, he was placed in the nursery class of an assessment centre for children with special needs, most of whom were showing severe developmental delay. Initially he attended for one day a week and also spent some sessions in a local playgroup. However, this was changed to full-time attendance at the assessment centre when he was three years old. At this point it became apparent that there was some cause for concern. He was mimicking the behaviour of less mature children and becoming aggressive towards others. He would frequently sit in a corner rocking, and he was echolalic. His mother thought that the repetition of language showed that he was learning, and did not know that this behaviour was no longer appropriate to his age.

On the other hand, a professional opinion was being formed that the child had complex difficulties.

When Robert was three and a half the paediatrician asked a recently appointed advisory teacher of the visually impaired to see him. She took the view that there were signs of normal development, and that he was being held back by not receiving the developmental stimuli which are necessary to compensate for blindness. In co-operation with his family and using the Oregon Project materials, she began an intensive programme of work with Robert directed particularly towards language and concept development. This was an uphill struggle, and it was nearly six months before Robert made the first breakthrough and began to use language meaningfully. From that point progress has been maintained. However, it is a sobering thought that, without this teacher who persevered on the basis of her intuitive assessment of the child, he might have remained in an environment of severely delayed children. Moreover, had she in fact been proved to be wrong in her "hunch," she might well have been criticized for spending a disproportionate amount of time on the child during those months. She was therefore taking something of a professional risk in following her hunch.

School placement

In order to extend his experience of normal language, Robert was placed in the nursery class of a mainstream school for five mornings a week, and the peripatetic teacher worked with him in the afternoons. A school was chosen which is at some distance from his home, because it already received other nursery children with special needs and was therefore experienced in catering for them. Robert was not however placed in the special group.

Once Robert began to make progress, the echolalia ceased and, although for some time he tended to use irrelevant language, this was gradually eradicated. His mobility improved and he was soon moving about with confidence both in the classroom and in the playground where, amongst other activities, he was riding on individual large-wheeled toys alongside his peers. He had become a happily integrated member of the class, relating well to adults and children.

From the age of four and a half, he attended the nursery full-time with full-time ancillary support. This is provided by someone who had already known him at his playgroup and who also serves as the taxi escort for his journey to school. In the following term he joined the reception class of the school for part of the day whilst remaining in the nursery for the remainder of the time. This arrangement is giving him the opportunity to fill any remaining gaps in his early learning experiences whilst also making a start on his more formal education.

Basic skill development

Robert now has clear speech and a good vocabulary. He readily initiates a conversation when introduced to a visitor, and quite confidently took me on a tour of the classroom. Indeed he set about organising the provision of a cup of tea, saying firmly: "You stay there!" while he went in search of a cup. He does however tend to chatter along his own line of thought rather than responding to a question.

His scope for spontaneous learning by imitation is obviously limited by his blindness, and his ancillary worker therefore structures his learning experiences very tightly. In these one-to-one teaching situations he concentrates well and is able to work for up to half an hour. In freer activities, he is well motivated, can make his own decisions about what he wishes to do and asks for toys or equipment which he cannot find for himself. He plays imaginatively with table top toys, play dough and in the house corner.

Robert's tactile and fine motor skills are developing well. He can balance up to five bricks, build with construction bricks, post shapes into a sorting-box, thread large buttons and screw and unscrew nuts and bolts. He can hold a pencil correctly and use a paint brush. He can cut with scissors if they have been guided to the edge of the paper. He is now being given individual teaching in pre-braille skills for about 10% of his curriculum time. In view of his earlier difficulties, his advisory teacher would see possible dangers in introducing him too early to more formal work, and it is likely that he will not actually begin to learn braille until he is six years old. In advance of that, however, increasing emphasis is being placed on tactile discrimination and fine motor skills.

With regard to cognitive development, he is learning to classify shapes and to understand comparison of size and shape, and he has started on basic number work.

He already has quite good self-help skills. He uses the toilet without assistance and washes his hands. He eats with a spoon and fork and drinks from a cup. He can undress himself, and hang his coat on a peg, but he sometimes needs a little help with dressing. There is a slight abnormality in his gait, and he may need a shoe building up to counteract this. He has good auditory skills for location and discrimination, and he is being given an initial introduction to orientation skills. Since the advisory teacher is qualified in mobility, he will be able to move on to pre-cane skills as part of his regular training as soon as he is ready for this.

Robert is beginning to talk to his peers and to relate to them in play activities. They know that he cannot see, and some of them are quite attentive to his needs without fussing over-much. He is out-going and friendly with a good sense of humour, and other children respond to this warmth of personality. At home, he has a happy, relaxed relationship with his younger brother. He also has some contact with two partially sighted children who live in his village.

He is showing some interest in music. The authority has an advisory teacher for music who will arrange for him to have instrumental tuition if this seems appropriate.

Current and future plans
Robert is theoretically working in the age-group below his own. However, since he was born on 31 August, it is obviously far more appropriate that he should be one year behind, and he is in fact close to the chronological age of others in his class. Although he was initially placed in a school which was experienced in special needs, it is not the long-term plan that he should remain there. His parents would like him to attend his neighbourhood village school, and the move is likely to be made within the next six months. His ancillary worker will transfer with him, which will provide continuity, and the staff of his new school are receiving preparatory training.

In view of Robert's earlier developmental delay, it is considered important that he should be allowed to progress at his own pace without undue haste. Initially he will certainly need full-time ancillary help to provide extra basic skills and to ensure his safety in the environment. The amount of support may be reduced later if appropriate. He will of course also continue to require regular visits from the advisory teacher , who will organise the provision of specialist equipment as this becomes necessary in addition to providing teaching in braille and mobility and overseeing his general progress.

In his new school, Robert will have full social integration and will be integrated for lessons whenever individual tuition is not needed. It is now expected that the mainstream curriculum will be appropriate to his needs. He is a strong-willed child who is likely to make the most of his abilities despite the handicap of blindness.

2. Emma G. aged 5

Emma, who is five and a half years old, is blind. She attends her neighbourhood infants school where she is a full member of the middle class and is also supported by a peripatetic teacher. Her educational progress is at present uneven, but she appears to be of good average ability.

Emma's blindness was caused by retinopathy of prematurity followed by infantile glaucoma. She therefore has no memory of having any sight. She wears a shell in one eye and is also totally blind in the other eye.

Emma is tall for her age and sturdily built, though not plump. She is an attractive child with half-open eyes, full cheeks and neatly styled, light brown hair. She gives the impression of being alert and thoughtful, and is very ready to chatter.

The early years
Emma's parents have made considerable efforts to give her as wide a range of educational experiences as possible. From the age of eighteen months, she attended an Opportunity Centre on three mornings a week, initially in the company of her mother and then travelling by taxi. Four of the 18 children attending this centre had either a sensory, physical or mental handicap. This experience made a useful contribution to her early development, but her parents wanted her to have contact with a more normal environment, so from the age of three years she also joined a local playgroup.

It is important to note that, at this stage, the LEA did not have a visual impairment service. Emma was seen by an educational psychologist who had had no training in visual impairment, and the parents were told that she was likely to be mentally handicapped. Mr and Mrs G. were convinced that this was not so, since her behaviour in many respects seemed to be similar to that of their older children at that age. They thought very carefully about the education they wanted for her, and visited special schools where they were particularly impressed by the confidence and freedom of movement of the children. They decided, however, that they would like Emma to attend a mainstream school at least for the early stages of her education. When the case was transferred to a psychologist who had experience of visual impairment, it was decided that integration should be attempted.

School placement

This decision was considered to be a feasible option because a service for the visually impaired was at that point about to be established in the authority. The first advisory teacher took up her post in the September as Emma entered the reception class of the infants school. Since the child has a spring birthday, she was in fact under four and a half years old at that point and therefore a young member of the reception class.

It must be said that the integration project did not get off to a very good start. The advisory teacher had not been in post long enough to be closely involved in the preparatory stages, but the school had been prepared for Emma's entry by an educational psychologist who was a qualified teacher of the visually impaired. There were many natural anxieties amongst the staff, and these were reinforced when Emma found difficulty in adapting to the change of environment, reverting to immature behaviour patterns such as toileting problems. The staff had never previously encountered this problem and were therefore very concerned. They asked her mother to keep her at home for a day while they decided how to tackle the problem, and the parents thought she was being rejected by the school which upset them very much. However, advice was given to both parents and school on how to handle accidents calmly and without any suggestion of criticism to Emma, and the problem soon disappeared.

The peripatetic teacher worked very hard to support the school, and towards the middle of the first term the whole staff attended an in-service training day provided for the authority by the RNIB. This had been planned during the summer, and a considered decision had been made that the training for the staff of two schools which were admitting blind children should be held after they had had a few weeks' contact with the children. It was felt that, when they had some understanding of the issues, the training would be more profitable, and overall this was shown to be so.

The reception class teacher took a great deal of interest in Emma throughout the first year and was delighted with the progress she saw her making in the group. From the start the advisory teacher visited the school on four mornings a week and withdrew Emma for a weekly total of five hours of individual teaching on each occasion. Since Emma had not previously had any specialised teaching, she needed to be taken through a range of early learning experiences such as matching and sorting, whilst steadily developing her auditory and tactile senses. At first she had difficulty in concentrating on a task, but the steady, regular tuition gradually produced results.

During the first year, a physiotherapist visited the school regularly and suggested exercises which would help to strengthen Emma's muscles and improve her posture and movement.

In addition to this supplementary help, a full-time nursery nurse was appointed to support Emma. She sometimes withdrew her from class to carry out work recommended by the physiotherapist or advisory teacher, but worked chiefly alongside the teacher. Emma therefore normally spent part of the morning and the whole of the afternoon amidst her peer group and followed as far as possible the same range of activities.

This pattern of work is continuing in her second year at the school. There was a slight hiccough at the start of the year, since the new class teacher left the school quite unexpectedly. Another teacher took over the class at extremely short notice, being in fact appointed on a Sunday to start work the following day! This would be daunting enough without the special factor of having a blind child in the class. This teacher has, however, responded very positively to the challenge and is quickly learning to cater for Emma's needs.

Basic skill development

Emma is brought to school by her mother, but leaves her at the gate, crosses the playground and meets the nursery nurse in the classroom. This element of independence was at her own request because other children were being encouraged to come in alone, and she did not want to be different. She is developing very good mobility skills in school and in the playground. She trails along walls and table edges and remembers where furniture is placed. Her mother says that in unfamiliar houses she asks where the kitchen is and then uses it as a focal point to recall the location of other rooms. She carries her head bent forward and her gait is not well-balanced, but the staff are working on this and she is making progress.

On the day of my visit, Emma was told that "Dr Dawkins" had come to see her and, after hearing my voice which is fairly deep, she said: "Are you a man doctor or a lady doctor?" Only a few months before, she did not even realise there was a difference between boys and girls. She talks fluently and with a very good command of language for her age. She tends to ask irrelevant questions in class and to want to stand near the teacher rather than remaining in her place, but this is of course only because she is seeking information and contact which others obtain through their eyes. For instance, she interrupted the teacher to ask: "Is Elizabeth back today? Where is she sitting?" This is far healthier than if she were to remain passive. She is quite easily distracted from her work. While she was doing an exercise, I turned the page on which I was making notes and she immediately said: "Are you reading a magazine?" She has to be kept on task, but her alertness to her surroundings must be encouraged. The teacher's approach at present is that, if she asks a question, she must be made to listen carefully to the answer and then get on with her work.

Emma is very musical. She learns tunes quickly, sings well and really enjoys music and movement lessons. She has keen hearing and auditory discrimination.

Literacy and numeracy

She therefore presents as a child of good general ability. However she is not as yet making very good progress in braille or number work. She does not seem to have fully grasped what writing is all about and she still needs a great deal of basic work in phonics. Her advisory teacher is concentrating on pre-braille and early braille activities. She is able to track the braille quite competently and to identify gaps or sudden irregularities in a line of braille symbols. She therefore has the necessary sensitivity in her fingers, and she shows good fine motor skills including page-turning and the use of a pincer movement with pegs. She is also beginning to match individual braille letters. She indeed seems to be on the brink of breaking through to an understanding of written language, and the teacher's patient perseverance will doubtless soon produce rewards. Emma is, after all, barely five and a half years old.

She is also having difficulty with basic number concepts. She can count readily enough, and distinguishes faultlessly between one and two, but can still not confidently distinguish between two objects and three objects. The problem is that she uses her fingers very competently to explore everything with close attention, but this means that by the time she has completed her examination of the third of three identical items, she has forgotten about the first! This highlights the difficulties which a blind child faces in basic learning compared to those of a sighted child who has all the objects constantly in view.

The head of the school is rather concerned about this slow development of literacy and numeracy skills. However, it is probable that Emma's difficulties are directly related to the situation of being blind from birth. Certainly, some blind children do make earlier progress in these areas, but in other aspects of educational development Emma is showing at least age-related progress, and her specialist teacher believes that she will be able to follow the normal curriculum. For instance, her present class teacher is finding that the national curriculum work in science is particularly suited to her. The work they have done includes feeling the difference between wet and dry objects, such as paper; tearing different types of materials; melting chocolate. Many of the experiments are thus tactile by nature and Emma is in some cases more adept than sighted children.

Social development

Emma is in a relatively small class of 23 children. Her classmates have quickly learnt how to behave towards her. They do not fuss over her too much, and one or two are particularly perceptive and kind in giving help when it is required. She clearly enjoys their company and talks about her friends,and they are undoubtedly benefiting from the experience.

She is becoming competent in self-care skills at home and in school. She goes to the toilet alone and washes her hands, dresses and undresses and can put in and take out her shell. She eats very competently with a spoon and fork. Friends invite her to their birthday parties. At first her mother accompanied her, but now her behaviour is so competent and mature that other parents are happy for her to go alone, and she receives many invitations. One mother reported delightedly that she was the only guest who said: "May I be excused from table?"

Mrs G. takes Emma swimming once a week, and she now swims quite well with arm-bands. She uses roller skates around the house and garden which encourages free movement. She has also been hill-walking with her father and has covered appreciable distances without needing to hold hands. She goes to Sunday School and sings lustily with the other children. When she is a little older, she will probably join a Brownie pack.

When Emma was a baby, her parents felt very alone with their problem and things were not easy for them. They had some differences of opinion with officials and felt somewhat vulnerable. Just after she started school, they attended a family week-end organised by RNIB and they found this very helpful. Emma and her elder brother joined in activities with other blind integrated children and their siblings, whilst the parents were provided with some formal sessions as well as opportunities to talk to each other. Mr and Mrs G. both feel that there is a real need for this type of opportunity, and they have indeed remained in contact with some of the other families.

Current and future plans

Her parents would like to see Emma progress through the mainstream for the whole of her education, but they are keeping an open mind and would be prepared to consider special school at a later stage, if this should be deemed necessary. It is likely that she will repeat her second year in the infants school rather than moving up to the third year. She will need this extra time to establish her basic skills, and since she is quite young in the age-group this should not present any social problems. Unfortunately, the class which she will then join is larger, and already contains another pupil who has substantial special needs, but as the school has only one class for each age-group, there is no way of avoiding this situation. Since both special children will have a nursery nurse, it is hoped that the difficulties will be resolved. Furthermore, the appointment of an additional teacher to the LEA's visual impairment service means that Emma will be able to have a specialist teaching session on five days a week instead of four as at present.

Emma's early path in the world of education has not been entirely smooth and it is difficult to predict the future with confidence. Her advisory teacher, who has had many years' experience of teaching in a special school, says that she has "a gut feeling" that Emma is making better progress than she would have done in special education. Certainly she is a well-adjusted little girl, with an outgoing personality and a streak of self-will which will be to her advantage if well-directed. If she can break through her early skills difficulties and learn to concentrate on the task in hand instead of being distracted by everything around her, she should soon be making very good progress.

3. Helen I. aged 6

Helen is a six year old girl who is totally blind. She lives in a village and attends the small Church of England Aided Primary School, where she has just moved up into the middle class. She is fully integrated and is of above average academic ability.

Helen was born three months prematurely, and had had a twin who was still-born. When she was five months old, her parents were concerned that she was not smiling, showed apparent nystagmus and did not seem to be responding to visual stimuli. When they were referred to an ophthalmologist, she was found to be completely blind. The cause was retinopathy of prematurity, and she does not even have any light perception. She is therefore one of the very rare people who have never had any sight at all and for whom visual concepts are meaningless. She has recently had one eye removed because of an inflammatory condition, and will shortly be fitted with a prosthesis.

Helen is an alert, friendly little girl who readily seeks information about what is going on around her. She is a neat, attractive child, prettily dressed and with good posture.

The early years
Mr and Mrs I. had found Helen to be a very difficult baby to manage. They had many sleepless nights because she was experiencing "day/night reversal," but of course at the time the reason for this was not known. She also strongly disliked being picked up and cuddled, which is a typical trait of blind babies, but caused distress to her parents. Mr and Mrs I. have two sons, one older and one younger than Helen. At the time of her birth, the older one was only eleven months old, and in the first few years he reacted badly to the extra attention which was given to his sister. This problem,

combined with the traumatic events of Helen's birth and the lost baby, made the first years of her life into a domestically stressful time.

When her condition was diagnosed, there was no referral to the education service or any specialised agency. The family were given the opportunity to attend a child development centre in a neighbouring town, but the other babies there were multiply or profoundly handicapped, and Mrs I. just felt out of place and upset. There was apparently no member of staff at the centre with any expertise in visual impairment. Mr and Mrs I. therefore had no idea where to turn for help. They went to the public library and found something concerning the "In Touch" radio programme. Through this they were referred to RNIB, one of whose education advisers then visited the family regularly until the case was passed on to the LEA peripatetic service. They therefore received skilled guidance from the early stages of Helen's development, but only because they themselves took the initiative in a field which was totally unknown to them. They also themselves made the move to have her registered blind, but the social worker who then came to see them was not used to working with children, and just said they should apply for anything they needed, such as a guard on the bath.

Helen seems to have moved through the early developmental milestones at a fairly normal rate. She rolled on the floor a great deal before beginning to crawl at about eleven months, and she then headed for open doors, apparently because she felt the change in air currents. She enjoyed movement and began walking only a little later than her brother had done, and initially using a "toddle truck." She was rather slow at toilet-training, but so also were her brothers. There do not seem to have been any problems with early language development.

From the age of two and a half, Helen attended the village playgroup with her brother, usually once a week. This was a voluntary group and Mrs I. always remained on duty with other mothers when her children were there. She would not have thought it reasonable to expect others to take responsibility for a blind child at that stage.

Arrangements were made for Mr and Mrs I. to visit the residential special school which it was assumed Helen would attend. They were very impressed with the school, and they found it particularly helpful at that stage to see older blind children, and to discover what sort of things their daughter might be able to do in the future. Mrs I. feels that parents of blind children really do need that opportunity to look into the future.

School placement

Despite their positive impressions from the visit, Helen's parents were very reluctant for her to go to a residential school, and were also worried about the week-end journeys by taxi with a driver unknown to them and on a busy motorway. Although they had no firm views about integration, they eventually decided, again on their own initiative, to invite the newly appointed head teacher of the village school to visit their home and meet Helen. He was immediately very interested in her and excited at the prospect of being able to have her in his school. This positive response gave the parents confidence to press their case for integration. The LEA and school governors agreed to their request, and arranged to participate in the RNIB Integration Support Scheme which helps to monitor such placements and contributes to staff training and the provision of equipment.

Helen entered the village school before her fifth birthday, along with peers who attended the same playgroup. A full-time non-teaching assistant was allocated to the school, and they were fortunate in obtaining the services of a braille teacher for ten hours a week. These staff work under the guidance of one of the LEA's advisory teachers for visual impairment who visits the school periodically.

In such a small school, there is a wider age-range than usual in each class and children work at their own pace. There is therefore no difficulty about Helen receiving her braille tuition and other special skill teaching within the classroom where her peers are working. Apart from this, she has always taken a full part in all class activities, from which she is withdrawn for not more than an hour a week for special quiet work. After four terms in the infant class, she was one of a group of seven children who were promoted to the middle class where she is now amongst the youngest.

The new class has two teachers with a "job share" post, who each work for half of the week. Shortly after Helen's change of class, the advisory teacher planned to spend a full week at the school in order to advise the new teachers, one of whom is a probationer, and to iron out any initial problems which may arise. One of these is that the new classroom presents an acoustics problem, and the possibility of improvements being made is under discussion.

Literacy and numeracy

Helen had been given excellent pre-braille training before entering school, and she has made rapid progress with learning braille. She has a full command of all forty-four upper signs, most lower signs and a good part of the dot 5 alphabet plus all of the simpler abbreviations. She uses her Perkins brailler fluently and is aware of the different dot patterns for compound signs, but she does not yet write double letter signs in the middle of a word, inverted commas or more complicated punctuation. She has excellent phonic skills, so that she can make herself understood on paper even when she is unsure of spelling. For instance, she wrote "treasure" as "tre-she-er." She is now aware of print spelling through using "Texas Speak and Spell" and through working with sighted pupils in class, and she is making good progress with spelling.

She originally learnt braille through "Braille for Infants," but she then moved on to brailled versions of the sighted reading schemes used by other pupils, including Ginn 360 level 3, "One, two, three and away" and "Pirate Readers." This means that she has the same reading experience as other children, and the class teacher hears her read in her turn alongside other pupils. The braille teacher is having to work extremely hard to transcribe all the material that is required. Helen really enjoys reading, and her parents also hear her read in the evening which compensates for any time which may be lost from braille skills at school in the interests of her taking a full part in what other children are doing.

The braille teacher is now in school on four days, since on Fridays the class goes swimming. Helen is beginning to do some braille work, such as writing her week-end "news" on Mondays, without direct classroom support from the braille teacher. She is just being introduced to the use of "Braille 'n' Print" which will give the class teacher direct access to her work and therefore make her more independent. This carries with it the disadvantage that she will have to move to a side table to use the equipment, whereas she has previously always been seated at a main table with her peers, but on the other hand the reduced dependence on adults will be socially advantageous. She has also tried using a "Braille 'n' Speak" which was borrowed for a short period, and now that her braille is so competent, it is suggested that she might be able to make effective use of this despite the absence of a braille output. She is also beginning to use a computer with a concept keyboard and speech synthesizer. She will start typewriting soon, and is being introduced to the idea of capital letters for this purpose and because some braille embossers use them.

In number work Helen has completed all the Ginn workbooks as far as Level 1 Book 3, the material being presented for her in an adapted, tactual form. She takes part with other children in all practical number work and verbal number games. She can read and write numbers one to ten, and is now being introduced to the concept of place value. Her only problem is that it takes her a long time physically to complete number work, and her new class teachers feel that she is in fact working below her potential. They are therefore looking for ways of extending her more, despite the time problem.

General skill development

For all practical activities, she likes to be doing the same work as other children, and is helped by the non-teaching assistant. When they do colouring or painting, she uses a template, and likes to do this even though she cannot see the result. She is encouraged also to make models as an alternative to two dimensional work. She is beginning to learn the colour coding buttons both at school and at home. Her teachers have to try to respond to difficult questions such as: "What is a shadow?" In this case, her ancillary helper astutely placed her in front of a wall in bright sunlight and showed her that her back became warm and the wall in front of her cold. Helen herself noted with surprise that the "shadow" was larger than her body.

In class discussion and in school assembly, she puts up her hand readily to respond to questions. She has taken part in outside visits with her class, for which the ancillary accompanies the group, and she has been very alert and receptive. As her peers begin to undertake enquiry work and to learn to extract information from a range of books, the staff are considering how Helen can have similar experiences. It is likely that her ancillary will serve as "reader" and train Helen to guide her to the material she needs.

Helen showed herself to be musical at an early age. She has music and singing lessons with her class and is learning to play the recorder. The advice of a music adviser has been sought, and the importance of fostering her talent will be borne in mind.

Helen particularly enjoys physical education. She plays football with a ball containing a bell, but she also joins in football games with an ordinary ball. In apparatus work, she is agile, well co-ordinated and very confident. At the start of the lesson, her ancillary takes her round the gym to show her the position of the apparatus, and she is attentive and thoughtful during this process. The ancillary then remains close to her throughout the lesson, for safety reasons, and helps her to carry out the same exercises as other children.

I observed Helen preparing for her PE lesson. All the children collected their kit from the cloakroom and returned to their tables in the classroom to change. She found the label on her shirt and shorts to be sure they were at the back, and noticed one sock was inside out, so reversed it before putting it on. She dealt with buttons with dexterity and was ready as quickly as other children. In fact, many sighted children of her age are less efficient at dressing. However she tossed her discarded clothing on the table and left it in a heap which would have made re-dressing a problem. Her mother says that she has the same problem of untidiness at home, and has yet to learn that blind people have to be highly organised. She also still insists on eating with her fingers, although she is able to use a spoon and fork. Unfortunately , all children in the school take packed lunches, so she has no occasion to be exposed to the reactions of her peers if she behaves incorrectly at table.

Mobility

At one point, Helen became "lost" in the classroom when she was particularly interested in getting to her next activity. Her teacher took her back to her starting-point, reminding her to concentrate on her learned route, and she then orientated herself attentively and thoughtfully by table corners and other landmarks and successfully reached her destination. With her family, she enjoys going to strange places, and moves about confidently, but she tends to become excited and headstrong and needs close control.

The authority is only able to provide the occasional bought-in services of a mobility officer. At present, the six-monthly visits are proving useful to the school and family. Helen shows good echo location and has been given a cane, not for real use yet, but so that she can develop a positive attitude towards it. She has given it a name, and is very interested in it. It is going to be very important that she should receive regular mobility training as she grows older.

Current and future plans

Helen's new class teachers are very happy to have her in the class. They report that she reads with great expression and feeling and produces promising creative writing and poetry. Her fine motor skills still need attention, but she is making progress. She shows a thorough understanding of topic work and asks relevant questions.

Helen's mother is encouraged to observe her daughter in class periodically, and at her last visit was very satisfied. She was pleased to see that Helen was disciplined in the same way as other children, that her work was displayed on the wall alongside that of others and that other children were helpful to her without being over fussy. Mr and Mrs I. are very happy with the integration scheme and they report that Helen "loves the school."

This is clearly a case of a very successful placement. Helen's rapid progress in academic skills places a heavy demand on resources both human and material, but she is clearly making optimum use of what is being provided. Her continuing progress will be monitored with great interest both by her own LEA and by RNIB.

4. Stephen T. aged 7

Stephen is a partially-sighted boy who is nearly seven years old. He lives in a housing estate in a large new town and travels daily to another large town ten miles away where a primary school is resourced to cater for visually impaired children. For a year he travelled alone by taxi, but his younger brother who is also partially sighted now accompanies him. Stephen is an alert, able child who is making good use of his very limited vision.

Stephen was sighted at birth, but when he was three months old his parents noticed a physical abnormality of his eye, and on investigation he was found to have retinal blastoma. It was too late to save his left eye which was removed; his right eye was successfully treated and he was initially able to see well with it, but by the time he was two and a half years old the sight was deteriorating as a result of a cataract. His distance vision is 6/36 and he can read N14 and N12 print, but finds N10 very difficult.

Mrs T has one artificial eye. As a child she was merely told that the other had had to be removed because of an infection, and it had never at any stage been suggested to her that she had a condition which might be passed on to her children. Her first child, a girl, is normally sighted, and it was only when Stephen's condition was diagnosed that doctors enquired into Mrs T's medical record and learnt that she also had had retinal blastoma. Had she known of the risk, she may still have chosen to have children, but the double shock of learning that her son had a handicap and then that it was inherited from her created feelings of guilt with which she is only now beginning to come to terms. Mrs T. is still a young woman in her twenties, and it is disturbing to find that even so recently doctors were apparently not taking any measures to ensure that genetic counselling was offered to a family in these circumstances.

The early years

When it was found that Stephen's remaining sight was deteriorating at the age of two and a half years, a home teacher began visiting on a fortnightly basis. At that stage, he was toilet-trained apart from an occasional accident, and able to eat at table with a spoon and fork. He had good gross motor skills and was beginning to give some help when being dressed, but his fine motor skills were rather clumsy. He had some vocabulary and was able to use two to three word phrases. The teacher worked with him and also advised Mrs T. on how she could help him with the development of language, socialisation, self-help skills, motor skills and cognitive skills. Arrangements were then made for him to attend a local nursery school part-time for two years before moving on to the primary school.

Mrs T. found this support helpful, but remembers feeling ill-at-ease and even overwhelmed at the frequency of home visits from a range of interested professionals. Some families suffer from a lack of support, but in other cases the amount of help offered may seem intrusive.

During this period and indeed subsequently, Stephen's progress was undoubtedly checked by his medical experiences. Frequent hospital visits were necessary in the early years, and when Mrs T. had to manage two small handicapped children and travel nearly twenty miles to the city hospital, the visits constituted a traumatic disturbance of family life. An attempt was made to fit a prosthesis for the missing eye, but unfortunately some medical difficulty arose, and Stephen endured considerable discomfort during attempts to insert and remove the artificial eye. The socket muscles were, or became weakened, and it was eventually decided that the prosthesis must be abandoned until he was rather older. This meant that the eye was closed and looked strange, which gave rise to some upsetting comments from other children. Some work was then undertaken on the remaining eye and, when Stephen came round from the anaesthetic, the eye was bandaged and he thought that it also had been removed, which of course caused him considerable distress.

These experiences have inevitably made him over-sensitive and nervous about anything concerning his eyes. Furthermore, he now appears to find bright light very painful. The doctor sees no reason why his condition should cause him to be photophobic, but nevertheless has no doubt that the discomfort of which the child complains is genuine. He holds his head bent and sometimes uses his hand to protect his eye. This has caused a posture problem, which makes him look different from other children, prevents him from observing what is going on around him, and is becoming a bad habit. He and his brother have now both been given very attractive, gold-rimmed spectacles and they are being encouraged to feel proud of these. It is reassuring to know that this has led to some improvement in Stephen's posture. Furthermore, Stephen has recently started inserting his artificial eye before going to school in the morning. It was his own decision to practise doing this, and he does not manage it every day, but he is becoming quite proud of his "magic eye."

School placement

When Stephen reached the age of five, Mr and Mrs T. were not happy at the prospect of his having to travel a distance to school, but they realized that he needed more help than could be provided in the neighbourhood school. The resourced primary school which he attends has had some years' experience of receiving visually impaired pupils. There are three specialist teachers of the visually impaired, but two of these also undertake peripatetic work in the area. The school also has an additional teacher on its mainstream establishment to compensate for the extra demands made on the staff. The support service is based in two temporary classrooms, one of which is used as a teaching area and the other for administration and the preparation of materials. There is some part-time ancillary help. The school as a whole has over four hundred pupils, and there are currently nine visually impaired children.

In the past, the usual practice was for the visually impaired children to spend a high proportion of their time in the special unit. However, at the point when Stephen entered the school, it was decided that new entrants should be based in a mainstream class and withdrawn for special teaching as little as possible. Staff preparation and support for this new approach was therefore required.

In his first year at school, Stephen was in a class of 23 children. The teacher was initially very concerned about how to cater for his needs, but she took a considerable interest in him and has been very pleased with his progress. Quite by chance, she retained the same class when they moved into their second year, and this fortuitous continuity has been very beneficial to Stephen.

The class teacher says that the child's full-time integration has only been satisfactory because of the high level of support provided. In the first year, his specialist support teacher spent most of every morning in the class. In the second year, this has been reduced to a three-quarter-hour session each morning. It was possible to allocate this amount of time because there are other visually impaired children in the class who also have learning difficulties. It was also judged to be important to give substantial support at this stage, since the full integration of such pupils was a new experience for mainstream staff.

In the first years, the support teacher worked particularly with the visually impaired children to develop their basic skills and ensure that they had access to the work being done by the class. For instance, she copied blackboard work on to a small board immediately infront of Stephen. She also took every opportunity to convey information which would heighten the class teacher's awareness of the specific needs of the visually impaired pupils in her class. However, increasingly she has worked with a wider group of children and readily takes over the teaching of the whole class in order to free the class teacher to work with individuals. There is a very fruitful relationship between the two teachers.

Literacy and numeracy

Stephen has made extremely good progress with his school work. He reads well and can manage the print size of the infant readers with his glasses. He has a hand magnifier and, when books with smaller print begin to be used, the material will be enlarged for him. His writing is quite large, but neat and well-aligned. He is left-handed and unfortunately it is his left eye which is missing, which obviously makes writing more difficult for him, but he manages surprisingly well. The content of the teaching is quite formal, including a substantial amount of written work, but the children have individual programmes of work for each day and have to find their own materials as required. Stephen moves confidently about the room, and is generally able to select the books and materials which he needs, but other children readily help him if he is in difficulties. His number work is very good. He initially used black card with large yellow numbers, but he is now able to cope with the class's number scheme with a little help.

General skill development

He draws well and confidently and much enjoys this. Despite having only one eye, he has had no difficulty in learning to interpret pictures and he has now overcome his initial problem in perceiving depth when he wished to grasp something. At the age of six, when he had been at school for six months, he was tested with the "Look and Think" materials. He was able to name most three-dimensional objects and models and succeeded in all the 3-D discrimination and matching tests. He also did all but one of the two-dimensional matching tests, and tracked the maze with a high level of accuracy.

Much of his progress is attributable to the fact that he is a very serious, hard-working little boy. He does sometimes need to be kept on task, and he can be disorganised with his personal belongings, but he is capable of sustained concentration and attention to detail. He is also being given deliberate training in listening skills. He is a perfectionist, and this carries with it the problem that he tends to be over-anxious and becomes tearful if things go wrong. For this reason, he is working in the middle group in the class to protect him from the stress of seeking to compete with the most able children.

When the teacher uses the blackboard, Stephen and another partially sighted child now go and stand by the blackboard so that they can see. Since Stephen still holds his head bent, he has to be lifted to see wall displays, or allowed to stand on a desk. At his own table, he often works standing up or he sits with his head propped on his hand so that he can see the work without raising his head. This posture problem is continuing to cause some concern.

Social development

Socially, Stephen has a good relationship with other children, and has one particular friend. There has been some name-calling from children in other classes, but this has been dealt with by the school. Stephen seems happier now that his brother is in school. They are both small for their age and have very quiet voices, a problem which is compounded by Stephen bending his head down. Other children, however, are very good at listening to him and he is readily chosen as a partner for activities. He is friendly with his own working group in class and this is important to him. In the playground, he has difficulty in locating his friends and will often be found standing alone in a shady spot, particularly on a sunny day.

His frequent tenseness contrasts with very relaxed, happy behaviour in the gym. The room is poorly lit, which suits him, and in this secure environment he runs about, with his head raised and a broad smile. When new exercises are introduced in physical education, he needs guidance with his perception of depth, but he is very active and really enjoys the lessons.

At home, his parents are concerned about the social isolation created by going away to school. For instance, it is not possible for him to go to other children's parties, and his friends would not be able to come to a party at his home. He does now play out sometimes with local children, under the supervision of his elder sister.

Current and Future Plans

The support teacher is maintaining close contact with the family in order to help them to reinforce the educational progress which he is making at school. There is a regular exchange of telephone calls and occasional home visits. The support teacher attaches considerable importance to maintaining this link with the family, so that the parents can be fully involved in their children's education.

Stephen is clearly an intelligent, determined little boy who has the potential to achieve a great deal. Life has not been easy for him so far, and he is clearly going to continue to need support and guidance. He is the sort of child for whom, without special help, expectations might have been low and he would have responded accordingly. Sights are being set higher because of the early progress he has made, and he has the opportunity to achieve his true potential.

5. Jennifer K. aged 8

Jennifer K. is an eight year old girl who is blind. She attends a village primary school where she has full social and functional integration. She is of above average academic ability and has no other disabilities, or areas of special need apart from those arising from her visual impairment.

Jennifer was identified as suffering from bilateral micro-phthalmos shortly after birth. Her mother was told by the medical consultant that she should not worry about the future, since the child would be sent away to a special school as soon as she was old enough. The mother was deeply shocked by this approach and by suggestions that she should try not to become too attached to her baby. She immediately resolved that the child should not be sent away from home, and she began enquiring into other possibilities.

The early years

There were two older daughters in the family, so the mother had experience of the various early phases of child development, and she did everything in her power to help Jennifer to develop as normally as possible. Since the local education authority at that time had no support service for the visually impaired, the only specialized guidance she received was occasional visits from an RNIB adviser. The health visitor and GP were very helpful, but had no specialist experience in this field. The doctors believed that Jennifer had no sight whatever, but, like many mothers in this situation, Mrs K. persevered in trying to identify some response to visual stimulation. She became convinced that Jennifer had some light perception and was able to see certain strong colours. The consultant was reluctant to believe this, but eventually acknowl-edged that, in completely arbitrary testing, Jennifer was able to name colours correctly. She is now no longer able to perceive colour, but the memory of her early experience has remained with her and she has a mental concept of colour.

From the age of about 18 months, Jennifer attended an assess-ment playgroup organised for handicapped children by the dis-trict health authority. Initially she attended once a week accompanied by her mother, but later went twice a week some-times without her mother. When she was about three and a half, Mrs K. decided that her case for integration might be stronger if Jennifer had some experience of an ordinary playgroup. She approached a local Methodist group, where there was initially some concern for Jennifer's safety, but they eventually agreed to let her attend if her mother went with her. Their fears were quickly set at rest because Jennifer mixed confidently with the other children, was very agile on the climbing-frame and trampoline, and took a full part in all the activities.

As school age approached, Mrs K. raised with the local education authority her objection to residential placement, and asked that Jennifer should at least be given a trial in a mainstream school.

She was informed that she would herself have to find a school which was prepared to admit Jennifer. This represented a major ordeal for Mrs K. who had not herself had a very successful school career and did not feel at ease with professional educationists. However, she was determined to fight for what she saw as her child's right.

After encountering reluctance in several schools, she went to a small Church of England school in a neighbouring village. Here she received a warm reception and genuine interest. The head teacher says that she never had any hesitation about accepting Jennifer as a pupil, and was indeed thrilled at the prospect of taking on this challenge.

School placement

The LEA therefore agreed to the placement, and Jennifer entered the school at the age of five, together with a group of children who had attended the same playgroup.

This small village primary school has only two classes, one for infants and one for juniors. Since the authority has a mixture of educational patterns, some children transfer to a middle school at 10 whilst others remain until 11 and then move to secondary education.

The school is a traditional, homely school building with just two classrooms. Lunches are prepared on the premises, and children eat these or packed lunches in the classrooms. The only area available for withdrawal teaching is the staffroom, which is in fact little more than an entrance lobby. There is a hard play area and the bonus of a small open-air swimming pool which is used by the children almost every day when the weather is reasonable. A field is available for games, and the neighbouring church is used for school assemblies and concerts. All this provision is on the same compact site, but there are changes of level and direct access only by rugged paths, slopes and steps which present something of a challenge for a blind child.

There are now 20 pupils in the junior class and 18 in the infants class. When Jennifer first entered the school, there were only 12 infants, which was an advantage. For the first term she attended half-time only. By this time, the local authority had appointed a qualified advisory teacher of the visually impaired, and he visited the school every day in the early stages in order to begin teaching braille to Jennifer and to guide the staff in their work with her. He now visits approximately twice a term. An ancillary helper was appointed initially on a half-time basis, but she became full-time once Jennifer was in school all day. She had had no previous experience of visual impairment, but she has learnt braille and developed her expertise whilst working with Jennifer. This post is financed centrally, but she was appointed by the school governors. It is a temporary appointment which is renewed annually, but will terminate when Jennifer leaves the school.

The infants teacher who was in the school when Jennifer first arrived had difficulty in accepting Jennifer as a member of her class, and in adapting to the circumstances surrounding the presence of a handicapped pupil. She left the school after one term. Her successor accepted the post knowing about Jennifer's presence and, in common with all other adults in the school community, is very supportive of the integration scheme. There have been no adverse reactions from parents of other pupils.

Communication skills
Since Jennifer entered the school, she has always participated fully in all aspects of the curriculum. She moved to the junior class two terms before the normal age for promotion. She has become very competent in braille, her work being transcribed by the ancillary for the class teacher. It is displayed along with other children's work together with the transcription. Her language work is well developed for her age, and she shows imagination in creative writing. She uses a cassette player regularly, both for general listening, and as a means of recording. She is quite proficient in taking notes from the cassette player, and listening to questions or instructions and responding on her brailler. She sits at a central table together with other pupils, although she occupies a double space because of her equipment. The other pupils are well accustomed to her special study methods and do not appear to be in any way distracted by them.

Jennifer does not yet use technological aids. A Braille 'n' Print has been provided, but she is not using it because she is thought to be too heavy-handed, and possibly also because the ancillary lacks confidence in the use of electronic devices. There is also some concern that the use of more equipment would tend to cut Jennifer off physically from fellow pupils in the classroom situation. She does not yet have any "Qwerty" keyboard skills.

General skill development
Jennifer has some co-ordination problems and in particular finds cutting difficult. She has some problems with art and craft work,

and the school is still trying to find appropriate media in which she might experience success in this area.

Number work has presented some difficulties, both because of the visual aspects of some concepts in practical mathematics and because the ancillary is not proficient in the use of the braille code. However, the school is now fortunate in having two visits a week from a support teacher who is qualified in maths and science. This teacher has been working on a part-time, temporary basis in the authority's visual impairment service. She has learnt braille and is now studying to obtain a qualification in visual impairment. She will now be a permanent member of the team. Jennifer is therefore able to benefit from specialist teaching in maths and science, which will be a significant bonus as she grows older.

The head teacher takes the junior class and she is of course well accustomed to Jennifer's needs, and to ensuring that she participates in class discussion. When outside visits are organized as part of the curriculum, Mrs K. goes too, to provide extra support. Jennifer works conscientiously but, when she dislikes work or finds it difficult, she does tend to put up barriers and to persevere less than she might. She needs encouragement and gentle chiding to ensure that she works well and achieves her full potential.

Jennifer is very musical and enjoys playing the piano and the recorder. The local Lions club paid for her to have piano lessons. She takes part in school concerts and nativity plays and is very enthusiastic about this.

She has two close friends, who help her in a relaxed, but sensitive way. When I arrived, she and one of her friends took me on a guided tour of the school campus. They both told me something of the history of the school as we walked through the churchyard. Jennifer found her way confidently, and was not worried by the steps, bank or rough ground. In the church, her friend put the lights on and Jennifer told me about the building, and where she had stood during the nativity play. As we walked back towards the school, it was Jennifer who remembered that we had forgotten to turn out the lights!

On the school field, Jennifer demonstrated her running skills. She has good natural movement and is able to follow a reasonably straight course. She enjoys sport and had been disappointed that she had not been allowed to take part in a regional competition, for which there is an admission standard. It had not been thought appropriate that she should be treated differently from other children, but this was difficult for her to accept. At the school sports day, she took part in the relay race, and she is now learning to skip, which is a particularly difficult skill for a blind child.

Personal and social development

Jennifer has good posture although she tends to hold her head a little bowed, and to one side which is understandable since she has some peripheral light perception. She is a tidy, pleasantly smiling child, but a little overweight. A physiotherapist sees her once a month and gives her relaxation exercises. She used to flutter her hands a great deal, but this is improving and really only occurs now when she gets excited. Her family and the school staff are very persistent in trying to correct this.

Jennifer has good spatial awareness and is able to dress and to look after herself independently. She has not yet received any formal mobility training. The authority has to call on the services of a mobility officer in the Social Services department who has not been accustomed to providing support for children, since in the past they have generally gone to residential schools. This matter is being investigated, since Jennifer is obviously reaching an age when she will need to be independent in the community.

Jennifer has two sisters aged 16 and 11. The eleven year old was in the same school for three years, and Jennifer missed her when she left. She goes to the Crusaders with her sisters on Friday evenings. There have been some instances there of bullying, but Jennifer has just been told that she must learn to stand up for herself. She also goes to a country dancing class.

Out of school she has contact with peers. Her mother looks after some other children until their parents return from work, and they all play together. She does not have much involvement with other visually impaired children, but she knows a blind girl of her own age with whom she corresponds, and the family are in contact with the family of a younger blind boy who lives in the vicinity.

Jennifer is a contented, friendly child, who is alert and interested in the world about her. She has good academic ability, she is musical and also very much enjoys physical activity. She is not without a streak of stubbornness, and as she grows older it will be important for her to be stimulated to give of her best.

111

Mrs K. hopes that she will move on to the local middle school and then to secondary school. The LEA officers have some doubts as to whether they can provide adequately for her needs at secondary level, particularly in some subject specialisms, and they may well recommend a special school placement at that stage. Mrs K. may still have further battles to fight if she wishes Jennifer to remain in integrated education.

Undoubtedly, a small village school has many advantages for a blind pupil. Jennifer readily became a full member of the school community, and her needs are being catered for without detriment to other pupils. However, the staff involved had no previous experience of such work, and it is greatly to their credit that they have made such a success of the placement. The Advisory Teacher has many other commitments which limit the time he can give to the school, and it is of course difficult for staff in such a small school to be released for in-service training.

It would seem important that Jennifer should begin to make more use of technological aids, if only because the amount of transcription required of the ancillary is becoming prohibitive. She should also receive formal mobility training. However, at this stage she is certainly functioning very well and making highly satisfactory progress in both academic and social development.

6. Martin N. aged 9

Martin is a nine year old boy who is blind apart from minimal peripheral vision in one eye. He attends a middle school where there is a special unit for visually impaired children.

When he was three years old, the health visitor identified visual abnormalities during a regular test, and referred him to an eye clinic. Here he was tested again, but his sight was reported to be normal. The health visitor and Martin's mother continued to think that he was not seeing properly, and he was repeatedly referred to the clinic. Mrs N says that this occurred seven times and each time they were told that there was nothing wrong. She recalls that the person undertaking the testing was unwittingly prompting his responses. For instance, she showed him a picture of a dog and urged him on: "Come on! It's an animal that people keep as a pet at home." When he guessed: "A cat?" she replied that this was near enough.

Eventually, when Martin was five years old, he was referred to an ophthalmologist at Mrs N's insistence and with a letter which referred to her as "an hysterical mother." The ophthalmologist found that Martin had retinitis pigmentosa with gross macular dystrophy and optic atrophy. At that stage, he had tunnel vision and could see up to the distance of his hand stretched out before him. He was then registered partially sighted, and the consultant explained to his family that he was likely eventually to become blind, but this could be a very slow process. In the event, the deterioration was unusually rapid, and within six months he was registered blind and his remaining sight was fading quickly.

School placement

Before the condition was identified, Martin had entered his neighbourhood first school. Not surprisingly, his progress was poor and he was reported to have discrimination and co-ordination problems. When he was known to be visually impaired, the head of the school was very sympathetic and would have been willing to keep him there. However, it was clear that he would need to learn braille, and he was therefore transferred to a first school in a neighbouring authority which has a visual impairment unit.

The family lives in a densely populated urban area where several local education authorities are within easy daily travelling distances of one another. One of these authorities had, until recently, a special school for the visually impaired which included the surrounding LEAs in its catchment area. In the late 1970s units for partially sighted children were introduced in the same LEA, these units also providing for children from the surrounding authorities. In 1985, a decision was made to close the special school and to extend the unit provision to cater for blind as well as partially sighted pupils. The traditional relationship with the cluster of surrounding LEAs remained in force, and they have continued to take up places in the units. It was therefore almost automatic that Martin should be placed in the primary unit which is only about eight miles from his home, transport being provided by taxi.

Martin entered the unit when he was just six. He was then a boisterous, rather noisy child, enjoying the company of his peers in a physical way. He had good language development and practical ability, and emphasis was placed initially on developing his tactile and auditory skills. He worked well in a one-to-one situation, but tended to be disruptive in group work.

113

Literacy and numeracy

He was based initially in the special unit, but within a year he was being integrated into mainstream classes for some activities. He developed a positive attitude to his work and progressed quickly through the braille pre-reading scheme and the family books, working on his own initiative in the evenings and at week-ends to achieve this. His haste tended, however, to lead to inaccuracies in writing braille and this has continued as he has become more fluent, so that his writing is now seriously marred by poor spelling and inaccuracies.

He has never found number work easy, but some progress has been made. He is able to concentrate and work with determination, but he is easily discouraged when faced with difficulties and tends to be slapdash in organising and presenting his work. He has been more successful in practical mathematics, such as measuring, than in theoretical work.

Personal development

Towards the end of his years in the first school unit, Martin was being integrated for social activities, science, environmental studies and some aspects of physical education. He took a lively part in the lessons and clearly enjoyed them. However, he did need to be kept on task, and in less formal learning situations he would tend to lose interest and roam from task to task.

During this time Martin was progressively losing his remaining vision. Being an active, sociable child who really enjoys all physical activity, it has been very difficult for him to accept the limitations which blindness places upon him. He has continued to enjoy athletics and, at the age of eight gained a silver medal in the "Milk Athletics Awards." He still enjoys kicking a football around, and is an ardent supporter of his favourite team, even though he can no longer play team football.

Martin began informal mobility training at the age of seven. The authority where he was attending school has the regular services of a mobility officer, an advantage which is sadly lacking in so many areas of the country. Martin has indeed also had some help from the mobility officer in his home LEA. He has found mobility difficult because, as his sight was deteriorating, he was never sure how much he could see from day to day and this inevitably made him feel very insecure. At one point, he said he could see a vague mixture of light and bright colours , but when told it was a line of parked cars, he was able to count them. He was therefore unsure as to whether to use his unreliable vision to find his way around or to depend on non-sighted clues. He was at one point given some training under blindfold to help him with this. His insecurity makes him react nervously to sounds and tactile sensations even if he really knows their origin. He has now begun formal "long cane" training, in which he has initially had some difficulty with hand-foot co-ordination, but he is making progress.

Mobility problems are a serious concern to Martin, because he is naturally a boisterous child. He tends to rush about and bump into objects and people, and the resulting encounters have led to aggression towards peers. His reaction unfortunately incites some teasing and troublesome peer group relationships which upset him a great deal because he really wants to be friendly and peer group pressures matter to him. As he lost his sight it was a blow to his self-esteem to discover that he could no longer find his way around a familiar area.

When these difficulties are seen in the context of a child who is experiencing the emotional trauma of progressively becoming blind, it is no wonder that Martin began to show disturbing behaviour patterns. His aggressive and disruptive behaviour at school led to some curtailment of his integration programme, and his parents reported frequent nightmares and other signs of distress. Martin was clearly not coming to terms with being blind.

The move to middle school
This was the situation when he transferred to the middle school unit where, at the time of writing, he is in his second term.

The middle school unit admitted its first blind pupils in 1985. It is staffed by two teachers and three ancillaries, and there are currently nine partially-sighted and five blind pupils.

The unit is housed in two large, well-equipped classrooms, which are in a central position in the body of the school. The partially sighted pupils are all integrated for 100% of their time. Most need materials enlarging for use in class, and six of them have the support of a member of the unit staff for most lessons. Two blind girls are integrated with the two top years for 90% and 95% respectively. They have accompanied support for English, social studies, mathematics, science, French, religious education and craft. The only lessons they do not attend are art and games, when they have mobility and typewriting lessons.

115

The other three blind children, including Martin, are in their first year, having transferred from the First School unit. These three children join their class group in the morning for registration and go with their class to the school assembly. In the unit they are prepared for integration. It is considered to be important that they should re-inforce their command of braille and other basic skills so that when they are integrated they should be able to benefit fully from the lessons. They are taught by the unit staff and follow as closely as possible the main school timetable and curriculum. They are all integrated for music and physical education and two are integrated for English and social studies lessons. It is hoped to increase this by integration into religious education and science later in the school year.

It should be noted that the authority has a strong policy commitment to functional integration, and this is monitored closely at each child's annual review.

A period of adaptation

Martin entered the school with a reputation for disruptive, aggressive behaviour, and an apparent falling away of his academic achievements. He is at present very much in need of one-to-one teaching and a calm atmosphere away from classroom distractions. He seems to have settled down well and to be working very hard. He is following a remedial spelling programme and his braille is becoming more accurate. He is now learning to type and is very enthusiastic about using the computer. He will be using a Vincent Work Station or Braille 'n' Print when he is integrated.

The senior teacher in the unit has discussed his attitude to blindness with him and he is becoming more willing to talk about his problems. He has established a firm friendship with the other blind boy in the unit. His relationships with sighted pupils are still unsteady and he is very sensitive to teasing. He is looking forward to being integrated into more lessons and hopefully this will provide a spur for him to increase his self-control in peer group contacts.

Social development

Martin is a sturdy young boy with an alert manner and a pleasant smile. He holds his head typically to one side in order to make use of his peripheral light perception in one eye. He is still very enthusiastic about all sporting activities, including apparatus work, running (for which he is matched with a sighted boy) and ice-skating which is provided weekly for the unit children. On

Saturdays he goes horse-riding with his brother and they also ride a tandem which was given to them by the local Rotary Club. They are both also learning judo together. Martin's brother is only about fifteen months older than he is, and the two boys enjoy friendly rivalry and often heated competition in all forms of activity. Martin tends to become too intense about this, but he can outdo his brother in some things.

Apart from his brother, he now has few friends in the neighbourhood, and his movements are very restricted because there are no easily accessible play areas. His mother is concerned that he is likely to be very lonely, particularly when his brother ceases to be willing to spend so much time with him.

At home Martin listens to taped books with great enthusiasm and shows good listening skills. At school, he is being trained to use the talking encyclopaedia which is in the unit. He has retained his visual memory, as was apparent when "The Sound of Music" was on television and he said he could see it in his mind with the "Christmas trees" on the hills. At school, however, he has not shown much sign of making use of this visual memory.

He is continuing to make progress in formal mobility training and is learning to use raised maps. Some of the training takes place in the high school to which he will later transfer, and he very much enjoys this. He recently attended an RNIB vacation scheme, and the mobility work undertaken there showed he has good orientation and is able to make effective use of echo location.

Current and future plans

Martin's emotional problems have undoubtedly caused a setback in his progress at school. He seems to be of good average ability, but by temperament he is unlikely to achieve his potential unless he is handled firmly. This is certainly a case where the unit provision has been particularly apposite. It has made it possible for him to move in and out of integration in accordance with his emotional needs and for him to receive a great deal of one-to-one teaching whilst still having the opportunity for social contact with sighted peers which is important to him even if sometimes difficult to handle.

He seems now to be emerging from a difficult phase in his development. He is finding it easier to talk about his worries both at home and at school, and hopefully he will be able to continue to build on his undoubted strengths.

7. Tracey Y. aged 13

Tracey is a thirteen year old blind girl. She attends her local comprehensive school where she is fully integrated, and is making very good progress. She went to residential special schools until she was eleven years old.

Tracey was born prematurely and when she was about five months old her parents were told that she was blind as a result of retinopathy of prematurity. It appears that until that point it had not been realised that her sight had been affected. Her parents had been sitting her infront of the television where she laughed (doubtless in response to the sound), and it was in fact the health visitor who became aware that she could not see. She now has a little light perception in one eye, but no other useful vision and no perception of colour. Her eyes are open and she is a pleasant, attractive girl, rather on the plump side. She has no other disabilities.

The early years

Tracey was not referred to the education authority as a baby, and Mrs Y. received no guidance as to how to cater for the special needs arising from blindness. As Tracey is the elder of two children, her parents had no previous experience of child-rearing from which to gauge her progress. However, she quickly showed herself to be an independent, determined child who explored her surroundings freely in the house and seemed contented. There were no problems over toilet-training or over other basic developmental milestones.

When she reached school age Mr and Mrs Y. were informed, without any preliminary consultation, that their daughter would have to attend a residential special school. They were very upset about this, and certainly did not want her to go away from home, but they were told that there was no alternative. She was therefore placed at one of the RNIB Sunshine House Schools on a Monday to Friday residential basis. The head teacher visited the family before Tracey was admitted. They do not, however, remember receiving any guidance subsequently about how they could work with their daughter at the week-end.

Special school experience

Tracey was very unhappy each week when she had to leave her parents to go to school, and when she arrived back on Fridays there seemed to be so little time for her to settle down again before she had to be preparing for the following week. She remained at the Sunshine House School until she was seven, and then transferred to another special school for the visually impaired where she was again residential from Monday to Friday. The school was at some distance from their home and the parents had little contact with it.

The staff found her to be a self-willed child, and she did not seem to be making very good progress in her education. Looking back on the situation now, Mrs Y feels that most of the pupils in the school were less able than Tracey or had additional problems and she was therefore not being stimulated sufficiently.

The family became more and more concerned about her having to go away to school, and she was feeling increasingly lonely at home because she had no friends in the neighbourhood. Mrs Y. then discovered that, in the area where her parents lived, it was the practice for blind children to attend mainstream schools. After further enquiries, the family made the major decision to move house in order to secure for Tracey an educational placement which would be more acceptable to them.

The move to the mainstream
Tracey was now eleven years old, but she was initially placed in a primary school near the family's new home so that she could adapt to mainstream life before moving on to the secondary school.

In the primary school, a full-time ancillary worker was appointed to support her and she had additional lunch-time supervision. A teacher of the visually impaired provided peripatetic help. It was found that, at this stage, Tracey had made little progress in braille, not yet having mastered any contractions. She had learnt no maths braille, did not know her tables and had no understanding of place value. Initially her attitude to studying was poor, and it was difficult to keep her on task. She was withdrawn for three sessions a week of intensive tuition, but otherwise she was fully integrated into the class.

Tracey herself was very happy to be living at home again, and quickly adapted to being in a mainstream school, even though this was of course a totally new experience for her. She made friends readily. There was indeed initially some teasing, but she responded in kind and rapidly earned the respect of her peers. By the end of the school year, she seemed well-adapted and ready to move into the secondary school.

119

The secondary school

Although the LEA has some years' experience of integrating blind children, each attends his or her neighbourhood school and it is therefore always a new venture for the school concerned. In this case, the head teacher and staff were initially very concerned as to whether they could provide Tracey with an appropriate education. Full consultations were held and awareness training provided, and a number of teachers attended an RNIB training day. Many of the staff, however, still had considerable reservations about the placement.

When Tracey entered the school, she had a full-time ancillary helper who moved up from the primary school with her and the support teacher of the visually impaired spent nearly every morning in the school. This was considered necessary because teaching materials had to be prepared for all subjects and the staff needed the reassurance of having regular access to a specialist teacher. Lunch-time supervision was also provided, because the head teacher considered it unsafe for Tracey to be left unattended at any time. She is now in her second year in the school, and the lunch-time supervision has been withdrawn. The involvement of the support teacher is also being reduced as Tracey becomes more independent and the school grows in confidence.

Tracey has made very good progress with her braille, now that she realises its importance to her as an everyday communication tool. She reads in braille readily in her leisure-time when she finds topics of interest to her, and she does sometimes listen to books on cassette, although she finds aural concentration quite difficult. She has a Perkins brailler at home in addition to one at school, and she uses a microwriter at school and at home. She will shortly begin to receive typing lessons. At present, she produces her work in braille and it is underwritten for the teachers by the ancillary, who has recently learnt braille, or by the support teacher.

Because of the late move to integration, Tracey is one year below her normal age-group, but since she has a summer birthday she is not significantly older than other children in her class. She is integrated for almost the whole of the curriculum. The only exception is technical studies, for which pupils follow a programme of modules in computer studies, technical drawing, woodwork, metalwork and design. She has, however, done some tactile work in art and she does home economics.

Most of her mainstream teachers acknowledge that they had considerable reservations about having Tracey in their classes, and some are still concerned that they may not be offering her as much as specialist teachers of the visually impaired would do, but they are all most impressed with the way she has settled down and with the progress she is making. Tracey herself is very happy in the school, and Mrs Y. has no doubts whatever that they made the right decision in seeking integration.

Progress with the secondary curriculum

Tracey speaks confidently and has wide general knowledge. In *English* she shows a good command of language and style and her creative writing is imaginative and fluent. She understands new concepts and concentrates well. Her sharp listening skills and good memory help her in *history*, in *religious education* and in *geography*. She has been unable to take part in the section of the geography course which is concerned with ordnance survey and mapwork, and for this reason may not choose the subject as an examination option, but she is very interested in geology.

In *mathematics*, Tracey was starting from a low base and the head of department was very concerned that this fact, combined with the presentation difficulties associated with the subject, would constitute insuperable obstacles. He is, however, now fully converted to the feasibility of her integration. For the first two years in the school, pupils are in mixed ability groups for maths,and work through the scheme at their individual rate, which has been a considerable advantage to Tracey. Her problem is that there are gaps in her basic skills, but she grasps new concepts readily, and is certainly not expected to be placed in the bottom set in the third year. There is a system of awarding "certificates" as pupils master various skill areas, and Tracey is progressing through this in number work, algebra, graphs and two and three dimensional work. There are some assessment targets which depend on vision and are inaccessible to her.

She is making particularly good progress in *French* for which she is in the top set. She excels in oral work, and is likely to start learning German in the third year. She and her ancillary are both beginning to master the contractions for French braille.

In *science* her teachers are delighted with her progress. She shows a good grasp of scientific concepts, and her powers of observation with senses other than sight have set a standard for other pupils to emulate. Although she obviously cannot use a microscope, she quickly learnt how to set it up and taught her peers how to do this! She is following a modular science course, and there are likely to be problems with some of the assessment targets in chemistry which will not be accessible to her. She has mastered the use of a bunsen burner, a clampstand and reading scales, and can manage filtering and the handling of tongs and test tube holders. For some skills, such as using a balance, measuring cylinders, a thermometer and a microscope, the teacher is at present merely recording that Tracey understands their use. As she progresses in science, it is to be hoped that she will be provided with specialised equipment which she can use. She is being encouraged to maintain well-organized braille accounts of her work for future revision.

In her *textiles* course, Tracey is competent at threading and using the sewing machine, and she uses a variety of textures to help her with design. She needs more time than other pupils, but her teacher believes that she would be able to take the subject at GCSE level.

In *music* she uses her listening skills well and has a good sense of rhythm and understanding of melody. She performs competently and is a valued member of the school choir.

She takes part in some aspects of *physical education*, including gymnastics and athletics. She has difficulty with co-ordination and ball skills, but her determination is described as being an inspiration to others. In place of games lessons she is taken swimming which she very much enjoys.

In her first year school report, she was marked in the 'good' or 'very good' category for effort, organisation, presentation and homework in virtually every subject, except where presentation is impeded by her handicap. There were no adverse comments about her behaviour.

Social and personal development

Socially, Tracey mixes happily with other pupils. She had an established group of friends with whom she moved up from the primary school, so she now has friends in the neighbourhood of her home. She plays with them on the nearby beach and rocks, but at this stage her mother still keeps a close eye on her. She moves about confidently in school but a major problem from the point of view of her growing wish for independence is that she has not as yet received any formal mobility training. A member of the visual impairment team will, however, shortly be undertaking the mobility officer course, and Tracey will then be able to receive appropriate instruction.

Tracey is still receiving a very high level of personal support at school, but this was rendered necessary by the school's initial concerns and her late move into integration. With growing confidence on all sides, and doubtless with an increasing use of technological equipment and other specialist materials, she is likely to be able to dispense with some of this support. She is certainly achieving a very promising standard, and may be expected to make a success of her school career.

8. John K. aged 14

John is a 14 year old boy who is educationally blind. He has been integrated throughout his education, and is at present in his first year at a 13-18 high school. He has good academic ability, and may be expected to go on to higher education.

John has optic atrophy arising from Lebers Amaurosis. He has no sight at all in his left eye and no central vision in his right eye. There is some peripheral vision in the top right-hand quadrant of his right eye which he is able to use for orientation by holding his head to one side, but the sight is of course of no use to him for close work.

Mr and Mrs K. were told that John was visually impaired when he was eight months old. They had known that this would be a possibility because their elder son was partially sighted. John seems to have had a significant amount of vision as a baby, but he was effectively blind by the age of two years. He does not himself remember having had any more vision than he has at present.

The early years

When he was three years old, arrangements were made for him to attend a nursery, initially on a part-time basis and later full- time. His elder brother was then at a special school with Monday to Friday residence. Mr and Mrs K. had been very unhappy about their first son going away from home. His impairment had only been identified at the age of two and a half years when a relative noticed that he seemed to be unusually clumsy. The ophthalmologist then told them he would have to go away to school, and they were never given any option. When John was approaching school age, a visual impairment service had been introduced in their LEA, so the peripatetic teacher went to see them and said they could choose whether their second son went to the same residential school or to a local school which had a special unit. They were of course overjoyed at this and chose the local school. At this point the family moved house and John attended a neighbourhood nursery for a term before moving to a resourced school shortly after his fifth birthday.

First and middle school education

The 5-9 primary school had a well-established unit for visually impaired pupils, and at that point in time the usual practice was for children to be based in the unit, and integrated from there into classes as appropriate. The unit was housed in a large, well-equipped classroom at one end of the school. The children joined other pupils at play-time and lunch-time, and groups of mainstream children would sometimes join the unit children for particular activities such as story time. There was a full-time teacher in the unit who, when John joined the school, was studying by distance learning for a qualification in visual impairment. There was also a nursery nurse.

John began to learn braille at the age of five. He was a quiet, shy boy, but he worked well and made good progress. Initially he spent most of his time in the unit, but was gradually integrated into a range of lessons with teacher support in the classroom. When he transferred to the middle school at the age of nine, he changed to a pattern of almost full integration with occasional withdrawal for specific purposes.

The middle school also had a resource base for the visually impaired. Here once again there had originally been a teacher in charge of the unit but by the time John went there the arrangement had become more flexible with various members of the LEA's visual impairment team providing support as required. One particular member of the team had overall responsibility for John from his second year in the school, but others also helped in certain specialist areas. The mainstream staff had long experience of having visually impaired pupils in their classes, including a small number of blind ones, and John was often able to work alone without any individual support. There was an established practice of having textbooks brailled well in advance, and materials required at short notice were prepared by the service's braillist. She worked in the team's base which at that time was on the same campus as the primary and middle schools, and so readily available.

John used his Perkins brailler and his work was transcribed for teachers. He began to take typing lessons and also increasingly used a variable speed cassette recorder and a mini-recorder for note-taking. He also had a talking calculator and was introduced to the use of an electronic braille writer. He followed the full range of the curriculum, with individual support in practical lessons. One of the members of the visual impairment team is a French specialist, and so taught him the special braille code and provided individual teaching in this subject. He went on a school educational visit to France. It is doubtless partly as a consequence of this special level of support that John is hoping to make a career in languages.

He has always enjoyed physical education. He participated fully in apparatus work with individual support, and also played football. He made very good progress in ball skills, and showed good co-ordination, and was indeed able to participate in team games.

John established good relationships with his fellow pupils in the middle school. Since he was travelling to school by taxi, it was not easy for him to maintain these friendships outside school hours, although this was sometimes made possible by the parents of his friends arranging to take him home by car. In fact his home was not far from the school. He also had many friends in the neighbourhood of his home and played outside with them. His mother recalls that this was very different from their experience with his brother who had been the victim of teasing and bullying. However, this is likely to have arisen because of the boys' very different personalities rather than from their differing educational experiences.

The move to secondary school
When John was approaching the age for transfer to high school, the family again moved house and it was generally felt that it would be better for him socially to be in his own neighbourhood rather than travelling daily to the resourced high school. Indeed, since he was the only blind child in his age-group, and since there were currently no blind pupils in the resourced high school, it would be no more demanding on resources to support him in the neighbourhood school.

An approach was therefore made to this school which had already had a partially sighted pupil and a number of physically disabled pupils. It is a Community School, with an enlightened approach to special needs, and the response of the staff was overwhelmingly favourable. In the summer term prior to his transfer, John spent two full days in the school, attending lessons with the teachers who would be teaching him in the autumn. He was accompanied by two members of the visual impairment team who spoke to the teachers about the specific issues which would arise in their subject, explaining how John worked and what type of support would be provided. The mainstream staff were also shown a video of John working in the middle school and taking part in out-of-class activities. This use of video is a regular practice in the LEA,and is found to be a very helpful way of introducing a handicapped child to a new school. The summer term visits were also used to plan routes around the school building so that John would be able to circulate independently.

At this point it should be recalled that John had spent the first eight years of his education in two small contiguous schools to which he was taken daily by taxi. The move to a large comprehensive school could therefore have been quite a traumatic experience for him. His mother was very concerned about this, but he is now a confident, self-assured young man, and he took this change in his stride. He walks to school, usually with a friend from the same street, crossing a major road where there is a crossing patrol. He received regular mobility training from a member of the team while he was at the middle school, both in the school and home environment and is now very competent, using a long cane and making excellent use of his limited peripheral vision. This means that, from a social point of view he is completely independent, and indeed he has travelled into the city and to football matches by bus.

Two members of the visual impairment team at present share the task of supporting John. At this stage, one or other of them is available most of the time in the school, and as far as possible they fit this into their schedule of work in such a way that they support him in their own areas of competence. They are likely to reduce their involvement as he becomes settled in the school and as the staff gain confidence in working with him. Their role is to ensure that he has the necessary materials for his lessons, to interpret visual information for him and to tackle any specific problems which may arise.

Access to the curriculum

John's main tool of communication is a Braille 'n' Print Mark 3, which includes a four-part computer memory. He therefore carries this to lessons and merely needs an electric point. He has access to an instant braille output for his own use, and can subsequently obtain a print copy for teachers, using a different memory for each subject if he needs to maintain continuity between lessons. The English teacher finds that the nature of the work makes it desirable for her to have immediate access to what John writes, so he takes the printer on its trolley to that lesson. Fortunately that particular classroom is close to the secure area where he stores his equipment. The use of a device such as Braille 'n Speak or a lap-top computer has been considered, but at present John feels that he needs to have a direct braille output when he is working.

He is continuing to learn to type on a computer. His work is very accurate, but rather slow, apparently because he is pacing himself by the response of the speech synthesizer. He at present has a practice session for typing during a weekly design lesson in which the work is inaccessible to him. He is however undertaking other parts of the art and design course. It is intended that, instead of taking him out of any course on a regular basis, the support staff will use incidental opportunities of free time to reinforce communication skills, mobility and living skills. There are indeed situations where he cannot realistically benefit from what his class is doing, and he should then have the chance to use his time more profitably.

The secondary curriculum

Each year the new third year intake at the school spends the first term in mixed ability groups. They are then re-arranged in sets for mathematics, science and French, but remain as mixed ability for the rest of the curriculum. John is now in the top set for all three streamed subjects, a fact which in itself illustrates how well he has adapted to the school.

He now normally works without any support in *English, drama, religious education, music and French*. He was initially supported in languages by the French specialist on the team, but he himself made the decision that he could manage without the extra help. He is finding the *German* rather more difficult than French, but he certainly wants to continue with it. He sometimes needs help in *music*, and his support teachers keep in touch with the staff for all these subjects to ensure that everything is going smoothly.

He particularly enjoys *humanities*, which is taught in an imaginative, participative way with the use of original documents, museum exhibits and real-life experiences. Worksheets are often used and need to be transcribed for John, and since there is a great deal of group work, the support teacher is sometimes involved in team teaching, working with a number of pupils as well as John.

127

In *mathematics*, he needs help because of having no access to the blackboard, but there are already occasions when the teacher is saying that he can manage without support. Once John has mastered the basic layout in braille of a new type of exercise, he often does much of the work orally with his support teacher, which enables him to cover more ground than if he were delayed by having to commit it all to braille. German film is used extensively for diagram work. He has done bar charts in braille, and his work has been displayed alongside that of others, but once he knew how to do it, it was better for him to concentrate on the mathematical content of the course.

In the *modular science course*, his support teacher works with his group for practical activities, and John plays as full a part as possible. He knows where to find equipment and carries out all activities except any which would be dangerous, such as pouring acid. He can observe a chemical reaction by feeling the heat of the test-tube and listening for bubbling or the "pop" of a glowing taper, and only when the change is specifically visual does he have to rely on information from others. He has studied the nature of the microscope, prepared a slide, applied stain to it and drawn a cell on German film. On a first approach to the examination board, the science staff were told that he would just score nought for skills which are inaccessible to him. They consider this atti-tude unsatisfactory and the matter will be pursued further.

He is supported in *housecraft* lessons, and the opportunity will be used to improve his living skills. He and his mother now live alone, so she does not feel the need to expect him to help her at home, but she is being encouraged to let him undertake some domestic tasks.

John is still very enthusiastic about all forms of *physical education.* He enjoys swimming and apparatus work and plays football with the support of his teacher. He has good close skills, and can manage to focus the ball with his peripheral vision up to a distance of five yards.

His year group are now selecting the options for their examination course. English, English literature, mathematics and science are compulsory for all pupils. For his three open options, John is at present thinking of doing history, French and German. There is also a modular, pre-vocational foundation course for everyone which ensures that they have some experience of curriculum areas which they are not taking for GCSE. For John, this will include art and CDT, in addition to personal and social education and work experience. He should therefore have a well-balanced curriculum with the academic bias which is appropriate for him.

Social and personal development

John has one particular friend in school, and a wide group of general friends. He has rapidly won the respect of his peers, and they are helpful to him in a relaxed way. He is completely unsupported during the lunch-hour, and there have been no problems. He will have the same group tutor for three years, and this teacher is pleased with the way he has settled into the school. He finds that John is a self-contained boy whom it is difficult to get to know, and he certainly tries to sort out his own difficulties rather than turning to others for help. He readily joins in activities such as arranging the furniture for an Open Day.

John is a good-looking, well groomed boy whose growing poise may give the impression that he has had greater social advantages than is in fact the case. Mrs K. has had to contend with many personal and family difficulties and has not always been able to give John as much support as she would have wished. When he was younger, many would have said that here was a boy who would be better off in a residential school. However, they are a close-knit family. John is in regular contact with his siblings and other members of the extended family, and the community in which he was brought up is important to him. It is by no means certain that he would have been equally happy in a totally differ-ent environment.

Apart from his interest in sport, he is a keen reader and is only restricted by the limited range of modern books available in braille which are suited to his age. He has contacts with family and neighbours, but otherwise he does not go out very much, and it has been suggested to his mother that she should encourage him to run shopping errands for her. The school visit to France was his first experience away from home,and he also attended an RNIB vacation scheme which he greatly enjoyed.

Current and future plans

John will still need some support in gaining the confidence to become fully independent. He is likely to need progressively less direct teacher support in class, largely because he is using tech-nological equipment which can give him independent communi-cation skills. He is of course in the early stages of his secondary education, but he is building on long experience of integration and at present prospects are very favourable.

9. Imram K. aged 15

Imram is a 15 year old partially sighted boy who has useful vision in only one eye and a severely restricted visual field. He attends a mainstream comprehensive school which has a resource base for visually impaired pupils. He is of good academic ability and is currently studying six subjects for public examinations.

It became apparent that Imram had a visual problem when he was about three years old, and retinitis pigmentosa was diagnosed. His parents were told that he might become blind by the time he was twelve. He himself only remembers being aware of not seeing well from when he was aged about eight, and it was particularly at night that he had difficulties. He is now totally blind in the dark, and he has tunnel vision with a reducing field. There has also been some deterioration in the quality of the remaining central vision. When he transferred to secondary school, his vision when corrected with a telescopic aid was 6/9. However, he now has only 1/60 vision in the left eye and 6/60 in the right, and his functional vision is monocular. He is able to read N10 print.

Early education in mainstream and special schools

Imram attended his neighbourhood primary school for four years. As his sight was then deteriorating, he transferred to a junior special school for the visually impaired to which he travelled daily by taxi. The school's usual practice was followed of placing a new entrant in the class a year below his own age-group. This was intended to give him the opportunity to make up ground lost by the late transfer. He remained in the special school for three years in a class of six to eight pupils. His progress was good, but he was not happy in this restricted environment, and he recalls that he found school less stimulating than when he had been in a large mainstream class.

At the special school, he received a good grounding in making competent use of the vision he had for close work. He used large print and had the benefit of considerable individual attention from his teachers. He was not introduced to keyboard skills, and he does not recall being given any overt training to develop auditory or tactile skills, doubtless because his close vision was still adequate for educational purposes. His difficulties did however deter him from reading for pleasure and this, combined with the fact that English is not his first language, caused his attainments in English to lag behind those in other subjects, particularly mathematics in which he was making very good progress.

Secondary education in a resourced school

When the transfer stage arrived, the options for Imram were a senior special school which catered for physically handicapped as well as visually impaired pupils, or a mainstream comprehensive school with a resource base for the visually impaired. The latter was thought to be more appropriate to his needs and was certainly his own preference. His transfer was delayed because he had repeated a year on entering the special school, but in that region there is some flexibility in the age of transfer. He is now in a year group in which other pupils are of a similar age to his own and he will be taking his public examinations when he is sixteen.

The resource base in his present school has three teachers, two of whom have a qualification in visual impairment. All three had substantial experience in secondary teaching before becoming involved in special education. Where possible they provide support teaching in subject areas in which they are experienced, but they have obviously had to extend their areas of expertise. The unit is currently housed in a temporary classroom at one extremity of the long school campus. This is, however, a provisional arrangement because a major rebuilding programme is under way in the school. The unit was originally near the main entrance and it will eventually return to a more central location.

This service was set up six years ago to cater for up to eighteen visually impaired pupils. There are currently thirteen in attendance. They are all partially sighted, and the unit has in fact not yet received any braille-using pupils. The authority docs, however, have a blind child in a primary school who may in due course transfer to the resourced secondary school. All visually impaired pupils in the school are full members of class groups and attend mainstream classes. They are withdrawn for additional support as required, but they all experience a high level of integration.

Imram settled well in the secondary school and has made very good progress in his academic work. In accordance with an established practice, he chose six options instead of the seven normally followed by mainstream pupils so that some time is left available for support teaching in the resource base and for training in living skills. Imram is now taking English, maths, physics, chemistry, history and computer studies.

Access to the curriculum

He uses enlarged print for most of his work. Wherever possible, material is enlarged in advance, but if teachers need to use other printed work unexpectedly, the pupil takes it over to the resource base to be enlarged. The staff in the base arrange for one of them always to be available in the unit to do the photocopying and to respond to any other emergency needs which may arise during lessons. There are no ancillary or secretarial staff, despite requests for such appointments, and this means that the teachers spend a great deal of time on work which is not appropriate to their expertise.

Imram uses his remaining sight very well for close work. He does, however, have difficulty in reading his own handwriting, and he has therefore learnt to use a microwriter. He finds this particularly helpful for note-taking in history and English. He is learning to type and will soon be receiving additional evening tuition, but he is not yet sufficiently competent for it to be a useful working medium.

His restricted visual field means that diagrams and maps cannot be made more accessible to him by enlargement. Since he cannot have a global view of a large area, he actually finds it easier to struggle with seeing the smaller version. The base now has a Minolta machine, and Imram is beginning to use tactile diagrams for some purposes. He also finds graph work difficult and the staff are experimenting with various devices to help him with this. In common with many visually impaired children, he chose to give up studying geography in which the mapwork presented him with considerable problems.

Imram is not able to see the blackboard, but on the whole teachers are able to make suitable arrangements for him to have access to printed versions of the material in use. This is not the case in mathematics where regular use of the blackboard is a fundamental part of the teaching. He therefore now uses a closed circuit television with a camera and this is kept in the room where he has his maths lessons. More general use of this type of equipment is not feasible because the school is composed of several different teaching blocks and a series of temporary classrooms. Hopefully, when the building programme is completed, it will be easier for pupils to have access to technological equipment in the classroom.

Progress in curriculum areas

Imram is expected to achieve very good examination results in *mathematics* and *science* for which he is working for the highest grades. For practical lessons, he works with a partner, and a support teacher is normally present. Some activities such as using a pipette present him with problems. Now that the assessed curriculum is broken down into specific skill areas, there is concern about how he will be able to master some of those which are fundamentally visual and discussions are under way with the examination board. In chemistry, the presentation of course work and the examination paper give rise to some difficulties. Pupils are required to use two texts simultaneously , referring from one to the other. This gives most pupils useful experience in cross-referencing and selecting relevant facts, but it puts Imram at a disadvantage because he has difficulty in finding his place.

Imram has continued to have rather more difficulty with *English*, although he should achieve an acceptable standard. He uses tapes for longer reading material and also for revision. He has developed good auditory skills and learnt through regular practice how to use this medium effectively. This is of course an important skill for an academic boy who is likely to be using a great deal of written material.

The only subject which has been omitted from Imram's curriculum is *technical studies*. A major part of the work is concerned with technical drawing, and it was felt that he would have too much difficulty in seeing his own work and that, having only monocular vision, he has a perceptual problem in understanding perspective. In the practical part of the work, there was no serious concern about his using tools, but the level of precision required would make him very dependent on teacher support. This is clearly an area of the curriculum where further work needs to be done to ensure that it is accessible to the visually impaired.

Personal and social development

People who suffer from retinitis pigmentosa often have more difficulty with distant than with close vision. A major concern for Imram and his family is that he feels very insecure in the community because he tends to knock things over on the meal table, to stumble on steps and to be unable to find anything which he drops. He has effectively no sight at night and therefore does not go out after dark. He goes to local shops alone, but is accompanied by his mother if he goes into town to larger shops. He does not look as if he is visually impaired, and feels that people, not realising his problem, are making fun of him if he stumbles or is unable to find what he wants in shops. He is determined to be as independent as possible and does not find it easy to tell people that he has difficulty in seeing.

Unfortunately, the service does not have a mobility officer. Visually impaired pupils are given basic indoor mobility training by the resource base staff and they receive help with living skills, but Imram would certainly now benefit from receiving some more formal mobility training.

The resource staff take the pupils for residential week-end activities such as skiing, and Imram is shortly taking part in a visit to France with a mainstream group, for which the staff will include the teacher in charge of the unit. These activities give the staff the opportunity to observe their pupils in social and domestic situations and to help them to develop appropriate coping skills. Imram enjoys skiing and takes part in as much physical education as possible. The school has a multi-gym which provides a very valuable alternative source of physical activity for the visually impaired students.

Imram has an older brother and sister who are fully sighted, and a younger brother and sister who have the same condition as he does. They are a closely knit family who enjoy many activities together and with their cousins who live next door. They do not, however, have many other friends in the locality, largely because the visually impaired children all travel some distance to their schools. Mr and Mrs K. are reluctant to let them go out much alone, as they feel that people do not understand their problems and will be critical of any difficulties or mishaps which may occur. Imram is now of an age when he needs to be more independent, and the school expeditions will perhaps help him in this.

Future plans

Imram is a determined, hard-working boy who is making very good progress in his studies. He says that he is interested in a career in accountancy, and he may certainly be expected to go on to a university. He makes very effective use of the sight which he has for close work, and he is also able to supplement this with the use of auditory and tactile media. He will continue to need training in mobility and help in developing more confidence in the wider community.

10. Kathleen L. aged 15

Kathleen is a 15 year old girl who attends her local comprehensive school, having received her primary education in a special school. She is visually impaired as a result of optic atrophy and an alternating divergent squint with nystagmus. Her visual acuity is 2/60 in the right eye, and has been recorded at 2/60 in the left although at times she has only been able to count fingers with the left eye. She is registered blind.

The early years

When Kathleen was born, she was identified as having dislocated hips and a squint. With appropriate medical oversight, the hip condition was corrected and has caused her no further problems. She was taken to an ophthalmic clinic for exercises and treatment for the squint, and visits continued on a regular basis, but Mr and Mrs L. have no memory of being told that the condition was anything more serious than a squint. It was therefore a considerable shock to them to be told, when she was four years old, that she would need to attend a special school. They knew nothing about special education and did not realize that there were different types of special school, so they assumed that they were being told that Kathleen was generally retarded. Kathleen had attended a local playgroup, and they were aware that she was not developing as quickly as their older son had done, but this is scarcely surprising since they had no idea how little she was able to see of the world around her.

It was only at this stage that the medical officers referred Kathleen to the education authority. The council had just appointed its first peripatetic teacher of the visually impaired. After meeting Kathleen, he also recommended that she needed to go to a special school, since the new support service had not at that stage developed sufficiently for her to receive the necessary help in the mainstream.

Fortunately, the family live within daily travelling distance of a special school for the visually impaired, so there was no need to consider a residential placement. An educational psychologist took the family to visit the school, and Mr and Mrs L. were immediately impressed with the caring, friendly atmosphere.

Special school experience

Kathleen settled down well and, now that full account was being taken of her visual difficulties, she began to make good progress across all areas of the curriculum. The only problem which developed with her work was that she had not mastered keyboard skills prior to entering the secondary department at special school and was therefore initially relying on handwriting, making the re-reading of notes taken in class very difficult. She was, however, provided with an electronic typewriter by the LEA as soon as she began to have typing lessons in school.

Kathleen enjoyed school greatly and made many very good friends there. Some of the pupils were residential and Kathleen chose to stay overnight about once a week so that she could take part in the extra-curricular activities. Mr and Mrs L. were very happy with the education she was receiving, but they became increasingly concerned about her social isolation. She was leaving home by taxi soon after 8.30 am and not reaching home until 5.00 pm. She knew no other children in the neighbourhood and her brother, who had played with her readily when she was small, was no longer the sort of companion she needed. In the evenings, at weekends and holidays she just sat at home with little to occupy her.

When she was due to transfer from the junior to the senior department of the special school, a review meeting was held in accordance with the local education authority's established policy. The advisory teacher of the visually impaired who was now in post raised the possibility of integration, but at that point Mr and Mrs L. thought it was better for her to remain in the special school. She therefore transferred to the secondary department.

However, a doubt lingered and grew as they became increasingly concerned about her social development. After discussion with Kathleen, it was agreed that a trial in a mainstream school should be arranged.

Planning the move

A problem then arose in that Kathleen had no hope of coping with mainstream classes unless she had appropriate technological equipment, and in particular a closed circuit television and a personal computer. These were not, of course, available in the local high school. It was therefore decided that, before committing any extra resources to an integration plan, Kathleen should, just for a few days, attend a mainstream high school where equipment was available because of the presence of another visually impaired pupil. This would give her an opportunity to decide whether she really wanted to make this move.

Although her reaction to this trial was positive, it was nevertheless considered that a longer trial was required before a firm decision could be made to withdraw her from the special school. A one-term placement in her local high school was therefore arranged. A key factor in this was that the Council agreed to the purchase of a closed circuit television and other equipment specifically for her use even though the placement might prove to be only short-term. It was reasoned that she must be given a fair chance to make a success of the move and, if the placement was not made permanent, the equipment would be available for other children.

Furthermore, the Council agreed to continue to pay the special school fees during the one-term trial, so that the place would remain open to her if she wished to return. This generous approach overcame problems which all too often bedevil trial placements.

Although Kathleen had herself decided that she wanted to be integrated, when the time drew near she panicked, shut herself in her bedroom, and tried to have the plans cancelled. It was only with considerable persuasion and encouragement from her parents and the advisory teacher that she agreed to give it a try. In fact, the introduction to the mainstream went smoothly and her fears were put at rest.

In the event, the trial placement proved to be very successful and when the review took place it was unanimously agreed that Kathleen should remain in the high school.

Mainstream secondary education

The school is relatively small, having some 620 pupils. The original building has been enlarged by the addition of new blocks, so it presents quite a challenging environment for a visually impaired pupil. It is within easy walking distance of Kathleen's home and was therefore the obvious choice, but it so happened that there was already a partially sighted pupil there who had far less visual difficulty than Kathleen, but who was also hearing impaired. The staff therefore had experience of catering for a pupil with special needs. Some were initially concerned about how they would cater for Kathleen, but none of the staff seem to have shown any reluctance to take on this challenge.

In the special school, pupils normally transfer to the senior department at the age of twelve years. In order that Kathleen should not be at an academic disadvantage, she was placed in the first year which was a year below her chronological age group.

However, since her birthday is in July she is only slightly older than the oldest pupils in her school year group. She is physically fairly small, and the age difference is not noticeable.

When she first entered the school, the advisory teacher provided full-time support for the first two weeks. This meant that each situation in the school day was assessed and all members of staff received on-the-spot guidance. The support was then gradually withdrawn as it became apparent that each teacher was in control of the situation. For instance, in the case of English this was after two lessons, but for CDT support was provided for six weeks. This may seem to be an expensive use of extra teaching time for one pupil, but the long-term result was that the staff of the school saw that help was rapidly available whenever they required it and they therefore felt reassured and became independent of the support more rapidly than they might otherwise have done. In other words, the intensive initial input was counter-balanced by sub-stantially reduced support in the longer term.

The situation now is that a peripatetic teacher spends half a day a week in the school. He comes for a different half-day each week, so that he can observe Kathleen working in all areas of the curricu-lum and have contact with all the teachers who are involved with her. This helps to cope with the range of contacts which is a problem peculiar to secondary education. He liaises with the deputy head teacher of the school, and provides a link with the advisory teacher for visual impairment if any major issue arises.

Access to the curriculum

Kathleen has no visual access to normal print. She reads only with a closed circuit television which she must have with her in the classroom. Because of the nature of the building, four CCTV's have been provided for her use. They are on trolleys, and are kept in a suitable secure location in each block or floor of the building, from which Kathleen wheels them to her classes, with the help of a friend if necessary. She has also been provided with a CCTV for home use. With this equipment she can read from books or worksheets, and teachers are asked to provide her with a typed copy of work which they are doing on the blackboard. For impromptu blackboard work, they are asked to speak as they write, so that she at least has oral access to the lesson, since she cannot see the blackboard at all.

For recording, Kathleen uses a Keynote word processing system with an Epsom printer and an electronic typewriter. She uses these both in school and at home. There is speech output so that she can check her work.

Until recently, she has not wished to use a cassette recorder as an alternative to reading, but she now realizes that, as more extensive reading is being required in some subjects, the CCTV is too slow a medium, and she is therefore to be provided with a variable speed tape recorder.

Progress in curriculum areas

Since Kathleen entered the school, she has experienced the full curriculum, with the exception of some aspects of physical education. She has consistently been in set 1 or 2 out of 5, but it should be noted that the ability levels in the school generally are skewed rather below the average. She has now selected her seven GCSE options, which are English, mathematics, modular science, religious education, French, home economics and information technology. Issues relating to specific areas of the curriculum are considered below.

She copes well in lessons which involve a substantial amount of written material, provided the work is available in good quality print. She has difficulty if teachers give her hand-written sheets or thin paper typed on both sides, when a reflection from the second side is thrown up by the CCTV. She can read a teacher's corrections and comments on her work with the CCTV if they are written in black or dark blue, but not red. With this equipment, reading is inevitably very slow, and this is going to be a problem for her. It is of interest that, whereas the *English* teacher told me that they have started on the GCSE texts, but she has given them "only twenty pages to read for a week's homework," Kathleen herself told me that she was worried about how she could possibly get through twenty pages before Friday! It is clear that she will need to use a cassette player for this type of reading. She admits that she has difficulty in concentrating when listening and this is a skill she will need to develop.

Kathleen is reported to have good understanding in comprehension work. She has a wide vocabulary, shows imagination in her writing and structures her ideas well. She found *geography* very difficult because of the mapwork, and has not selected this as an option.

For *mathematics* she uses handwriting because of the problems involved in recording numerical work on the computer. Her writing is difficult to read, and the recording of her work does hamper her. No suitable large-print scientific calculator is available, and she therefore relies upon viewing the calculation display under the CCTV. Practical mathematics has presented problems, in that pupils are required to make three-dimensional shapes, and her poor sight makes it very difficult for her to handle the materials accurately. Such activities are an assessable part of the course, and discussions with the examination board may be necessary.

The *French* teacher was just beginning her probationary year when Kathleen entered her class, and found the prospect of using an audio-visual course with a blind pupil somewhat daunting. However, she was determined to make a success of it, and relied largely on whispering translations or explanations to Kathleen as she taught. Where necessary, she provided written descriptions of pictures. The teacher quickly learnt to adapt both curriculum materials and teaching style, and the success of her work is demonstrated by the fact that Kathleen came at the top of the whole year group in the French examination. Kathleen really enjoys French. Her classwork and homework are of a high standard, and she is confident in oral work. Unfortunately, her computer keyboard has no accents on it, and she has difficulty in adding them by hand, which leads to errors.

In *science* pupils do practical work in pairs, and they share out tasks, so Kathleen manages quite well with the help of her partner. She is unable to use a dropping pipette, and she is going to have difficulties in taking accurate measurements. Here again, discussions with the examination board may be required, and special equipment may be needed for her GCSE work. It is also difficult for her to benefit from teacher demonstrations to the class as a whole. Despite all this, she is doing extremely well in theoretical and practical work. One advantage is that the school has a closely structured science curriculum with detailed modules, so it is relatively easy to make necessary modifications for Kathleen in advance of lessons.

In *other practical subjects* Kathleen works very competently despite her difficulties. She achieves consistently high marks in *home economics*. When she was doing *CDT*, she managed quite well with the design side of the work, but had some difficulty in using the tools and equipment. Nevertheless, she persevered so long as it was a compulsory subject. Similarly, she was at a disadvantage in *art and design*, but she came into her own when the class undertook a module on ceramics and then achieved highly. She very much enjoys *music* and plays the piano, receiving piano lessons through the LEA's peripatetic service.

Physical education has always been a difficult area for Kathleen. She misses the regular opportunity for swimming which she had at the special school. She has made good progress in running, and is pleased that sailing is now being included in the curriculum.

The school reports include a section on "Attitudes to learning" which gives a four-point score for each of the following:

> Brings necessary equipment
> Is positive in approach to work
> Works well with others
> Can work independently
> Is pleasant and co-operative
> Attempts homework conscientiously
> Maintains good level of classwork
> Responds well to constructive criticism

In many subjects Kathleen's last report records the highest score in all these areas, and in no case does she have less than the second highest score. This represents a very positive attitude to her work. Many of her teachers indeed acknowledge that they find it easier to take account of her special needs because she is such a pleasant pupil to have in the class. The efforts made by Kathleen and by her teachers are leading to good progress, with most recent examination marks in the 55-90% range.

Personal and social education

Socially Kathleen is a very well adjusted member of the school community. She does not want to stand out as being different, and is often irritated by the encumbrance of all her equipment. She also disliked being "fussed over" by well-meaning peers when she first went to the school, but they have learnt now that this is not necessary. Initially, she was the victim of some animosity from one or two children who resented the special attention she was receiving, but these were children who themselves had developmental problems, and there are no signs of these difficulties now. One friend has been a particularly valuable support and has herself benefited from this role. Kathleen is learning to be tolerant of the sometimes misguided reactions of others, and has developed a keen sense of humour in responding to them.

Her parents were delighted to find that she quickly made friends with local children once she was attending the same school. They accept that she wants increasingly to go out independently, although they of course worry very much about her safety.

Kathleen is a very attractive young girl who is interested in her personal appearance and does not look visually impaired. She uses the sight she has very competently, and her parents feel that the special school had helped her a lot in this respect. It does create the problem that strangers are unlikely to realize the difficulty which she has.

She quickly lost contact with most of her former friends at the special school. However, she recently attended a vacation scheme organised by the RNIB, and has become very friendly with another visually impaired girl whom she met there and who lives a short bus journey away from her. They go out together regularly and enjoy being able to share their experiences and laugh over their difficulties. This has not, however, taken her away from her friendships with local sighted children.

The school describe her as being far more self-assured and out-going than when she joined them. She herself says that some situations do provide her with problems but she is sensible about asking for help if she needs it. For instance, some teachers do not always provide materials in an appropriate form for her, and her dependence on technological equipment is an irritant.

Future plans

Kathleen wishes to move into a career in which she will be able to help other visually impaired people. She says that she would like to teach, but she is of course likely to come up against the continuing reluctance of the teaching profession to accept visually impaired colleagues. For the present, however, Kathleen shows every sign of having the academic ability and attitudes to take her into mainstream higher education.

11. Peter R. aged 16

Peter is a 16 year old, partially sighted boy. He is in the fifth year of a secondary school which has a special teaching facility for visually impaired pupils. He is integrated for 90% of the time, but he also receives some special support. He is entered for seven GCSE subjects.

Peter suffered retinal haemorrhage at birth in his right eye, which left him with reduced vision, and he has since had a number of further haemorrhages in this eye. Optic atrophy in the left eye at two months left him with no useful vision in this eye. He wears spectacles, has 3/36 vision in the right eye and can read N14 print. He is a sturdy young man, over six feet in height, and has no other disabilities.

The early years

Mrs R. suspected that her son was not seeing normally when he was only three weeks old, and this was medically confirmed when he was aged three months. The family received guidance from an RNIB adviser from the time when Peter was about a year old and a local teacher for pre-school handicapped children became involved when he was three and a half. At that stage, the local education authority had no service for the visually impaired.

It was suggested to Mr and Mrs R. that Peter's sight might deteriorate further, and they therefore deliberately sought to give him as wide a range of experiences as possible whilst he was able to benefit. He rode a bicycle at the age of three and was given ample opportunities for contact with other children.

After a year in a nursery school, he spent three years in his local primary school. There was still no specialist service in the authority and, although some peripatetic advice was given to the school and an ancillary assistant appointed in his third year, the staff were not able to cater adequately for his needs. His parents were concerned about his slow progress in reading and spelling and, when he suffered a further haemorrhage, they began to think that a residential special school placement might be more appropriate. However, it was at this point that the local education authority set up a visual impairment service and opened a "special teaching facility" in one of its primary schools. Peter therefore became one of the first intake into this facility, at the age of eight years.

Resourced primary school

The facility had two teachers and a nursery nurse. It was equipped with special lighting, a closed circuit television, magnifiers, desk stands, large print books and similar items. Peter was placed in a mainstream class of his own age-group with 32 pupils, but was initially withdrawn for about 40% of the time. This time was used for special teaching in perceptual skills, mobility, computer work, English and topic work, and at a later stage for touch typing. The concentrated help which he received enabled him to make up some of the ground which he had lost when he was not receiving regular support, and the proportion of integration was gradually increased to reach 80% by the time he left the primary school.

143

His school reports show that his achievements in reading and English remained rather below average, but he received an average score for effort and was gradually making some progress. It is recorded that, to improve his spelling, he needed more experience of reading and should try to read for pleasure. This highlights a central difficulty for a child for whom the physical activity of reading is laboured. In maths he readily grasped new concepts, but once again was somewhat held back by his difficulty in handling the written language associated with mathematics.

Peter worked enthusiastically in other areas of the curriculum. He played a full part in class discussions showing good general knowledge even if the follow-up written work was more difficult for him. He showed ability in music, drama, art and physical education. It became increasingly difficult for him to take part in team games, chiefly because contact sports put him at greater risk of retinal haemorrhage, but he was an enthusiastic runner.

In the primary school, Peter very quickly became well-liked by fellow-pupils and adults. He was a self-assured child with a positive approach to life, and he was already showing initiative and leadership qualities. He says himself that, in his neighbourhood school and sometimes at later stages, he was the victim of some teasing, but he seems to have taken this in his stride. Looking down now from his six foot two inches in height, he flexes his muscles and comments wryly that he no longer has any problems of that sort!

Mr and Mrs R. were by now pleased with the progress which Peter was making. They were a little concerned about the long taxi journey which he had to undertake each day, and protested strongly when the escort was suddenly changed for no apparent reason. They are insistent that, if a long journey is necessary, it is important for the peace of mind of both child and parents that there should be a stable relationship with the escort. The original person was, in fact, reinstated in accordance with their wishes. The change of school did mean that Peter lost contact with friends in his immediate neighbourhood. However, as he developed wider interests of his own, this ceased to be a matter of special concern to him.

Resourced secondary education

At the point when he reached the end of his primary school years, a "special teaching facility" was introduced in a secondary school in the authority, and he was therefore amongst the first visually impaired children to enter that school. The special facility consists of two teachers and a non-teaching assistant, and has a physical base in a central position within the school. This originally consisted of just one room which provides administrative support, reprographic facilities, storage space and an area for withdrawal teaching. Now that educationally blind children and a higher overall number of visually impaired pupils are attending the school, an adjacent room has been allocated for the use of the service.

Peter has moved through the school as a full member of a class of his own age-group. There were approximately thirty pupils in the class in the first three years, but in years four and five he has been in subject option groups of various sizes. In years one to three, Peter was integrated for 85% of the time, with 5% being devoted to learning touch typing and 10% to subject support and basic skill reinforcement. In the final two years, typing became one of his option subjects, but he has continued to spend about 10% of his time on skill reinforcement and private study. Despite this element of withdrawal, he has had some experience of all areas of the curriculum. The arrangement for visually impaired pupils in the option years is that they select one less option than other pupils, in order to leave them with some time for extension work.

Access to the curriculum

Peter needs enlarged print for all his school work. The material is prepared by staff in the special facility and since the school has now had regular experience of visually impaired pupils over a number of years, teachers are fully accustomed to making their requirements known in advance. The teacher who is in charge of the facility has been in post since the initiation of the scheme with the result that routines are well-established and smooth-flowing. Problems do inevitably arise and, as in any community, some people are better organised than others, but overall the visually impaired pupils are well supported. Each year an induction session is provided for newly appointed staff, and this includes exercises with simulation spectacles.

In addition to using large print, Peter has a monocular viewer which he in fact rarely uses, and the closed circuit television is of help to him for certain activities such as reading ordnance survey maps. For mathematics and science he is provided with specialised equipment including a clear calculator, protractor and ruler, a digital thermometer and voltmeter.

For recording his work, he uses handwriting, typewriting or word processing at his own choice and the decision depends on the type of exercise. His typewriting is not yet really fluent and his spelling requires further improvement. This is of course related to the fact that his reading is still slow and laboured and he does not have the experience of reading for pleasure which would improve his command of written English.

Progress in curriculum areas

The subjects for which he is entered for GCSE are *English, maths, geography, physics, technology, office studies* and *typing.* He will have 50% extra time for the examinations in maths and geography. Some difficulties are being encountered in preparing him for the *office studies* examination because of the design of the question paper. Students are asked to type from a handwritten draft and from a text with handwritten random amendments shown in "balloons." This is of course a relevant exercise for students preparing for secretarial work, but visually impaired people have great difficulty in reading handwriting or random alterations. On the other hand, if the working text were presented for Peter in neat, typewritten form, this might seem to defeat the whole point of the exercise. This is a matter which has to be further explored with the examination board.

In practical work for *physics and technology*, Peter works with a friend who is also partially sighted. The two boys have moved up through the school together and are firm friends. They tackle problems together and show considerable initiative and ingenuity in finding solutions. Their closeness has in some measure restricted the development of friendships with fully sighted peers, but they do nevertheless provide valuable mutual support to each other. This is one of the advantages which Peter has found in being in a school where there is a concentration of visually impaired pupils.

Although he is managing to hold his own in academic work, it is particularly in practical and physical activities that he excels. He is still not able to take part in contact sports because of the risk of haemorrhage, but he participates fully in *outdoor pursuits*, including running, rock climbing and pot-holing. He has done sailing, cycling and tandem riding - on one occasion in partnership with a blind boy! He has been skiing with disabled groups and he is able to play snooker and bowls. He in fact makes very effective use of the sight which he has.

Peter is interested in mechanical things and particularly cars, despite the knowledge that he will, of course, never be able to drive. He recently undertook some *work experience* in a garage and performed satisfactorily. He once assisted teachers by repairing the school minibus.

He had considered some form of mechanics as a career, but is now proposing to apply for a catering course at a local college of further education, where peripatetic teaching support would be available to him.

Social and personal development

He received mobility training whilst at primary school, and at that stage used a symbol cane. However he does not like to use it now. He has good co-ordination and as a result of the regular training which he has received, his mobility is quite good. He is therefore able to circulate quite confidently, and goes into the neighbouring large city alone or with a friend. He has a sensible attitude to his difficulties, and when walking with others frequently asks for information about things which he cannot see clearly.

Peter has a good relationship with his elder brother. Their parents have been careful to treat the two boys as equal, but different. The older one enjoys shooting and model car racing. Peter has an electric organ and goes skiing.

Peter is an outgoing, friendly boy who is very popular with both fellow-pupils and staff. He is determined to live as normally as possible, and is a well-adjusted confident young man. His bent is practical rather than intellectual, but he is expected to achieve an average set of results in his GCSE examinations. There can be no doubt that this will be attributable to the regular support and training which he has received throughout his education.

12. William G. aged 17

William is a young man of 17 who has one artificial eye and severely impaired vision in the remaining eye. He attends a comprehensive school which has a resource base for visually impaired pupils. This is a case of a boy who was not referred to the LEA's visual impairment until late in his education. However, he achieved some passes in public examinations in his fifth year, and is now spending one year in the sixth form before going on to seek employment.

At birth, one of William's eyes was unformed and he had microphthalmus in the other. It is thought that the cause is likely to have been rubella, but evidence of the mother's contact with the disease was never established. The doctors at first thought that he was totally blind. When his parents noticed that their baby was aware of the Christmas tree lights, the doctor attributed this to wishful thinking, and it was some time before it was acknowledged that he had some sight. He was provided with a prosthesis for the missing eye, and he soon learnt to manage this himself. He now has 1/36 vision in the remaining eye, the condition of which is static.

The early years and primary education

The medical services did not refer William to the education department, and his parents had no idea that any special support or advice might be available to them. They were relieved to find that he had some sight and did what they could to help him to use it. They live in a housing estate on the outskirts of a major city, and William went to the neighbourhood primary school until the age of twelve. The classes were quite large and no additional staffing support was provided. The teachers knew that he had poor sight and he recalls that they were all very understanding and helpful to him. However, written material was not enlarged and he could not of course see the blackboard. He managed as best he could and became quite adept at disguising his problems because he did not like attracting attention to himself. At that time, schools were less aware of special educational services, and the need to seek guidance.

During his primary education, William made slow progress in basic skills, but his teachers will not have known how far this was attributable to the visual impairment. His own memory is that he generally tried hard with his work, but if he found it too difficult he just did nothing, but kept quiet. He is now a self-contained calm young man, and it is easy to believe that he would have attracted little attention in a large, busy class. Despite his very restricted, monocular vision, he is quietly competent in mobility and self-help skills. He socialised well with his peer group in and out of school. He recalls that he was sometimes the victim of teasing, but he accepts philosophically that most children are likely to suffer from this at some stage, and certainly he also did his share of teasing others! He took part in games with other children and also rode a bicycle on the quiet streets of the estate.

Mainstream secondary education

William transferred to the local comprehensive school alongside his peers. He was withdrawn from some lessons for general remedial support and the ophthalmic clinic had now provided him with a telescopic aid. However, he used this very little since the teachers were not at that stage doing much blackboard work. By the time he reached the second year, he was having serious difficulties with most of his work, and it was decided that he should repeat the second year. He could well have drifted on through school in a failing situation, but the deputy head teacher suspected that his visual impairment might be a more significant factor in his difficulties than had previously been realised. He referred the matter to the education office, and the visual impairment service then learnt of William's existence for the first time!

It was proposed that he should transfer to another comprehensive school which had a resource base for visually impaired pupils. He himself was reluctant to do this, because he was well-adjusted socially and did not want to leave his established group of friends and move out of the neighbourhood community. However, Mr and Mrs G. were very concerned about his low achievements at school and welcomed the opportunity for him to have extra help. William eventually agreed to a trial placement in the other school. After the trial he was persuaded to remain at his new school, but he was not happy about the move and it took him a long time to settle.

Resourced secondary education
He was placed in a mainstream class most of the members of which were a year younger than himself. He was integrated for most subjects, but had some withdrawal time to improve his basic skills. The resource base in this school has three teachers who undertake withdrawal teaching, classroom support and the preparation of materials as required.

William had some experience of all curriculum areas except technical studies. He has difficulty in understanding perspective because his vision has always been monocular, and his teachers therefore felt that he would gain little from doing technical drawing. In practical work he would have had problems in achieving the detailed accuracy required. For a boy who had many gaps in his education to make good, the use of time was critical and some choices had to be made, but it should be noted that some partially sighted children undertake technical studies successfully.

When the time came to select options for public examinations, William gave up history and geography, both of which he was finding very difficult. Nevertheless, he had at least had some introduction to the subjects. He eventually achieved basic, "general level" passes in English, home economics and social and

149

vocational studies, although he did not pass the other subjects which he took. For a boy who, at the age of 14, had been failing dismally in all his school work, this represents a quite noteworthy achievement. He clearly benefitted from the increased individual attention provided by the resource base, and the specialist understanding of the nature of his difficulties.

Access to the curriculum

William normally uses enlarged print for his school work. He can read small print if he holds it close to his eye, but only very slowly. He has begun to learn to type, but is not really fluent. He uses a computer in the resource base, and also has one of his own at home, but does not often use this for school work. He is not an academic boy, and reading and writing are unlikely to play a significant part in his working life, but he has now mastered strategies for overcoming the barrier to learning which his visual impairment created.

Post-sixteen education

He is now spending a year in the sixth form, taking non-examination modules in media studies, communication skills and computing. He also spends one day a week on a catering course at a local further education college, and is greatly enjoying this.

Personal and social development

William is a good-natured, quietly confident young man, well over six feet tall and very slim. It can be seen that he is visually impaired, but this might not be apparent to strangers. He has very good self-care and independence skills. Although initially he travelled to the resourced school by taxi, he now goes independently using a bus and train. He readily goes into the city alone or with friends. He has been away from home on short skiing and other holidays with a group of visually impaired young people, and he generally has relaxed, happy relationships with his peers. Having been in neighbourhood schools for most of his education, he retained his friendships in the local community even when he moved to the resourced school.

For work experience, he helped with ground maintenance at a golf course, and worked so well that the manager would have been happy to employ him on a permanent basis. He hopes to undertake some form of outdoor work, but has encountered the problem that for farmwork he would be required to drive a tractor which is obviously an impossibility for him.

150

William feels ready to leave school now, but he is pleased that he transferred to the resourced school and appreciates the achievements which have resulted. The teachers in the base have been amazed and delighted at the progress he has made from a very poor starting-point. Mr and Mrs G. are understandably aggrieved that they received no support or guidance when their son was young, but they are very pleased that he has developed so well.

13. Khalid F. aged 24

Khalid is a young man aged 24 who is totally blind. He experienced full integration at secondary level before going on to a specialist residential college, and he now attends a mainstream college of higher education. His qualifications include five CSE's, seven 'O' levels and a BTec General, and he has almost completed an HND course in business and management.

At birth, Khalid was blind in one eye and had very little sight, described by doctors as 25%, in the other, as a result of glaucoma. At the age of eleven, an operation was performed with the hope of improving his sight, but sadly it was followed by a retinal haemorrhage and he became irreversibly blind. He now wears attractively shaped dark glasses. He is a tall, good-looking young man with a relaxed, out-going manner.

A late start

Khalid's family first came to England when he was ten years old. At that time, there were no local educational facilities for severely visually impaired children in the area where they came to live, and his family were told that he would have to go away to a residential school. They were not prepared to agree to this, and some home tuition was therefore arranged, but in the event this seems to have been rather spasmodic. After about a year, Khalid returned to Pakistan for twelve months, and then at the age of twelve, he settled in England on a permanent basis.

At this point, the LEA in which the family was living had just appointed their first peripatetic teacher of the visually impaired, and it was possible to consider local provision for Khalid. He of course spoke virtually no English and had had no training in the skills he would require. Initially he was placed in a school which served as a language centre for newly arrived immigrants, providing intensive tuition in English. There was another blind Asian boy in a similar situation to Khalid, and an additional part-time teacher was therefore appointed to work with these two boys. She was an experienced special needs teacher, but had had no previous experience of visual impairment, so she worked under the guidance of the peripatetic teacher, concentrating on teaching the boys English and developing their tactile skills.

The other boy had additional special needs and was eventually transferred to a special school. As Khalid made progress, he began to learn braille and was introduced to mobility training. The Social Services mobility officer provided him with a full training over a substantial period of time, covering indoor and outdoor mobility, the use of public transport and even coping with visits to an unfamiliar town. Khalid himself is sure that this early and comprehensive training in mobility was a major factor in enabling him to experience full integration in his secondary school.

The move to secondary school

The LEA had a 13-18 community high school which had facilities for physically handicapped pupils and had recently admitted partially sighted boys. When the head mistress was approached with a request to receive a blind boy, she was initially somewhat daunted. However, the teacher in the school who had overall responsibility for the physically handicapped pupils had some personal experience of blind people and knew a little braille. It was this factor which tipped the balance in favour of responding to the request. Khalid then presented as a confident, extrovert boy who was anxious to learn. Since his parents spoke little English, contact with the family was through his elder brother, but it was clear that they were a close-knit, supportive family, that they realised Khalid had ability and were determined that he should make a success of his education.

Khalid was therefore admitted to the third year, with the normal 13+ intake from middle schools. He was in fact in the age-group above this, and since his birthday is in September, he was almost fifteen when he entered the school. This delay had of course arisen because of his late arrival in England, his need to learn English and the recent onset of total blindness, and it was obviously unavoidable. However, the age difference never seems to have presented him with any difficulties in his peer group relationships.

From a physical point of view, the school presented many potential difficulties. It had been built to a forward-looking "community" design, as part of a shopping complex, with the public library and a theatre being incorporated into the school building.

Access was via broad flights of steps or ramps, and internally there were ramps alongside staircases for the wheelchair pupils. Most teaching areas were open-plan, the only place for withdrawal teaching was a screened area of a landing, and the internal structure of the school was very complex.

In fact, the school could have been seen as a most unsatisfactory environment for a blind boy. In the event, the inherent problems were turned to advantage, since there was never any suggestion that he should experience anything other than total integration, and for four years he had daily exposure to all the complexities of a real-life environment. The school has not proved to be as satisfactory for blind pupils who have additional special needs, but Khalid's ability and personality were such that he derived full benefit from the environment.

It is important to note, however, that he was not always an ideal pupil. He has always found some difficulty in persevering with academic work and, because he was so anxious to be independent, he tended not to ask for help when he needed it. These factors, combined with his deficient command of English and poor braille skills when he entered the school, put a brake on the progress which he should have made. He was popular with the other pupils and readily got into mischief with them. On the first serious infringement of a school rule, when he was given a "detention," he said smugly: "I can't stay for a detention because I go home by taxi!" The time of the taxi was promptly changed, so that he could stay for the detention, and Khalid still remembers this clear signal that he was to be treated exactly as other pupils.

Access to the curriculum

Khalid studied the full range of the curriculum in year three, but had some withdrawal time to improve his English and braille, the content of the work being selected to reinforce his mainstream lessons. The regular support was given by the special needs teacher, but peripatetic staff also visited the school frequently in the early stages. The school had an additional allocation of staffing to take account of the needs of disabled pupils and, in view of the resulting smaller classes, it was the accepted practice that pupils with special needs were full members of the classes and only had individual support in lessons when the particular activities necessitated it.

They were eventually able to appoint an ancillary worker who had a qualification as a technician for the blind. She supported Khalid in some practical lessons and prepared his materials, including raised maps and diagrams and braille required at short notice. All his text books were transcribed into braille by prison services, but advance notice of several months had, of course, to be given for this. Khalid used a brailler, typewriter and cassette recorder for classwork and homework, and where necessary his work was transcribed for teachers.

When he moved into the fourth year, he selected two fewer options than other pupils, so that he would continue to have time for further skill training and reinforcement work. The subjects he took were English, mathematics, drama, science, environmental studies and art. He was later to drop science, but he achieved CSE passes in the other five, with a Grade 1 giving him an 'O' level in mathematics. This was all after an additional year of study, because at the end of his fourth year the lag in his basic skills was still hindering his progress, and he therefore repeated the fourth year course, whilst remaining with his class group as a fifth year pupil.

Curriculum provision

Khalid particularly enjoyed *mathematics*, and coped very well with the course despite the problems of braille notation. He was less interested in *science* and therefore did not take it as an examination subject, but he nevertheless studied most of the course, including the practical work.

He continued to have some difficulties with written *English* and spelling, but he made sufficient progress to pass the examination. He took an enthusiastic interest in *drama*. Much of the course was concerned with improvisation and self-expression, and this was very valuable for his developing confidence and independence. He took part in plays, and recalls that, if he forgot his words, he just improvised, and the producer once asked him if he would please leave the writing of the play to the author!

The *environmental studies* course included a substantial amount of mapwork, and the school soon had its own thermoform machine to help with this. There was a regular element of outside visits associated with the course, including a range of outdoor pursuits. Khalid took a full part in all of this, the group having an additional member of staff, in some instances the head mistress. She well remembers the difficulty she had in keeping pace with him in walking and hill climbing. He particularly enjoyed a midnight walk when he had the advantage over other pupils.

He also showed some ability in *art*. As in other subjects, early negotiations took place with the examination board, and the CSE syllabus was adapted so that he did clay work and pattern work on his brailler.

Personal and social development

Khalid had good tactile skills and quickly became competent in braille. He also used his auditory skills well, and became adept at recognising voices and footsteps. He was completely independent about the school, and had many friends. His home was several miles from the school, but if he wanted to stay after lessons for extra-curricular activities or just to socialise with friends, he found his way home by bus. If he stayed late in the evening, friends' parents would take him home by car. His social development was therefore not impeded by going to a resourced school at some distance from his home. He also had friends in his own neighbourhood, because he was just not prepared to let his blindness impede him. He had been a cyclist before he became totally blind, and he admits that he continued to ride his bicycle in local streets, orientating himself by sound and echo location.

Post-school special education

Khalid thus completed his examination course at the age of eighteen. It did not seem appropriate for him to remain longer at school, but he wanted to continue studying. It was therefore suggested that he should go to a specialist residential college, where he could take courses with a vocational bias and gain experience in independent living with some formal training in living skills. He accordingly went to college for three years, but he feels that, in his particular circumstances, it was a mistake. He had been accustomed to full integration and a high measure of independence, and he found it very difficult to settle in a residential community. He was too out-spoken, not over-zealous with his studies and rebellious about the accepted structures. He became very active in the students' union, and developed difficult relationships with the staff. He readily acknowledges, however, that this was probably largely his fault.

In his first year at the college he achieved a pass level in the BTec General. In the following year, he took 'O' level courses with a bias towards business studies and achieved four passes. In the third year, he began 'A' level geography and also took three more 'O' level subjects. He was therefore building up a very respectable bank of qualifications despite feeling ill-at-ease in the college. At the end of the third year, he applied to spend a further year in the college, but he had to go on an extended visit to Pakistan for domestic reasons, and on his return he decided to make a break with the college.

Mainstream further education

He was then accepted as a mature student on an HND course at a local college of higher education. He was their first blind student, but there were also some partially sighted students in the college. There was a lecturer appointed to support visually impaired students, and they had the services of a braillist to transcribe work as required. Khalid was provided with a Eureka, a braille embosser and other general equipment such as a cassette recorder.

With the help of this technology, he had ready access to the HND course. His support staff had substantial difficulties with the element of the course concerned with finance, because of the problems of presenting the layout of accounts in braille,and because Khalid had a perceptual problem in understanding this. They also found that he continued to be too independent in his approach to study, and not always to ask for help when he needed it. He in fact completed most of the course satisfactorily, but failed one examination which he is about to take again.

Current and future plans

Khalid wants a career in business and would like to study further. The reason that he has not always been successful is that he has too much zest for life and other interests which distract him from his studies. He at present works for the Citizen's Advice Bureau, is taking a course in counselling, and also works for a local radio station.

Khalid is now married and has a baby son. His wife and child and all his friends are sighted, and he believes that blind people must themselves make the effort to help other people to get through the "sensitivity barrier" in relationships. He says that both blind and sighted people should stop referring to each other as "they," and sighted people should be made to understand that the blind are not embarrassed at the use of vocabulary related to sight. He has grown up in a sighted world, and is himself completely relaxed. His friends become equally relaxed by contact with him, and this highlights one of the side benefits of having blind children in mainstream schools.

14. Ashraf B. aged 21

Ashraf is a tall, seemingly self-assured young man of 21 with an out-going personality and a strong sense of humour. To a stranger he would not appear to be visually impaired, although he does not have much direct eye contact when in conversation. He has retinitis pigmentosa.

Ashraf's perspicacious appraisal of his own experiences offers some salutary lessons to all those who work with the visually impaired. This study therefore takes a rather different form from the others. Extracts from a conversation with him are presented in his own words, and are interspersed with a commentary designed to pinpoint what may be learnt from them.

'The doctors always knew I had retinitis pigmentosa, but I don't know how much they knew about it at school. I had no extra help or special equipment.'

The school undoubtedly knew that Ashraf was visually impaired, but were probably told that his loss of vision was not severe. However, with a deteriorating condition, there should be regular monitoring of actual visual functioning as well as medical examination. It seems that this did not happen.

'When I was little, I really loved reading. I used to go to the public library every day after school and come back with one or two books which I read from cover to cover. I could see to read then, and anyway, they were children's books, so the print was quite large. Then reading started to get more difficult and I lost interest. Reading was such hard work and so slow.'

Many children are slow or reluctant readers, but if a child who has been a fluent reader becomes less competent, alarm bells should start to ring.

'I always suffered from night blindness. I used to go to the cinema with my cousin. I remember I couldn't find my way to the toilet. He said: 'It's over there,' but I got lost. When we came out, I used to bump into things and stumble off the pavement. One of my mates told my parents, but they didn't think it was a serious problem. They had been out with me (in daylight, of course) and knew I could see then.'

Parents ought to be told what signs to look for in their child's condition. Even if they have received advice, they may not fully understand, particularly when language and cultural differences set up a barrier between them and their advisers. In fact, in Ashraf's case, he did not begin to visit the eye clinic regularly until he was about eight years old, so his family had no access to advice.

'I couldn't see anything on the blackboard, but my friends let me copy from them. Some of them knew I had problems, but I didn't want to say anything to the teachers. I don't know why. Partially sighted people often just don't want anyone to know.'

Indeed some children go to amazing lengths to conceal their difficulties. If they are asked if they can see something, they will say "Yes," and teachers need to ask more specific questions and test such children carefully in order to check on their sight.

'My strongest memory of the middle school was cricket lessons. I tried so hard. You see, I have tunnel vision, and when I was fielding I could see the ball coming towards me, but when it got near my feet, it disappeared! I reached out and missed, and everybody laughed. The teacher got angry with me, or sometimes he teased me and said: 'Why don't you borrow my glasses if you can't see?' He knew I was "partially sighted," but I don't think he understood what it meant. I'll never forget that third year in the middle school. Time and time again I watched the ball coming, and just when I was going to catch it, it disappeared!'

Teachers who are in contact with visually impaired pupils should be given very specific information about the nature of a child's difficulties, including practical experience using simulated spectacles, where appropriate. Ashraf's PE teacher probably thought it was best just to "laugh off" his difficulties, and doubtless had no idea that his lessons were to remain a haunting, grim memory of the child's middle school years.

'I did not do well in the secondary school because the reading was becoming more and more difficult. I said nothing about it, though, and I was put in the CSE classes. Then, in the fifth year, there was a set book which we had to read for CSE English, and the teacher made us read in turns round the class. I was horrified. I knew I couldn't read it and they would all laugh if I stumbled along from word to word.'

It is worth bearing in mind that, after primary school, pupils may not often be required to read aloud. A visual difficulty may therefore more easily remain unidentified. A pupil may well pretend to read silently and use other devices to gain access to the content.

'When my turn to read came, I said: 'I don't want to read.' The teacher was furious. 'Everyone is reading and so must you!' she said. I repeated; 'I don't want to read' and then mumbled: 'I can't see it.' She was still angry, but then she suddenly seemed to understand. She must have talked to her colleagues, because things started to happen.'

Teenagers can often be obstinate and unco-operative, and teachers can understandably be irritated by their behaviour. This particular teacher was sensitive enough to pause and listen to what the boy was finding it so difficult to say.

'When it was realized how bad my sight was, the careers teacher saw me, and it was decided that I should go away to a special residential college for three years. I didn't want to go, but they said I had to. I wanted to stay at school and do 'O' levels and 'A' levels.'

We now place considerable store by involving parents in discussions about their child's education, but it is equally important to involve the young person. Ashraf certainly has the impression that he had no say at all in where he was to go. From this point it was almost predictable that things would not work out well.

'For the rest of my fifth year, I went to a local special school for the visually impaired for one day a week to learn braille before going to the college in the September. I didn't need braille then and I soon forgot it. I have started taking lessons again now, as I realise that I shall need it some day.'

It may well seem sensible to provide a child with a skill he is going to need later, and indeed some children are left struggling with print when they would make far better progress with braille. However the time spent in teaching braille may not be justified so long as print is still a possible medium of communication, and a short concentrated course of training at the optimum time may be more effective.

"I did not really enjoy the time I spent at that college. All I remember about the first year was learning ironing and

braille! I had wanted to start on the 'O' level course, but they insisted on my doing the foundation course first. I felt that much of this was too basic for me. I do not remember having any mobility training.'

It is possible that he appeared not to need it, and once again did not admit to the difficulties he was having in the dark. In fact, although he was given a formal medical examination and sight test, it seems that his functional vision was not tested.

'At the college I passed 'O' levels in English, maths, commerce, sociology and information processing. I then started on an 'A' level course in history and sociology.'

Despite his dislike of the college, he was clearly making up for the time he had lost at school when his difficulties were unrecognised, and he was showing that he had more ability than had been apparent.

'I had had lots of friends at school. When I first went to college, we used to write letters and meet in the holidays, but it only lasted about six months. Then we just lost touch. I was very lonely in the holidays.'

This is an inevitable problem with residential placements. Teenagers with disabilities find it difficult enough to mix easily with their peers, and once they are outside established groupings, the chances of breaking into them are small.

'The LEA had sponsored me for three years at the college, but after two and a half years I left. When I had told them I wanted to go to university, they told me that they did not consider me capable of university work.

There often seem to be a tendency for educators to set their sights too low for visually impaired students. Many of the problems arising from their disability, such as lack of confidence, slowness and poor handwriting are associated in the teacher's mind with low academic potential, and the young person's true ability is often under-estimated.

'After leaving the college, I went to our local technical college and did a BTec course. I passed it with overall merit, and my name was even put forward for a special award, though I didn't in fact get one.'

160

Ashraf was clearly resolved to prove that he was able to achieve more than was expected of him, and he was continuing to build on the confidence which his residential experience had given him.

'I find studying quite hard-going, because even with the CCTV, reading is so slow. I have tried using books on cassette, but I hate it. It's so difficult to concentrate, and I fall asleep.'

Cassettes are invaluable for extended reading, but they are not easy to use. Visually impaired children should be given regular training in their use so that they develop the auditory skills which will later be so valuable to them.

'By now I was using low vision aids and also closed circuit television with a camera to help me see the blackboard. I was promised this equipment when I first went to the local college, but it was a year and a half before it came, so I only had it for the last 6 months. There were then difficulties because they didn't provide a trolley, there wasn't room for the equipment on my desk and it was difficult to get it from room to room. But I solved that problem! I got to know someone who works for a crematorium; he makes those trolleys they push the coffins about on. So he made me a similar one , and I had the CCTV at one end, the camera at the other, and a good working space in between. It was ideal!'

Top marks for ingenuity, but this is yet another example of the world of special education lagging behind developments in technology. These students really should have more efficient technical support. Ashraf was in fact then receiving regular visits from a support lecturer, whom he found very helpful, but the college had no previous experience of visual impairment, and it took them some time to adapt to his needs.

'After the BTec, I moved to a college of higher education, where I am in my first year of an HND course. I also do some part-time voluntary work now. I want to go into marketing. I should still like to gain a university degree, but I am already 21 and must get going on a career. The degree will have to be by part-time study. I am going to end up with a collection of certificates which will look funny, as it starts with CSE's and a certificate in English as a Second Language. I was told then that any little qualification might be of some use to me.'

This range of certificates will convey a graphic message in spanning the gulf between what was expected of him and what he has achieved. Ashraf's English, incidentally, is faultless and a certificate in it quite irrelevant.

'There is an ancillary helper in the college. She works with me particularly in the accountancy course, because I can't read the material on the computer. There is a computer programme which enlarges the print, but no-one seems to know how to use it properly. You have to keep changing discs, and it's all so complicated that we don't bother.'

Technology has the power to resolve so many difficulties for the visually impaired, but their teachers and supporters must first master the technology!

'The HND course has core modules for which we do integrated assignments. This is a group exercise and I enjoy it, because a lot of it is discussion and we share out the reading. My ancillary helps with the research work as we have to consult library books and so on.'

Group learning is obviously particularly accessible to a visually impaired student. This can equally well be used as a technique at school level. Most of the assignment work for GCSE is individual, but there is some scope for group projects, in which the handicapped student must make a fair contribution, but with a bias towards the skills which are most appropriate to him.

'When I first went to the college of HE, I was desperately unhappy. All the other students were in groups and I sat alone. They knew I could not see very well. I wished I had never gone there. I decided I had to get to know the others somehow, but how do you start a conversation? One day, there was another boy sitting alone, so I went and sat by him and said: 'Where do you come from?' He told me, and I said it must be a long journey. He laughed and said: 'Oh, I don't come every day. I am in a hall of residence!' So I asked what that was like, and we were into a conversation. It was just how to get started. When his friends came in, they just accepted me in their group.'

People generally ought to be more welcoming and out-going towards anyone who has a disability. Since they frequently are not welcoming, those who have the disability often have to make the first move, and overcome their own inhibitions. Ashraf now has the maturity to do this, but he has learnt the hard way.

'I use a symbol cane, but it is not much use in a crowded building, as people just jostle me like everyone else. I have still had no formal mobility training, so I was delighted when I was told that the mobility officer from the Social Services Department would see me at the college. She showed me the routes around the building, and said: 'Is that all right?' so I just said: 'Yes, OK.' I am still silly like that. It wasn't all right at all, and she obviously didn't realise that I needed more help, but I don't like to make a fuss. When I told the lecturer for special needs about this, she said I was being silly and I must go back and ask for more help.'

'I went to see the mobility officer, and started by saying: "I don't like using the long cane." She became angry, saying I was being 'stroppy' and it was for my own good. This time I persevered and explained that I had never had any mobility training and I really needed help. Now we have started from the beginning and I am doing a proper mobility course.'

One is left wondering how many visually impaired people are deprived of help which could be given because of misunderstandings and a failure to perceive needs which are poorly expressed.

'I have plenty of friends at college now. One boy used to irritate me because he was always saying: 'Careful!...Mind that post... There's someone coming ... Don't bang into that!' and he kept grabbing hold of me. He was trying to be helpful and I knew I ought not to be irritated, but it got on my nerves, and it was going to spoil our friendship. One day I made up my mind and said to him : 'Look, we're mates, aren't we? You mustn't mind me saying it, but I don't like you doing that. Can you stop, please?' He said: 'Oh, I see. OK.' Now everything's fine and we're great friends.

I have another friend who just treats me as he would anyone else. He once parked his car in an area marked "Private" and someone parked another car where it blocked us in. They wouldn't move it because they said we had no right to be there. We had to get out, so my friend said: 'Come on! Do you know how to bump a car?' Between us, we moved it and got out. Then he said: 'Let's bump the other car back again, so they won't know how we got out.' So we did, and then off we went laughing. I remember that incident, because we were just having fun together, and my friend treated me as if I was no different from anyone else.'

He clearly remembered the incident because this friend completely disregarded his visual difficulties, whereas other people found it so difficult to behave so naturally with him. It is not easy for anyone to strike the right balance between giving help where it is needed and seeing the true person beyond the disability. We all have to try to be more perceptive about this, but visually impaired people also need to learn how to help themselves and guide their friends to what is required. Ashraf has obviously learnt how to do this, but some people never learn unaided and suffer continual social unease which could be relieved if they were just given a few techniques for managing the situation. If you go about it the right way, it is possible to ask someone to behave differently without causing offense.

'I like being with sighted people, but I also have some good friends who are visually impaired. It's good to be able to talk about our problems and laugh about them together.'

One difficulty about integration is that a child may feel very lonely, and need at least some contact with others who have similar difficulties. RNIB's vacation schemes for integrated children provide such an opportunity, and have shown that teenagers in particular welcome the chance to meet each other.

'I know of course that I shall eventually go blind. I depend so much on my sight. What will it be like to be totally blind? From the age of thirteen I went for my hospital appointments alone, and when I was about fourteen, the doctor told me that I would be blind before I was twenty. I worried so much about it, and here I am at twenty-one and the condition seems to be stable. Now they say I'll be blind at 35 or 40. They don't really know. I have been reading about RP. There are twelve different sorts. The doctors don't really know, so why tell me they did? I was so upset.'

Children are sometimes not told that their sight will deteriorate. They can generally cope with the truth better than adults expect, and there is a case for saying that they are entitled to know the facts. However, where there is uncertainty, surely hope should always be fostered in the young.

'I don't like going out at night in the town now. I stand at the edge of the pavement with my cane, and five, ten, twenty people go by before a man or woman says: 'Can I help you?' Why don't the others offer to help? They don't seem to know

what to do. I think integration is good for sighted people. Children will grow up knowing how to treat a blind person.'

This should undoubtedly be one of the advantages of having more people with disabilities in the community but we still have a long way to go for our society as a whole to become more understanding.

Sadly, this account reveals that we have a long way to go in many areas if we are to give a fair deal to visually impaired children. It is not all negative, however, because Ashraf has come through his problems and is able to make a success of his life. His experiences highlight what can be done and what should be done to support those who may not have the qualities of personality which have been a strength to him.

Section III: Commentary

Section I of this study set out to describe eight different approaches to the provision of visual impairment services, and section II provided a series of individual case studies. It will have become apparent to readers that the differences lie, not only in the nature of the local authorities and the history of their services which were basically the reason for their selection for study, but also in many details of the way in which services are provided. There are various reasons why this is so, and an attempt will now be made to identify the constraints within which local authorities have to operate, some common trends in the type of problems which may arise, and the relative effectiveness of the various approaches adopted to overcome them.

The identification of visually impaired pupils

Statistics

The original intention was to provide more specific statistical information about the numbers of visually impaired pupils in various categories. This did not prove to be feasible because the information is not available in a comparable form in different areas. There are in fact no easily definable boundaries between blindness and partial sightedness, or between a level of visual impairment which justifies inclusion on an LEA register and a level for which no significant special support is required. This is partly because the relationship between an ophthalmic condition and its implications for visual functioning is a very complex one, and also because, in the case of a sensory handicap, its impact on the child's education is influenced by factors such as general academic ability, other areas of special need, personality and social factors. This means that no form of classification of visually impaired children is totally satisfactory, and the diverse figures encountered for the incidence of the handicap may be at least partly attributable to this fact.

The number of visually impaired children recorded in the authorities studied varies between 1.5 and 4.2 per thousand which is too wide a range in a small sample for any conclusion to be drawn about statistical probabilities. At least if any authority believes it has either significantly less or more cases than these figures, there may be a need to re-examine its assessment procedures.

Statements of special educational need

It might have been expected that the procedures for providing children with Statements of special educational need, introduced by the 1981 Education Act, would have ensured that visually impaired children were identified and the educational implications of any visual defect fully analysed. In authorities where the statementing procedure is fully operative, this has in fact happened. In an authority with a really well-developed statementing system only 41 out of 4000 children with Statements are visually impaired. This figure does highlight the extent to which we are considering a low incidence handicap. In another authority there are 32 visually impaired children out of 2,200 with Statements, and in a third there are 146 out of 2300. These variations again raise many questions. Of more concern is the fact that some authorities are still experiencing considerable delays in carrying out assessments for Statements and this may well mean that some children's difficulties are remaining unidentified. This is probably not as serious a problem in the case of children who are obviously visually impaired as it is for those children who have less clearly determined needs and whose educational progress may well be undermined by an unidentified visual defect. Unless the teachers of such children themselves identify the root cause of the problem, the children become incorrectly "labelled" as slow learners.

Severe learning difficulties

This issue is a particularly relevant one in relation to children with severe learning difficulties. At national level it is well established that nearly half of the total number of visually impaired children have severe or multiple learning difficulties. Against this figure, the authorities in the study recorded between 19% and 42% of visually impaired pupils as being multiply handicapped, and some were not in fact able to provide figures.

This does suggest that there may be many children in schools for severe learning difficulties whose learning programme does not take full account of visual difficulties.

Undoubtedly substantial problems arise because peripatetic teachers of the visually impaired may have no experience in the field of severe learning difficulties and may be ill at ease in that environment, whether it be in the area of designing valid means of assessing such children or in drawing up a suitable educational programme. Some teams have a member of staff who has developed expertise in that specialism, and this is one solution to the problem. Another is that the staff in special schools should receive the necessary elements of additional training so that they can provide for the needs within the framework of their own specialised work. At present it seems clear that some PMLD children are not receiving the stimulation of their minimal vision which is desirable, and that some children may appear to be more mentally handicapped than they really are because a defect in their vision has not been identified.

Educationally blind children

Most of these comments apply particularly to partially sighted children. Blindness is of course more easily identified, and the main issue of interest in this case is the sharp fluctuation in incidence. Overall numbers are so low that it is possible, as in the case of one large authority, for there to be little experience of blind children. Another established a good service, only to find a sudden trough in numbers with no children in one age-band needing to use it. On the other hand, the presence of a visually impaired family in an area can completely transform the level of need. It is clearly essential that, whatever may be the budgetary constraints, local authorities should seek to build into their services the flexibility to respond to these fluctuations in need.

The placement of visually impaired children

The use of special schools

All the services under consideration had their origin in a system in which severely visually impaired pupils were placed in special schools, whether within the authority or outside it. With the possible exception of the authority which provides a regional service, they are all moving increasingly towards some form of integration for most pupils.

In four of the LEAs for which comparable figures are available, there were some 158 children placed in special schools a decade ago. There are now only 40, and of these just six have been placed there in recent years. This does show the scale of the move away from special school placements, although it must be recognized that this is in areas where support services are well developed. All the authorities hold fast to the belief that special school placement should remain an option for certain children, although the reducing rolls of the remaining special schools must raise questions as to how they can be enabled to continue to cater for the needs of such children. There is certainly a danger that an able child may not find an appropriate peer group in a special school.

The distinction between blind and partially sighted children

Another quite general trend in developments is the blurring of the distinction between blind and partially sighted children. The previously promulgated view that the educational needs of the two groups were totally distinct can be said to have totally disappeared. Obviously, braille using children require special human and material resources, but none of the authorities provide separate locations. In a number of cases, units which were originally set up for partially sighted children have become resource bases for blind children with an increasing tendency for the partially sighted to be supported in their neighbourhood school rather than needing to go to the resource base. It is acknowledged that it is the level of educational need which is significant rather than the medium of communication. In any case, children are not necessarily exclusively braille-users or print-users, and a combined service is more acceptable to borderline cases, particularly if a child has deteriorating vision.

Neighbourhood integration or resource bases

Where severely impaired children are integrated, the major issue is whether this is in their neighbourhood school or at another school, possibly further from home, which is specially resourced. Examples of both approaches have been described in this study. In rural areas, a resourced school may not be a feasible proposition, but even in urban areas parental feelings sometimes run high in favour of neighbourhood placements. This applies particularly at primary level when most children attend a neighbourhood school and the one who travels away in a taxi quickly feels an outsider. The difference is rather less stark at secondary level when children in a given locality may anyway be attending a range of schools. There is no doubt that a resourced school can provide a good service more economically and make more concentrated use of skills which are often in short supply. Moreover, the mainstream staff develop experience in working with visually impaired children, and this cannot be replicated in a wide range of schools which have only ever encountered one such pupil. The children themselves at secondary level in particular appreciate the opportunity to have some contact with peers who have similar difficulties to their own.

Some authorities which have set up resource bases are now encountering increasing parental resistance. Parents often have to be told that they must choose between the best educational provision available, which is in the resourced school, and the social advantages of a local school combined with a less good specialist service. It is easy to suggest that the two options ought to be available at parental choice, but this is often just not realistic. If an authority opts to concentrate its resources in a named school, there may well not be enough funds to make equally good provision in other schools. This is a serious dilemma with which LEAs are faced, and there is no easy answer. In the last resort an education service should be concerned with education, and parents may have to accept a compromise which may not be ideal from a social point of view. Some authorities take the view that neighbourhood provision may be required at primary level, but may not be the best solution for secondary education.

Whichever solution is chosen, there will undoubtedly be advantages and disadvantages from a social point of view. LEAs could perhaps go further in acknowledging and seeking to counteract the disadvantages. Children who travel some distance to a resource base do feel isolated in their home community. There may be some means of establishing a contact with their neighbourhood school, and they ought to be enabled to take part in extra-curricular activities at the school they attend, even if it means making exceptional transport arrangements. The early provision of mobility training is also necessary for some children to feel confident in their local community. LEAs could also investigate the possibility of making more opportunities available for extra-curricular activities through their youth service. On the other hand, a child who attends a neighbourhood school needs also the companionship of children who have similar difficulties, and this can be achieved through local contacts or by participation in national schemes. There are problems associated with both neighbourhood and resourced provision, but they do not need to be insuperable problems.

The role of peripatetic support staff

Leaving on one side for the present the support which may be required in specially resourced schools, the main thrust of a peripatetic service is likely to be the oversight of a large number of children who attend many different schools. The study has shown that there are wide discrepancies in the way this service is organized.

Nature of their responsibilities

Different services hold sharply opposing views about what a peripatetic teacher should actually do. The extreme positions are the heads of service who state categorically that their staff are teachers and their role is to teach, and those who take the equally firm view that their role is to support and advise teachers and not to undertake direct individual teaching. Other services have an approach which lies somewhere between these two extremes, and combines teaching and advising in varying proportions. It is not possible to state dogmatically which of these viewpoints is to be preferred. A great deal depends on the level and range of educational need of the pupils who are being integrated, and on locally accepted practice in relation to other support services. However, one consideration is of the utmost importance, and that is that everybody concerned should have a full understanding of what the local policy is. The peripatetic teacher should visit a school knowing exactly what his or her role is to be; the school and indeed the pupil should know exactly what to expect from the visit. If the peripatetic teacher goes to a school "just to see how the child is getting along and to give any help possible," then it is unlikely that the visit will be productive or cost-effective. The visiting teacher should prepare each visit and have clear objectives in just the same way as a mainstream teacher should prepare each lesson.

Such an approach does, however, place an onus on the host school as much as on the peripatetic teacher. If guidance is to be offered to the mainstream teacher, some liaison time away from the class must be allocated for this to happen. If the child is to be withdrawn for individual teaching, once again an opportunity must be given for the peripatetic teacher to be briefed about the work required. If the visiting teacher works without reference to what has been going on in class, or indeed relies on the child to provide information, there is unlikely to be any real continuity in the work covered. Even if the visiting teacher is going to work alongside the class teacher, there needs to be close liaison so that the class teacher continues to feel fully involved in that particular pupil's education.

In the real world, it may be very difficult for this element of planning to be implemented. Nevertheless, in services where the head of service promotes a clear working structure, the time spent on organisation is fully justified, and the staff are likely to derive more satisfaction from their work, because they have definite objectives and can assess them. The individual child studies provide a number of examples of impressive educational achievement which has been made possible by highly structured, efficient peripatetic support.

Specialism within the team

A further issue with regard to which the services differ markedly in their approach is the extent to which individual teachers have a specialism within the team. All members of support services are naturally expected to extend their field of competence beyond the age-range or subject which they previously taught, but some element of specialism may nevertheless be to the advantage of the pupils receiving the service. A common practice in the larger services is for all members of the team to carry at least a small caseload across all age-groups and to be able to give general support in all subject areas, but at the same time for each member of staff to be the known contact point for one or two areas of specialist interest. These may either reflect their previous experience or be new areas of interest which they develop on the job.

Such an approach gives the service more professional respectability in the eyes of schools than the somewhat dilettante attitude of one person professing to be an expert in everything. In a large county, it may be cost-effective for each member of staff to have a main caseload concentrated in a geographical area, but this need not preclude consulting or calling in an appropriate colleague for certain topics. Indeed, each teacher may contribute to the team's work in his or her specialism by drawing up written guidelines, developing teaching materials and providing periodic in-service training sessions, not to mention personally keeping abreast of developments in that field, rather than by having face-to-face contact on all matters relating to the specialism.

All this may seem to have little relevance to a very small service of one or two teachers which is in no position to introduce such flexibility. The answer in some cases is that the staffing should be increased, but in an LEA with a relatively low population such an increase may be difficult to justify. It should be noted that a spin-off of increased integration may be that, in diverting finance from residential, external placements to additional internal staffing for severely impaired pupils, the LEA will incidentally be providing the extra numbers of staff which make some specialisation possible.

Flexible allocation of time

A further major consideration in the work of peripatetic staff relates to how their time is allocated between different children. It is all too easy for staff to feel that they should be fair to everyone and therefore to seek to divide their time equally amongst their caseload. However, this may well not reflect the level of need of the various children or the variations of need from time to time.

The services studied have resolved this dilemma in various ways. Some have clearly defined categories of support to which children are allocated, such as weekly, fortnightly or termly visiting. One service concentrates on intensive support for a small number of children, and uses periods at the end of term when it is often difficult to carry out a regular support role, to oversee the progress of the much wider client group. More than one service is prepared to give intensive, even full-time support to a child at the time of entry to a new school, in the knowledge that this will be justified by a very reduced need for help once the child is settled.

It is always possible to say that more help would benefit a child, and priorities therefore have to be established. If this is done in a positive, considered way, it may help peripatetic staff to resist pressure from those heads and teachers in mainstream schools who are adept at effectively fighting their own corner in an open market!

The management of the peripatetic service

The overall conclusion to be drawn from all this is that peripatetic provision really does need to be managed! All too often, a service has been initiated by one person being appointed who will gener- ally have received training in the education of the visually impaired, but who is very unlikely to have had any effective preparation for a peripatetic, let alone a management role. This is in fact an extremely complex role involving self-organisation, the management of resources, familiarity with many types of local services, and of course a complex network of relationships with head teachers, teachers, parents, officers of the authority and others. To this must be added the consideration that the service is almost certain to be under-staffed, and priorities therefore have to be established, which is a heavy responsibility.

The role of head of service
Where services are now well developed, the head of service will often have started his or her career without any specific prepara- tion, and will be well aware of the problems. There are now examples of well managed services where the leader of the team

has a clear concept of the nature of each team member's role, controls the work schedule of colleagues and plays a dynamic part in determining priorities.

This is a management task and it lies at the hub of an effective service. If peripatetic staff are just left to respond to crises and to help those who shout loudest, their work will never make any significant impact. However, it does need someone with experience, confidence, strength of personality and management skills to lead a peripatetic support service, whether it be for visual impairment or any other type of need. It is worthy of note that, in all the services described here, the head of service may be said to be a dominant figure in the local scene.

Line management

This does of course create a problem for local authorities which are new to the field of visual impairment, because the first person whom they appoint is unlikely to be ready initially to take on such a role. Most services are responsible jointly to an adviser or inspector for special needs and to an assistant education officer. These people have very wide responsibilities and will sometimes see themselves just as a point of reference or a channel of communication for a peripatetic service, and may not expect to have any day-to-day involvement in running the service. It must be said that this is not a satisfactory situation.

If a new service is going to flourish, someone in a senior position must accept that, for the first year at any rate, the oversight of the service will involve a major time commitment. This officer must have regular, preferably weekly, contact with the person appointed; must be readily available to provide support and to help the new colleague to grow in confidence, and the two must work in partnership to design a realistic framework for the service. The time commitment for this should be taken into consideration when the service is introduced.

Even in an established service, if a new head of service is appointed who does not yet have the appropriate experience, this type of support really does need to be available in the early stages.

Support staff in mainstream schools

Whatever may be the approach to integration, most LEAs will now acknowledge that there are circumstances in which some children need sustained, individual help in the classroom beyond that

174

which can be offered by a peripatetic service. We have seen that some LEAs seek to concentrate such children in particular schools which are designated resource bases for a particular type of educational need, whereas others are prepared to allocate quite a substantial amount of extra staffing to neighbourhood schools. Whichever approach is adopted, a number of considerations commonly arise.

Teacher or ancillary

The main decision which has to be made is whether to appoint a teacher or an ancillary without a teaching qualification. The reasons why opinions about this diverge is that some of the tasks which need to be carried out require a teacher and others do not. The advantage of setting up a resource base with a team of staff is that a combination of qualified and unqualified people can be used to cover an appropriate range of activities. In this situation, the child can benefit from appropriate teaching support when required, but routine tasks such as reprographic work and the handling of materials can be provided at less cost. The appointment of an individual support teacher is an expensive option and is usually only encountered in the case of blind children.

The role of a teacher

It is undoubtedly true that visually impaired children benefit from the support of a teacher who understands their particular needs, who can interpret the lessons appropriately and who can work in full partnership with the class teacher. However, it is as yet very far from standard practice for support teachers to have a qualification in visual impairment. In the two authorities where members of the visual impairment team work interchangeably as peripatetic or support teachers, all have the specialist qualification. Similarly, in the authority where resource bases replaced a special school, five of the nine teachers are so qualified. However, in the remaining authorities studied, only two out of eleven support teachers have obtained a qualification.

Support teachers often learn braille and they gradually acquire experience, but they may depend a great deal on internal training and support from the peripatetic service. It is only as more part-time training facilities become available that we are likely to be able to envisage the provision of fully qualified support in neighbourhood or resourced schools.

Important as this matter is, much of the success of a support teacher's work depends on personality and ability to strike the right balance between, on the one hand, taking over too much control of the child's education so that the class teacher no longer feels responsible and, on the other hand, confining the work to transcribing written material. Classroom relationships seem to be smoothest where the support teacher is involved with a number of pupils and works in a team teaching situation, thereby becoming an inherent part of the teaching team.

The role of an ancillary

The use of ancillaries to support partially sighted and blind children is widespread. These under-paid and unassuming aides are jewels in the crown of many integration schemes. Their role is not an easy one because their presence in the classroom may well be resented at times by both the teacher and the pupil. Particularly as a child grows older, he or she tends to regard the helper as at best a necessary evil, and it is extremely difficult to give effective support without becoming too intrusive. The ancillaries may learn, from experience or training, how to interpret the visual aspects of education, but can often only do this satisfactorily if they have a grasp of the teaching objectives. It is clearly essential that ancillaries should be given some preparation for their work and should have ready access to qualified advice. Those who work with visually impaired pupils frequently undertake more specific "educational" tasks than other ancillaries, and appropriate support for this role obviously ought to be provided.

Ancillaries are often appointed on the basis of termly contracts. From the LEA's point of view this is an economically sensible approach, since the system can then respond readily to changes in the pupil's needs. However, this is an unsatisfactory employment pattern for people who may be putting considerable personal commitment into improving their competence for the task they are undertaking. A far more desirable arrangement is for such ancillaries to be given permanent contracts to the authority, but with the understanding that their actual school placement may vary from time to time. Consideration should also be given to rewarding extra training by appropriate salary scales.

The national curriculum

At the time when these studies took place, the introduction of the national curriculum was a major preoccupation of all visual impairment services. It was too early to be able to report fully on the approaches to be adopted, since in all areas discussions were still proceeding, but some general trends are already apparent and the issues which the curriculum raises for integrated pupils are being identified.

An entitlement

A quite general starting-point for specialists in visual impairment is that the national curriculum is an entitlement and that, in principle at least, visually impaired pupils should not be debarred from any part of it on account of their handicap. The use of the "disapplication" concession for pupils with special needs receives very little favour. Some services are going to great pains to explain to schools how particular assessment targets may be made relevant. For instance, for a blind child colour discrimination may be represented by texture discrimination, and other "observation" skills may be interpreted through the use of senses other than sight. In other authorities, it is recognised that a very small number of targets may be inappropriate, and that the efforts required to give them a semblance of relevance may not be time well spent.

Modifications

In both cases, however, attention is being paid to the detailed analysis of objectives in each curriculum area. Some services are already drawing up booklets of guidelines for mainstream teachers identifying appropriate teaching methods and materials required for visually impaired pupils to follow the syllabus. Such guidelines are likely to be welcomed by teachers, and their introduction may raise the profile of the support service and reinforce the mainstream teacher's interest and confidence in responding to individual needs.

Apart from the question of the practicality of applying some assessment targets within subject areas, the broader question arises as to whether the full scope of the national curriculum can be applied in the case of all visually impaired children. The two reasons for doubt are the time factor and the need for them to learn supplementary skills because of their disability.

Inevitably, some of these children work more slowly than others, and need longer to complete tasks. They also often have to make a considerable additional effort of concentration and therefore find school work very tiring. It is sometimes possible to devise strategies for reducing the volume of work to be done whilst preserving the full range, but some services do set store by ensuring that children are not exposed to unreasonable physical strain.

Supplementary curriculum

A more significant problem lies in the fact that these pupils need time to master certain specialist skills. This is sometimes referred to as their supplementary curriculum, which should be clearly set alongside the national curriculum. Three aspects of a visually impaired child's educational development give rise to this need. These are the acquisition of specialist communication skills, mobility training and the teaching of living skills.

a) Communication skills

Whether a partially sighted child depends entirely on technological aids for written work or whether large-print can be read but handwriting is untidy, the ability to type competently is likely to be a major advantage. This should be regarded as a basic skill to be acquired during primary education so that full competence has been achieved before the secondary level. It may of course be argued that, in the age of computers, this should apply to all children, but that is a separate issue. Some LEAs buy in the services of a typing teacher as required, and it should be possible for an ancillary to ensure that the pupil practises regularly. An interesting approach has been noted in one LEA where the head of service has designed a teaching programme in typing for visually impaired children which can be implemented by whoever is available on a regular basis in the school.

For blind children, it has traditionally been assumed that braille is required for personal use, and typing for communication with sighted people. However, with the coming of the computerised transcription of braille, the need for typing skills is no longer so apparent. Competent use of braille and computer keyboard skills are of course required, but knowledge of the typewriter keyboard may no longer be an automatic requirement.

b) Mobility

Certain aspects of mobility training may be provided by a support teacher or ancillary helper if detailed guidance is given. This applies to general orientation within the school, the development of observation through other senses, the memorising of routes. However, professional training for outdoor mobility is absolutely essential for all blind and for many partially sighted children. All too often they are not receiving this, largely for the strange reason that it is not regarded as an "educational responsibility." Mobility officers in Social Services departments are generally fully occupied by work with blind adults, and anyway have generally had no training for working with children. Nevertheless there are still very few education departments which have established an explicit post of mobility officer. The best that can generally be expected is that one of the teachers in the authority happens also to have received training as a mobility officer.

This is an issue which requires urgent attention. Where in the country is there a primary school which does not provide road safety training? "Outdoor mobility" is merely road safety training for the visually impaired. As more and more of such children are integrated, they mingle socially with their peers and need to move freely in the local community. It is worthy of note that one of the young men considered in the study regards the early comprehensive training programme in mobility which he received as the biggest single factor which has enabled him to be so socially well-adjusted. At present all too many visually impaired children are at risk on our roads or are inhibited in their social development because their parents dare not let them go out unsupervised. Visual impairment services are well aware of this problem, but the makeshift ways in which they have been seen to be tackling it are not satisfactory. It is a national change of approach which is required.

c) Living skills

Visually impaired children should also receive a structured programme of basic living skills. This blends fairly easily into nursery and infant education, where the gradual development of self-care and independence skills is an inherent part of the curriculum, including the refinement of gross and fine motor skills. With guidance from a specialist teacher, the class teacher can readily adjust her approach to individual needs. The position is more difficult as children grow older and this ceases to be a significant element in the mainstream curriculum. The visually impaired child continues to need a structured programme in mastering a wide range of living skills as they become appropriate to his growing maturity. At secondary level, some services arrange withdrawal from an element of the curriculum to provide the necessary training; for others it is included as a discrete option in the curriculum; for others yet again it is an extra-curricular activity.

As the extent of integration increases, support services are very aware of the need for this supplementary curriculum. It is of course an area where special schools have the advantage, because they build it fully into their curriculum, though often at the price of a reduced exposure to other subject areas. It is certainly clear that some integrated pupils have been disadvantaged by inadequate attention to one or all of the three supplementary areas of communication skills, mobility and living skills, and it is important that this should feature in discussions on the curriculum; as should also a continuing programme for the development of visual, auditory and tactile skills.

Patterns of integration

In these studies the extent to which pupils are integrated has in many cases been expressed in terms of percentage integration into the mainstream curriculum. However, these figures do not really paint a full picture. It is possible for a child to be physically present in a mainstream classroom whilst following an individual learning programme, or to be receiving the bulk of the teaching from a support teacher rather than from the regular class teacher. Such situations are very different from one in which the child is a full member of a class and special support is brought in merely to give him access to the lessons. This is not to suggest that one approach is better than another, but rather that an integration scheme needs to be planned with detailed objectives in mind.

Catering for additional educational needs

Many visually impaired children have additional learning or emotional difficulties which impede their educational progress. They may not be able to benefit fully from mainstream lessons until they have mastered basic literacy and study skills. In two of the LEAs studied, it is found useful to withdraw such children for periods of individual teaching with the quite specific objective of placing them in a less distracting environment. Another approach, encountered in some cases where a resource base has replaced provision in a special school or unit, is for such children to be taught separately for a major part of the day until such time as they are able to participate fully in lessons. This can have some advantages, but it carries with it the danger that the child becomes more and more out of step with the range of educational experiences offered to his or her peers, so that there is an even bigger gulf to be crossed when he or she is integrated.

On the other hand, it may be of little educational value for children to attend mainstream lessons, as a token tribute to integration, if it is not an environment in which they can learn effectively. In this case, a modified curriculum or modified teaching approaches need to be designed in the same way as they would for a fully sighted child with learning difficulties, and this of course depends on the broader pattern of local policies in relation to children with special needs.

Apart from the child's actual needs, previous experiences are very relevant. At present many LEAs are transferring children from special schools or units to the mainstream at various ages. These children cannot necessarily be treated in the same way as young children who enter the educational system now and in the future with maximum integration being sought from the start. There must inevitably be a time-lag during which provision for certain children may fall short of the ideal, and this is apparent in the case studies of some of the older pupils.

Access to the curriculum

These comments concern visually impaired children who have additional educational needs. Children who are of average or above average ability and who have no handicap other than the visual impairment have been found in the authorities studied to be able to benefit from full integration. Their needs lie quite specifically in the area of access to the curriculum. They can develop basic literacy and study skills alongside their peers, with special teaching being provided within the classroom. They should then be building up a reserve of educational experiences similar to those of their peers. Some children will use a different reading scheme to learn braille, but they can be given the same language background as the class by listening to cassettes and moving on to a brailled version of the class readers as soon as practicable.

It has been seen that, whether blind or partially sighted, such children can benefit from all areas of the national curriculum. The teaching approaches or the detailed content of some subjects may need to be modified, but no major curriculum area needs to be neglected. In the later years of secondary education, the volume of work required may present problems if a visually impaired child works slowly or needs time for specialist skill development. In certain cases, it may then be necessary for some aspects of the national curriculum to be curtailed, but as far as possible a good breadth and balance of studies should be preserved.

Social integration

Particular emphasis has been placed on functional integration because this is obviously the central concern of an education service. Mention needs also to be made of social integration. It has been apparent in the study that children only mingle freely with their peers if they are full members of classes. This is now a quite widespread practice, except in some areas where units were established many years ago and it has proved difficult to change long-engrained procedures which were appropriate in their day, but are no longer so. Even where there is a physical resource base for the visually impaired, the pupils are now generally withdrawn to it for extra teaching rather than being based in it and feeding out from it to classes. It is important that they should attend registration with their peers, have lunch with them and have the opportunity to mix at playtimes, even if in the event some of them tend to prefer the company of other visually impaired children.

It is sometimes thought necessary to provide additional lunch-time supervision for a blind child as a safety precaution. If this has to happen, the supervision should be as non-intrusive as possible, but the child studies have shown that this is often not necessary, and head teachers are perhaps over-cautious.

The children should also be encouraged to participate in extra-curricular activities, and some LEAs now accept the costs involved in making special transport arrangements so that children can stay after school for some activities.

Any LEA embarking on a proposal for integration does need to be aware of all these complex factors which determine whether a scheme is satisfactory from an educational and social viewpoint. When all has been considered, it remains true that the factor which most clearly determines the level of success of a scheme will be the attitudes and ethos of the school involved. The LEA officers will know which head teachers and staff are most likely to be able to respond to a challenge which may seem daunting, but can also be highly rewarding for all concerned.

Equipment and resources

There can be no question about the impact which developments in educational technology are making on the opportunities available to visually impaired children. Some equipment may be expensive, but the costs have to be assessed in relation to the benefits to the child and in some cases compared with other headings of expenditure arising from an alternative form of provision. Some LEAs show an impressive commitment to taking advantage of whatever technology can bring, whereas others still need to adjust their scale of values to the realities of today's world.

Making an appropriate choice
Nevertheless, discretion is just as important as generosity. Some pupils can only participate fully in mainstream lessons if they have regular access to a closed circuit television. However, such large pieces of equipment do create a barrier between the child and the classroom environment and its presence will often be resented by the child. Low vision aids may be equally effective in certain circumstances and various types of computer with modifications may be appropriate. The question which an LEA should be

asking is not: "Can we afford the most expensive equipment?" but rather: "What is the most appropriate item for this child at this stage, and how can it be funded?"

The types of equipment required fall into the two broad areas of reprographic equipment and individual communication aids. Any area must now have ready access to enlarging photocopiers, and this was not examined in any detail in the study. It is for braille-using pupils that major items such as thermoform machines, Minolta ("swell paper") copiers and braille embossers are required. The production of raised diagrams and maps can also be of use to some partially sighted pupils who are not braille users. Now that this equipment is available and being introduced into many LEAs, it is obviating the need for teachers or ancillary workers to spend an inordinate amount of time transcribing braille, and it provides pupils with a wider range and better quality of materials. These advantages must be set against the expense involved.

The selection of individual communication aids depends very much on a pupil's needs at a particular time and on the "state of the art" in technological developments. Overall these studies have revealed that many visually impaired children do not yet have access to equipment which is available, and which would be very useful to them. There are some very noteworthy exceptions where the triumph of new technology has been seen to flourish, but these cases are still disappointingly rare.

Funding

Most visual impairment services have some form of annual capitation for regular expenditure, combined with a strategy for seeking funding for major items. This seems to be satisfactory provided that the capitation is high enough for its required purpose and if it is adjusted, for instance, when materials have to be provided for blind children. Where such children are integrated, the goodwill of the host school can be insidiously undermined if there is a continual struggle to obtain the materials which give access to the curriculum. With the introduction of the Local Management of Schools scheme, close attention will need to be paid to how any funds allocated to schools through a Statement will be used, and how these should be supplemented from central funds.

With regard to the strategy for obtaining large items, forward planning is essential. Finance departments do not respond happily to being told that it is impossible to predict how many thousands of pounds may be required next year, and yet this is often the reality of the situation. On the other hand, it is not acceptable to commit the LEA to purchasing items which are not needed immediately, if only because equipment can so rapidly become out of date. The only effective solution is for the LEA to acknowledge the need for building some sort of contingency plan into the budget. It is important that pupils' needs in terms of communication aids should be reviewed regularly, particularly at the point of transfer from primary to secondary education, for examinations and for transfer to further education. If children who would otherwise have been placed in a residential school are to be educated locally, then the necessary funds should be transferred to the appropriate budget head. Some LEAs now have an agreed system for making such virement, but this is not yet the case in all areas.

Equipment for home use

A further area in which there are considerable variations in practice concerns the provision of equipment for home use. This is a difficult policy issue, and account has to be taken of the treatment which equipment may receive in some homes. Nonetheless a child is going to be at a disadvantage if he or she has no access to written material or a communication system outside school, particularly in the light of the approaches to study which are encouraged by the GCSE.

Local fund-raising groups are sometimes happy to provide a specific item for a child's use at home, since they can readily see the tangible result of their fund-raising efforts. In some areas, of course, there is a clear policy standpoint on the issue of accepting voluntary involvement in provision which is a statutory duty of the LEA, but this again raises the question as to whether the provision of equipment for home use is a statutory obligation. It is therefore a problem which allows of no simple solution, but it does need to be tackled.

The competent use of equipment

Perhaps more important than all these questions about the provision of equipment is the issue of how effectively it is used. It is absolutely crucial that everyone concerned should know what a piece of equipment is designed to do, how to use it and where to turn for help when in difficulty. This applies not only to the pupil, but to the head of service, peripatetic teachers, support teachers, ancillary workers and mainstream teachers. This is obviously not easy for people who may feel insecure in handling any form of technological aid, but they should be given appropriate training so that they may gain confidence. The laughing response: "Oh, you know me. I'm no good with machines!" is just not acceptable in today's world. Nor should support staff be saying: "Oh, we leave it to the children. They know more about it than we do." A key role of the head of service should be to ensure that the whole visual impairment team keep up-to-date with new technology as it comes on to the market, that they understand all the possible functions of a piece of equipment, and that they are able to train a child in its use in a formal, structured way.

Mainstream teachers who have visually impaired pupils in their classes cannot be expected to give much time to mastering the subtleties of equipment in use, but they should at least know what purpose it serves, what constraints its use may place on the pupil's speed of working or ability to perform certain tasks, and where to turn for help if needed.

The services which have a forward-looking approach to educational technology have been seen to be providing appropriate training in its use, but this is far from being widespread practice. One may sympathise with those who find this aspect of their work particularly daunting, but at least they should be given suitable opportunities for training.

In-service training

The understanding of educational technology mentioned above is, of course, only one aspect of the training required by the staff of a visual impairment service.

The specialist qualification

LEAs have in recent years experienced varying levels of difficulty in attracting staff with a qualification in visual impairment or in enabling them to become so qualified. The current position in the services studied is that there are 39 members of staff working in a peripatetic capacity of whom 28 hold an appropriate qualification. With the introduction of new distance-learning and part-time courses, most of the remaining 11 are now studying for a qualification. This improvement in the situation is encouraging, but it is still a matter for disquiet that any staff who are visiting schools and families as "the expert" in their field are not in fact appropriately qualified. This applies to 30% of staff in a range of LEAs which have been selected because their services are considered to be of good quality. The position in some areas is considerably worse.

In these same authorities, 23 support teachers are in post, not including those who have a combined peripatetic and support role. Of these 23, only 10 have a qualification in visual impairment. Once again, this proportion is likely to be far more favourable than the national average. In some cases, particularly where partially sighted pupils are being supported, other qualities such as experience of the relevant stage of education, an understanding of special educational needs in general and an appropriate personality, may be just as important as a specialist qualification, but there is no doubt that overall provision will be enhanced as more of the staff involved become qualified.

INSET for visual impairment staff

The extent to which visual impairment staff participate in the shorter types of in-service training varies considerably from area to area. In one respect it may be easier for them to be released than mainstream teachers with their specific timetable commitment, but training still has to be funded. Some teams have regular training sessions of their own, and some have funds earmarked for training. All the staff certainly need to be able to update their skills to familiarise themselves with new technology, to have contact with colleagues from other areas, and to keep in touch with developments in the mainstream of education. There is an awareness of these needs in some areas, but all too often "inset" takes the form of individuals trying to seize the opportunity to attend courses which happen to be brought to their notice, rather than the head of service deliberately structuring the training provision.

INSET for mainstream staff

Apart from their own training, all services accept that they have a major role in providing training for the staff of mainstream schools. This is approached variously in the following ways:

- Individual advice during peripatetic visits.
- Awareness courses for the whole staff of a school when a visually impaired pupil is admitted.
- Contributions to sessional courses for special needs co-ordinators.

186

- Open, "twilight" sessions for interested teachers from any school.
- A regular annual meeting advertised widely to schools in the area.
- Response to invitations to participate in schools' own training days.
- The circulation to schools of a list of topics which may be covered on request.

Any of these approaches are well worth exploring in the search to disseminate good practice, and in particular to make teachers better able to identify poor visual functioning and to cater for it.

INSET for ancillary staff

The major blemish on the training scene remains the almost total lack of appropriate provision for ancillary, non-teaching staff. The core of the problem is of course the absence of national funding for this purpose, or of any requirement for training in the contract of such people. They are generally poorly paid and underprivileged in the education service, and yet the work continues to attract committed people of real quality who respond enthusiastically to any training which is given. Some of the LEAs studied have makeshift arrangements for providing some training for their ancillary workers, but all recognise that there is an urgent need for this problem to be tackled at national level.

Pre-five provision and parental support

Early parental contacts

It is apparent in the individual child studies undertaken that many parents received little or no educational advice when they first learned that they had a visually impaired baby. All too often doctors have seen their role as treating the condition if possible or more often having to tell the parents that nothing can be done. It is obviously crucial that parents should receive early advice about how to stimulate their child's normal development despite the visual problems, and peripatetic teachers are particularly skilled in providing this type of support, but they can only help when the case is brought to their notice.

In the case of most of the older children studied, they were babies when local peripatetic services had barely been introduced, and certainly there is now a far more fruitful understanding between child health and education services in many areas. However, some visual impairment services still have to strive to achieve full recognition by doctors of their particular area of expertise. Where good links have been established, parents gain reassurance and confidence, and the benefit to the child in his or her early development is sometimes very marked.

Early placements

It is a sad truth that some medical personnel and indeed educational psychologists still do not fully acknowledge that teachers of the visually impaired have particular skill areas on which they should draw if the children in their care are to receive the type of support to which they are entitled.

The provision of education outside the home before the age of five is very varied in nature, depending partly on local mainstream provision for this age-group. The "mainstream versus special" dialogue is in fact as much a live issue at this stage as it is for older children, but the decision reached is more likely to be opportunist. The options for placement are multi-disciplinary child development centres, social services day nurseries, mother and toddler groups, voluntary playgroups, "special needs" nursery classes, nursery units for the visually impaired, or mainstream nursery provision. Some strongly held views have been encountered favouring either maximum contact with fully sighted peers or the concentrated specialist teaching which can only be provided in a designated environment. There seems, however, to be universal agreement that some form of provision outside the home is desirable before the age of five.

Parental consultation

All LEAs studied believe firmly that parents should be fully consulted about a child's educational placement. In general, they hope to win the parents' support for the recommendation made by professionals, and if there has been sufficient early consultation and openness, this is generally achieved. However, in the last resort, all the authorities say that they, and their elected members, would not oppose strongly held parental preferences.

The parents interviewed in connection with the child studies are all happy with the current provision, but that was of course to be expected since it is examples of good practice which are being portrayed. Their main concerns relate to social development where the child is travelling a distance to school, and inadequate mobility training which is impeding the child's independence in the community. Many parents would welcome contact with similar families, both for their own sake and that of the child. Generally, however, they feel well supported and have a good relationship with their child's teachers.

Post-sixteen provision

It will have been noted that, in the LEA studies, sections on post-sixteen provision have been very brief. This is not because this area of work is considered unimportant, but simply because most visual impairment services play relatively little part in supporting students in colleges of further education.

Role of peripatetic teachers

The peripatetic staff generally advise school leavers on the selection of courses and liaise with colleges about equipment and resources required. One of the LEAs studied has staff specifically designated to work at the further education level, and in another the head of service provides regular weekly support for the more severely impaired students. Some others provide in-service training for college lecturers and continue oversight of the students during their further education course. Most authorities place some visually impaired students in specialist residential colleges, either because they need specific vocational training which cannot be provided locally, or because it is thought they would benefit from training and experience in independent living. The LEA visual impairment services do not generally seem to be involved with mature students or the adult education sector.

Trends in further education provision

Against this background of practices, attention may usefully be drawn to the findings of an RNIB survey carried out in 1988. A total of almost three hundred further education colleges responded to a questionnaire on provision for visually impaired students. The replies showed that in 1985-6, 512 visually impaired students attended 89 colleges, whilst in 1987-8, 783 attended 146 colleges. The increase in figures is reflected in an almost universally sympathetic and welcoming approach to admitting students with disabilities. These figures include both the 16-19 age-group and mature and adult students on full-time or part-time courses.

In 1987-8, 16.7% of all the students had additional learning difficulties, though in some cases these may have arisen from a late diagnosis of their handicap, and 7.4% had additional physical or sensory handicaps. Over half of the students were reported as using non-visual methods of study for at least part of their work. At the start of their course, 71.4% of the visually impaired students were over the age of 19.

These figures reveal that post-sixteen education for the visually impaired is a significant area of need. As may be expected, the resourcing of the students varies considerably. Most colleges have now designated a member of staff as responsible for special needs, but only 14 had someone responsible specifically for the visually impaired. However, fifty-four colleges had provided extra teaching staff for the visually impaired and almost half had provided some form of ancillary help. One particular area of concern was that colleges had often had difficulty in providing the training and support in mobility, which was essential to their students' independence.

Specialist equipment had generally been funded by LEAs, except where students were eligible for grants through vocational training schemes. There is of course some doubt as to whether such funding will continue in the light of changes in the financing of colleges.

The need for specific support

It is clear from this survey that the incidence of visual impairment in further education colleges is sufficient to merit some form of discrete service. The figures have grown insidiously and many LEAs may not be aware of the need. Much of the work required is in the adult sector, and it may therefore not be appropriate for existing peripatetic services to absorb support at this level into their generic caseload. Nevertheless, it is an area where an injection of specialist advice and support would be beneficial, and the decision of one LEA to appoint lecturers with a qualification in visual impairment as members of their service is worthy of note.

Current and future plans

All the services studied are well aware that they cannot stand still, but must continue to evolve in the light of changing circumstances and attitudes. Areas of growth particular to the various services have been highlighted in the individual studies, and they are mainly related to that area's stage of development. However, particular attention is also being paid everywhere to the implications of the Local Management of Schools scheme and the National Curriculum.

Local management of schools

The general trend, and certainly the preferred approach of officers and teachers, is that support services should remain centrally funded. There is understandable concern that, if individual schools had to buy in support required, the amount of help provided for visually impaired children might diminish. Where children have Statements of special educational need, funds may be allocated to schools to buy in the extra human and material resources required, but the peripatetic service may need to over-see the use of such funds. Where designated schools have resource bases or units, views differ as to whether these should also be centrally funded or financed as part of the host school. At the time of writing, most of the LEAs studied are awaiting the DES response to their proposed structure, and there is no doubt that it is an issue which could have a considerable impact on service delivery.

National Curriculum

The introduction of the National Curriculum has been greeted with rather more optimism. As a matter of principle, all services feel that the curriculum is an entitlement from which visually impaired children should not be excluded. An analysis of the various assessment targets clearly highlights the fact that visual impairment gives rise to a need for alternative means of access to the curriculum, but not to the need for a modified curriculum. Heads of service therefore see the National Curriculum as a tool in their hand which they can use to mould the attitudes of main-stream teachers. Several services are drawing up guidelines on methods and materials required to achieve the assessment targets. Faced with the need to implement the curriculum, teachers will welcome such help, and are therefore likely to be ready to accept guidance, the need for which they perhaps did not previously realise.

There are therefore some encouraging signs that support services may be developing a higher profile in the eyes of schools. This may well prove to be a considerable bonus at a time when they must continue to strive to retain or improve their share of scarce financial resources.

Individual studies of children and young people

However services may be described or assessed, their true merit is only to be seen, in the last resort, in how the individual pupil benefits from it.

The children chosen for study are believed to have benefited from the support available to them. However, it will have been seen that their experiences have not always been ideal. This is particularly true for some of the older children and young people, who began their education when services were less developed. Nevertheless, it would be too complacent to say that things are different now and the same mistakes or lapses could not happen today. Such things do still happen in many places, and the studies contain salutary warnings as well as models of good practice.

The children studied have achieved or are achieving success in their education. The circumstances involved are too varied for general conclusions to be drawn, but perhaps a common factor is that somewhere along the line someone has set their sights high for each child, and given him or her the stimulus to achieve as much as possible despite the disability. The question we are left with is: "Are our expectations sufficiently high for every child?"

The way forward

These studies lend themselves to be used in various ways. In LEAs where visual impairment services are still at an early stage of development, some errors or delays may be avoided by learning from the experience of others. On the other hand, well-established services may wish to reassess their work in the light of the examples given. It is remarkable how much LEAs still work in isolation from each other, and knowledge of practices elsewhere can only be beneficial.

The description of local practices and levels of service will of course rapidly become out of date. However, the rate of evolution of visual impairment services has been so varied around the country that the material is likely to continue to be of use even when it no longer accurately describes current practice. It is within this framework that it is hoped the studies will have a role to play in promoting increasingly good educational opportunities for visually impaired children.

Section IV : Guidelines for service development

In comparison with other areas of special educational need, visual impairment has a low incidence among children, with the result that models of practice in various situations may be less readily available at a local level than is the case for some other handicaps. Officers and advisers may therefore have little relevant experience to draw on when required to design a response to specific issues. The studies in this book provide the raw material to fill this gap, and this, combined with the extensive specialist experience of RNIB's officers and staff, enables us to offer guidelines to LEAs as a basic working tool in their development of services.

There are no definitive right or wrong answers to the questions which must be asked. That which is appropriate for one child may be inappropriate for another; a scheme which is both feasible and relevant in one geographical area may be unattainable or misjudged elsewhere. In the last resort, it is obviously only the officers and council of a local authority who can determine how their particular needs should be met, but it is hoped that these guidelines will help to direct the thinking and will serve as a checklist as a detailed local scheme is evolved.

1. Assessment of need

1.1 Incidence of visual impairment
An essential element in planning any service is to obtain a reliable estimate of the level of need. This has been seen to be particularly difficult in the case of visually impaired children on account of the low incidence of the handicap, which leads to sharp fluctuations in statistics in different areas and at different points in time.

National statistics provided by the Department of Education and Science suggest that the numbers of children in special schools or units in 1982 amounted to 1.12 blind and 2.41 partially sighted per 10,000 of population in the 5-16 age group. It was projected at that time that the figures would fall to 0.9 and 2.1 respectively by 1991 or earlier. These figures do not, however, include children integrated into ordinary classes on an individual basis.

Various statistical surveys of people registered blind or partially sighted have also been undertaken, but, for a variety of reasons, parents do not always seek registration for their children. The figures are therefore an under-estimate of the true situation.

In 1982-83, RNIB commissioned three demographic studies from Shankland-Cox. These drew on earlier work on the integration of educationally blind children, published in the *New Beacon* by Michael Colborne-Brown and Michael Tobin *(1). These studies considered "registrably" blind and partially sighted children as opposed to those who were actually "registered." The studies suggested that there were some 5,500 visually impaired children, not including those with severe learning difficulties. Their projections up to the end of the century suggested that there would be approximately one visually impaired pupil to every 1100-1200 in the 5-14 age group.

RNIB undertook in 1986 a nationwide survey of educational provision for visually impaired children. LEAs were asked to provide details of the number of children who had a visual impairment which necessitated some form of special provision. There are wide differences between authorities in policies with regard to special education, in assessment methods and in procedures for collecting statistics. The responses to the RNIB questionnaire therefore constitute a very imperfect research instrument. It is nevertheless worthy of note that some trends do emerge.

Eighty per cent of local education authorities in the United Kingdom responded to the questionnaire. Of these, 74 per cent recorded an incidence of visual handicap for school age children of between 0.5 and 1.6 per thousand. Fifty three per cent of the authorities gave figures in the narrower range of between 0.5 and 1.1 per thousand. These figures are notably lower than the range of 1.5 to 4.2 per thousand reported by the eight LEAs included in the present study, which, it should be recalled, were selected because of their well-developed services for the visually impaired.

It must be stressed that these figures have little statistical validity. Nevertheless they may provide some guidance in assessing the likely need for services, and certainly if an authority produces a figure which diverges widely from the findings at national level, the procedures used may merit some further examination.

*(1)*New Beacon* vol LXVI No.781; vol.LXVI No.787; vol.LXVII, No.795.

However, it is also important to note that the level of need for services cannot be established merely by counting the number of visually impaired children in the LEA. The educational implications of visual impairment vary widely, not only because of the nature and degree of the impairment, but because of other medical, social and developmental factors. The significant measurement is that of the special educational need and the extent of the support needed to meet that need.

1.2 Onset and evolution of visual impairment

Unlike some other handicapping conditions, visual difficulties may appear at any age and may change progressively over a number of years. An awareness of this factor is important in planning services.

It is certainly true that some children have a visual impairment from birth which is likely to remain constant in the long term and educational plans can be made accordingly. However, others may have a serious condition such as cataracts which is significantly improved by surgical operation, and others may have a minor impairment which is expected to deteriorate and to lead to a need for education by non-sighted means at a stage which may be unpredictable. Some children and young people lose their sight suddenly as a result of accident, the side effects of treatment for cancer, or other medical conditions. In the case of such a trauma, the sight sometimes returns partially after a period of time.

Quite apart from these factors, the needs resulting from the impairment will be influenced by such matters as the level of medical surveillance and treatment, social conditions, linguistic environment and educational background.

As a result of all this, the education service may expect to have to cater for children with a static visual condition, children who have to be prepared for future changing needs, and others who will need swift rehabilitation and personal and social support in the face of traumatic circumstances, as well as wide ranging patterns of special educational provision.

1.3 Additional handicaps

It is well known that visual impairment is often associated with other handicapping conditions. In any district it will be found that, of the total number of blind children, a significant number, possibly as many as half, will have profound and multiple learning difficulties. Of those who are partially sighted, many may also have minor hearing problems, physical disabilities associated with cerebral palsy, epilepsy, severe learning difficulties or other handicapping conditions. The reason for this tendency is that many of the specific causes of visual impairment have now been eliminated by medical advances. There are, however, still some children who have a specific visual handicap of hereditary, accidental or medical origin, without having any other disability.

Where a child has additional difficulties, the form of educational provision has to be determined on an individual basis, in the light of the balance of needs. If the visual handicap is not considered to be the dominant one, the child may be placed in some appropriate special school or unit which has the staffing and resources to cater for other needs. An appropriate input of support is then likely to be necessary to take account of educational needs arising from the visual impairment. It was found in the LEA studies that visual impairment services often have difficulty in allocating sufficient resources to support teachers in such special schools.

In assessing the level of service required for visually handicapped children, it is only too easy to fail to take account of those who are satisfactorily placed in some form of special education, but whose visual needs require attention alongside more dominant handicaps.

1.4 Level of service required
It will be apparent from the sections above that it is extraordinarily difficult to make any useful prediction of the number and range of visually handicapped children who may require special educational provision. However, in attempting to assess a local situation, the following points should be borne in mind.

- Children with a severe sight loss and no other handicap are likely to be known to the education service and easily identified.

- Special schools catering for other handicaps should know if pupils are visually impaired, but may not be aware of the full extent of the educational implications of the impairment.

- Similarly, teachers in mainstream schools may know that some children are partially sighted, but may not fully understand the educational implications and, in particular, may be attributing low achievement to general learning difficulties, whereas the specific handicap may be responsible.

- Despite the existence of supposedly fool-proof screening procedures, there are always some children whose problem escapes detection or who develop a new or more severe condition which is not immediately identified. All teachers need to be on the look-out for signs of poor visual functioning, and to have someone with specialist knowledge to consult in case of doubt. Furthermore, the staff in an LEA visual impairment service should seek to co-operate fully with the professionals in the health services in order to help ensure that full benefit is derived from the functions which are by law the health authority's responsibility.

- Although the needs of educationally blind and partially sighted children are different, there is no need to envisage establishing separate services for the two groups. Most special schools, units, resource bases and other services now cater for a range of degrees of impairment including both partially sighted and blind children. A frequent pattern of development is that an authority initially establishes a local service for partially sighted children and, as those involved gain experience, they begin to cater also for blind children.

  This trend has the advantage that appropriate provision may more easily be made for children with deteriorating or fluctuating vision.

- The practice sometimes encountered of placing visually impaired children who have no other disability in schools for physically handicapped children cannot be justified. The children do not normally have common medical, physical, social or educational needs, and the families often resent such a placement.

- Even though the incidence of visual impairment is low, every LEA in the British Isles (with the possible exception of some off-shore islands) is large enough to justify the provision of its own service for visually handicapped children. However, for certain elements in the service, it may be appropriate for smaller LEAs to develop co-operative schemes with neighbouring authorities.

197

2. Structure of the service

The Warnock Report and the 1981 Education Act promote forcefully the concept of special educational need as opposed to categories of handicap. This has necessarily encouraged the development of generic services, and it may therefore seem anachronistic to cling to the idea of a discrete visual impairment service. Nevertheless very specific requirements arise in relation to a sensory handicap in terms of assessment, links with medical services, staffing and equipment. It is essential that we should not lose sight of this, whilst also encouraging appropriate interaction with other branches of special educational provision.

Some LEAs now have a "sensory impairment service" which brings together the staff dealing with hearing and visual impairment. Others have a separate visual impairment service, which may be satisfactory if it is a fairly large department, but where there are only one or two teachers in post there is a risk of isolation. In either case the staff need to have a clear management line of responsibility, whether it be to an adviser/inspector or an officer, and an articulated policy for contacts with other branches of special and mainstream education. The practice found in several LEAs of having a named link person in the psychological service, who will take a particular interest in visual impairment issues may be worth considering. These people could form a team who would be involved in discussions on developments in the service and in case conferences and reviews.

The head of the visual impairment service may also be a co-opted member of the special school headteachers' group. Visual impairment is after all found in association with a range of other areas of special need, and it is important that the service should see itself as a coherent part of a more complex pattern of provision.

It has often happened that a new visual impairment service has been introduced initially by the appointment of one teacher, and has then been left to grow under its own momentum. This can result in a well intentioned advisory teacher making unilateral decisions or progressing along a path which is out of step with practices elsewhere in the LEA. However small an initial, embryonic service may be, it is essential that a longer-term blue-print for the service should be drawn up from the start so that lines of communication are clear and so that an officer at an appropriate level of seniority is in a position to manage the service effectively as it evolves.

It is hoped that the information and suggestions contained in this book will provide a framework within which LEAs will be able to devise such a blue-print and structure its evolution in response to the specific local situation.

3. Pre-school provision

LEAs are of course required to provide some form of educational support for children with special needs as soon as it is required. One of the most disturbing findings of the individual child studies was that many parents did not feel that they had had the help they needed when their child's condition was first diagnosed. (See for instance, the studies of Robert, page 85; Helen, page 96; and Jennifer page 107). Various support services are responsible for providing this help, and those who work in the field of education may have a valuable role to play in co-operating with colleagues in other services to ensure that omissions do not occur. In so far as the actual educational role is concerned, provision to be considered falls into the two main categories of support in the home environment and various types of pre-school placement.

3.1 Support in the home environment

Work carried out in people's homes is obviously extremely time-consuming, both because of the travelling involved and because of the need to move at the family's pace in establishing effective working relationships. The help given to children with disabilities in the early stages of development is of paramount importance, and all the LEA services studied set considerable store by this, but it may not always be necessary or even desirable for the day-to-day fieldwork to be undertaken directly by highly qualified, specialist staff. At the home visiting stage in particular, clear management decisions need to be made firstly about what support is required, and secondly about which person or agency should provide it.

Work which may need to be undertaken includes:

- Establishing an initial contact with the family of a visually impaired baby.

- Liaison with medical, paramedical, nursing, and social services staff.

- Provision of information at various stages on educational services available.

- Advice to parents on developmental programmes to be undertaken with the child.

- Monitoring of child's progress.

- Parent counselling and advice on behaviour management.

These and any other relevant tasks may be undertaken by:

- A qualified peripatetic teacher working directly in the home.

- Another professional or voluntary worker, with occasional visits from the peripatetic teacher.

- Someone who has received training from a peripatetic teacher relevant to particular tasks (such as the use of "Portage" or "Oregon," which is a teaching package designed specifically for visually handicapped children).

- A generic service for pre-school children with special educational needs, of which many have now been established, often on an inter-disciplinary basis.

A decision as to how each element in the home support service is to be provided can only be determined locally in the light of the children's individual needs and the many other demands on the time of a peripatetic teacher. It is important, however, to remember that the quality of support provided in the home environment can often have a considerable impact on the child's subsequent development.

Apart from the individual support, it has been seen to be generally recognised that parents need the support of families with similar difficulties. It is not easy to arrange local parents' groups for a minority handicap, but it is well worth exploring possibilities, even if it means looking to a wider area than the individual LEA. Emma's parents, for instance, felt that they benefited considerably from contact with other parents (see page 94).

3.2 Pre-school placements

It is generally accepted that most children with a visual handicap benefit from early school placement. They learn to model their behaviour on that of their peers, receive regular professional help

200

in attaining developmental milestones and often become more independent than in the home where the family may be over-protective.

In the case of a child whose only or principal handicap is a visual one, placement in an ordinary day nursery, playgroup, nursery school or nursery class is likely to be appropriate. All the younger children studied had some form of pre-school education. Most authorities provide additional nursery nurse time for children with special needs, and such time will be required to carry out visual stimulation exercises, to help with basic daily skills and to ensure adequate supervision if the child is blind. The amount of time required will depend on individual circumstances, but it is not likely to amount to more than a few hours per week. The child will be under the supervision of a peripatetic teacher who will design and monitor the programme to be followed by staff, which will be over and above the normal learning activities offered to the class.

There are obvious advantages in selecting a placement near to the child's home, particularly if attendance will initially be part-time. If such local provision is not available, transport to a centre elsewhere may have to be provided. The child will not then be mingling with other children from his own community, but he will at least be receiving some educational support.

Some authorities group children with specific handicaps in one nursery. This does mean that staff arc able to develop appropriate skills for catering for their needs, and resources can be concentrated. It does, however, have the disadvantage that the company of other handicapped children may present a less stimulating environment than a group of normal children. If the nursery class is attached to an infants' school which is a resource base for visual impairment, this can provide continuity for the child and also facilitate a flexible approach to the time of transfer to the main school. A child's general development is often delayed because of a visual handicap and it may be desirable to delay his admission to the reception class, or to provide some nursery class experience alongside reception class work. There are, however, disadvantages in allowing children to progress through school with an age-group younger than their own, and this should only happen after a full consideration of the later implications.

Children who are multi-handicapped may be appropriately placed in a local day special school even from the age of two years. There should be a structure for ensuring that the staff of the school receive advice and training for catering for the specific visual needs.

Some children with complex needs may be placed in special units linked to other pre-school provision or in isolation. A young child with significant developmental delay may need a great deal of individual attention and may seem to have little in common with chronological peers. However, it is always desirable to explore possibilities for integration, since even quite severely delayed children often benefit from mingling with others who are functioning normally. A tight, protective unit for children with special needs may be very restrictive and a rather sad environment if the child is able to benefit from a wider social context. Indeed the level of concentrated teaching may be more than the child needs or can benefit from. However, very severely delayed children who do not have internalised language are unlikely to benefit from the company of normal children if they are unable to see what is happening and therefore have no situational guidance for the language being used by other children. Furthermore, if the children around them are also very delayed in development and not using language, it is very difficult for them to establish any relationship with the visually impaired child, as was seen in the case of Robert (page 86). Their teachers need very specific training if they are to cater appropriately for their needs.

Pre-five provision may well prove to be crucial for the child's later development. The issues which have to be resolved concern not merely the volume of resources required, but the most effective form of provision from both a financial and an educational viewpoint.

4. Types of school placement

There is rarely a definitive answer to the question: "What is the most satisfactory school placement for this visually impaired child?" Many different factors interact to determine whether a special school or some form of integration is appropriate, and ideally, if each LEA is responding appropriately to the 1981 Education Act, it ought to be able to offer a continuum of provision from full mainstream placement to residential schooling, so that the child's needs and the family's wishes may be catered for at each stage of education. How far such a continuum can be offered must be a matter for local determination, and it would not be productive to attempt to offer an ideal service model. Nevertheless the 1981 Education Act does place a duty on all schools to cater for the special educational needs of their pupils, and a duty on LEAs to cater for pupils with special needs in mainstream schools wherever possible and to provide any necessary extra resources. The continuum of provision should be developed within these boundaries, and this has been seen to be happening in the LEAs studied where, even if there is a clear policy favouring integration, be it resource based or individual, there is also the in-built flexibility of allowing other types of placement if the need arises. It is suggested that officers should familiarise themselves with practice in other authorities, and seek to keep abreast of new responses to a range of needs which arise.

What is offered below is a suggestion of some issues which should be examined in relation to each of the main types of placement, and it is framed in the form of questions which LEAs should put to themselves. The five sections are not, of course, mutually exclusive, and issues raised in one section may well have some relevance to others.

a) Mainstream with little or no special support

- **How many pupils with a significant degree of visual impairment are attending their local school without any special support?** When a new VI service is created, the LEA invariably finds that there is a greater demand for it than had been expected. It will be found that the need is genuine and that many children have not been receiving support from which they could benefit.

- **How are statistics on visual handicap collected and how is the information made available to schools?** The 1981 Education Act rightly puts the emphasis on educational needs rather than handicap. Nevertheless it is essential, for purposes of planning as well as provision, that LEAs should know which pupils have a visual impairment.

- **Do designated teachers for special needs know where to obtain information and advice concerning visual impairment?** The frequency of visits from a support teacher and the level of awareness training provided for all teachers will vary according to local circumstances, but all teachers should have a point of contact to obtain the help they may need. It was the lack of such information a few years ago which prevented William from having the help he needed (page 148–9).

- **How does a school obtain finance for minor items of expenditure associated with a visual handicap?** (This may include heavy-lined stationery, large print books, a lamp or blinds at a window, improved blackboard lighting.) If funds are only provided in response to a Statement, children for whom the full assessment procedures are not deemed necessary may well lose out, particularly under the Local Management of Schools scheme.

- **Are special needs/remedial teachers aware of the implications of visual handicap for the development of basic reading and writing skills and gross and fine motor skills?** All too often children are assumed to be slow learners when a specific difficulty is in fact responsible for their problems.

- **Does a visually handicapped pupil have access to the full curriculum?** Although there are provisions for the National Curriculum to be disapplied in the case of children with special educational needs, this is rarely likely to be necessary for visually impaired children, whose main need is generally for access to the curriculum. Such pupils should not be excluded from physical education, practical subjects or external visits because of apparent dangers. If there are specific problems, extra support should be provided, or alternative activities arranged which fulfil similar educational objectives. (See section 7 below.)

- **Is the child receiving regular medical monitoring?** Visual problems can vary markedly over a period of time and, whether or not there is a Statement, at least annual medical examination is essential.

b) Individual integration with support

Individual integration in a neighbourhood school where there are no other children with similar needs may be **an appropriate choice of provision in certain circumstances.**

- Parents may be very determined that the child should remain in the neighbourhood school, particularly at primary level. There is growing parental pressure for the handicapped child's own school to have extra resources, and this may well become a significant part of an LEA's service in the future.

- A travelling time to school of more than an hour in each direction is likely to be undesirable, and in rural areas in particular it may not be possible to make grouped provision within a reasonable distance of home. This is certainly true in the case of Tracey (page 119–120).

- In some areas there is a strong community identity, and a child may develop feelings of alienation if educated outside that community. This can apply in villages, amongst ethnic minorities, in families with strong religious links, and even in some urban localities.

- If a child is well-settled and happy in a school at the time of onset of blindness, it may be socially and emotionally desirable for him to remain there.

- There may be other circumstances, such as terminal medical conditions, when the personal well-being of the child or family may need to take precedence over strictly educational considerations.

However, if such an individual placement is appropriate, **LEAs should be aware of the following disadvantages.**

- The provision of the necessary specialist support and resources inevitably involves higher per capita costs than if such pupils are grouped together.

- Even if extra expenditure is accepted, it is unlikely that the child will receive the same level of access to specialist teaching, because of problems involved in deploying limited manpower.

- The mainstream staff of the school are unlikely to have had any previous experience of visual handicap.

- The child may grow up with a feeling of isolation because he may never meet other children who are faced with similar difficulties. In some respects visually impaired children can learn from each other, and they should have the opportunity to do so. Special arrangements can, of course, be made for children who are individually integrated to have contact with visually impaired peers, as has been done for instance for Jennifer (page 111).

In determining the provision to be made in a neighbourhood school, the following questions may need to be addressed.

- **What is the role of the peripatetic teacher?** Whatever extra staffing is provided within the school, it is essential that the provision made should have the oversight of a qualified teacher of visually impaired children. Preparation of the scheme, the training of staff, the selection of equipment and monitoring of the pupil's progress are tasks which are likely to fall to the peripatetic teacher.

- **How much extra teacher time will the school require?** If the pupil is to learn braille, daily tuition may be required. Specialist teaching may also be required for daily living or independence skills. The pupil may need more attention from a teacher (not necessarily with a visual impairment qualification), but a real attempt should be made to determine how much help is actually required. It is not in the interests of the children or economy to overwhelm them with teacher attention.

- **Exactly what type of help is required from an ancillary or welfare assistant?** Such support may be very valuable where required for self-care activities, supervision and help in practical work and the preparation of teaching materials. A welfare assistant who is present during lessons should be working under the direction of the class teacher. An attempt should be made to allocate the number of hours' help which are actually required, and not more. A child cannot experience the advantages of integration if shadowed at all times by an adult. There are logistic difficulties in providing a helper at irregular times during the school day, but these problems can be tackled by combining the work with other classroom or clerical duties.

- **Is there a need to make other skills available to the pupils?** In particular, teaching in mobility and keyboard skills are likely to be required at some stage.

- **What preparation is required in the school?** Awareness training for all staff is obviously necessary, but also for other pupils and adults in the school community, including cleaners and dinner staff. Perhaps the most difficult part of the preparation is to ensure that everyone takes account of the pupils' special needs, but at the same time to enable them to be accepted as members of the community in their own right and as individuals amongst other individuals. It is where this has been achieved as in the case of John (page 129) that individual integration schemes have been seen to be particularly successful.

c) Resource base in mainstream

Children who need special help because of a visual impairment are sometimes grouped together in a school where resources can so be concentrated. The term "unit" which is often used for such an approach may lead to misunderstandings, as it can be interpreted as a separate entity from the main school, sharing the same premises but not really being an inherent part of the school. For this reason, the term "resource base" is being used here, though other phrases are used in some areas.

The **advantages** of using one school as a resource base are that it is more economic to concentrate human and material resources in one place, and therefore more educationally satisfactory because the level of resourcing is likely to be higher. The staff of the school as a whole develop experience and expertise in catering for the needs of visually impaired pupils, and will feel that it is more worth their while to devote time and energy to this aspect of their work if they know that they are likely to continue to encounter this type of need in their classes. The visually impaired pupils themselves have some contact with other children who are in a similar situation, and this can help to counteract the feeling of isolation which some children experience when fully integrated. Peter has certainly benefited fully from this type of placement (pages 144-145).

The **disadvantage** of concentrating provision in one school is that the pupils, though integrated, may be separated from their immediate local community. The significance of this depends on geographical and social factors and can only be assessed in the light of local circumstances. In some cases, of course, the travelling distance could be prohibitive. It has to be acknowledged that there is increasing parental resistance to resource base placement, particularly at primary level. The advantages and disadvantages of such placements are well illustrated in the case of Stephen (pages 104 and 106).

The choice of school

The choice of a school which should provide a resource base is obviously a crucial one. The following questions may help to determine whether a suggested school is the most appropriate.

- **Is the school accessible to all parts of the LEA?** It is of course not always possible to find a school in an ideal location, but initial planning should take account of the travelling times for pupils who may later be found in any part of the LEA, and the transport arrangements which will be required.

- **Is there suitable accommodation within the main body of the school?** The use of a mobile classroom or a room in a remote corner of the building does not promote a healthy relationship between the special service and the school. If a mobile classroom is available, it may be worth considering whether it could be used for some other purpose, so that the resource base could be more centrally placed.

- **Is the type of building structure appropriate?** Major building alterations are unlikely to be necessary. Visually impaired children will be living in the real physical world with all its hazards and they have to learn to cope with this. However, a building with poorly lit corridors, or frequent minor changes of level would present significant risks, particularly for young children. Suitable highlight painting or a differentiation of floor texture near the steps may be necesssary. An open-plan building is not a major problem, and may have the advantage that the presence of an additional adult who is helping a visually impaired child may be less obtrusive in the class. For blind children, however, some directional guidance may be required in the form of carpet strips or hand rails.

- **What minor modifications to the building or furnishings are required?** These may include improvements to lighting, the provision of additional power-points, attention to the surface quality and lighting of blackboards, highlight painting of stair-treads or edges of large furniture, venetian blinds at some windows. Pillars in open spaces or similar obstructions may need demarcating to prevent damaging collisions. In some situations, the use of a sound beacon to mark a dangerous opening may be considered. The work required is not likely to be expensive, but if qualified advice is sought and the changes are carried out in good time before a resource base opens, then much daily irritation and inconvenience will be avoided.

- **What arrangements are there for the secure storage of expensive equipment?** Integrated children will need to use equipment in their own classroom, and it should certainly not all be kept in one resource room. Some large items cannot easily be moved about and, depending on the level of risk of burglary and vandalism in the locality, consideration may need to be given to security outside school hours.

- **Does the nature of the school's intake make it appropriate for the role of resource base?** Parents are likely to be happier if their child is placed in a popular school in a pleasant environment rather than a school where there are many children with other forms of educational or social need. The quality of the linguistic environment is very important, since this contributes to the education of a blind child just as the visual environment contributes to the education of a sighted child. However, the parents of ethnic minority children may prefer them to attend a school where there are at least some other pupils of ethnic minority origin. It is important to select a school which has sufficient breadth of provision to cater for the educational needs of all children who may be placed there.

- **Is the present and likely future roll of the school sufficiently large to absorb easily the number of special needs pupils proposed?** A school is sometimes proposed as a resource base because falling rolls have made a classroom available, or because it already makes special provision for another type of special need, and the staff are happy to co-operate. It is not possible to specify an optimum number of statemented children who may be catered for in a school, but it may be useful to consider how many such children are likely to appear in any one class. It may be difficult for normal class activities to proceed unimpeded if there are more than two or three pupils with significant special needs, such as a sensory or physical impairment, in the group.

Nature of the provision

Once the school for a resource base has been selected, it is useful if a clear picture is established of the type of integrated provision which is to be developed.

- **How will the resource base be used?** There are various ways of developing the concept of a resource base, and the use of the term may evoke very different images in people's minds. The extremes are to regard it as just a store cupboard or as a home base where the visually impaired children will spend most of their time. Ample storage space will certainly be necessary. The teachers involved may need a working base, but it is to be hoped that they will also share working and social facilities with other members of staff. With regard to the pupils' use of the base, considered decisions need to be made as to when it is more appropriate for them to work in the base and whether there are occasions when other pupils should use it alongside them.

- **Do there need to be any limitations on social integration?** Ideally, the visually impaired pupils should be full members of classes and take part in registration, assemblies, playtimes, lunch-breaks and out-of-school activities alongside their peers. If it is suggested that this should not happen, the reasons need to be closely examined.

- **For what percentage of time will there be full functional integration?** For a variety of reasons, it may be necessary for visually impaired children to be taught in a separate group at certain times. However, Martin is a case of a boy who at present needs withdrawal teaching, both because of his deficient braille skills and because of his social adjustment problems (page 116). It should be borne in mind that, if a scheme begins with separate teaching and a proposal to integrate progressively, there is then an in-built tendency for the shift of emphasis to be very slow. Certainly if such a procedure is adopted, it is important to plan regular reviews in order to stimulate progress towards full integration.

- **Can a child be present in a classroom and yet not integrated?** It will often be appropriate for an additional teacher or ancillary to give support in a classroom where there is a visually impaired child. This adult may need to work individually with the child but it is sometimes possible for the extra person to work with a group or to co-operate in some other way with the class teacher. No child should need to be constantly shadowed by an adult, a procedure which inevitably impedes successful social integration. The secret is to give enough, but not too much help, and to be supportive without being intrusive.

- **In what special skills will the pupils require specific teaching, and how will this be provided?** The pupils may need to be taught braille, typing, mobility, the use of technological equipment, daily living skills. It is important that appropriate staff should be allocated for this. In particular, even a teacher with a qualification in visual impairment may not be able to teach mobility or typing. (See section 8 for a further discussion of staffing matters.)

- **What extra human resources will the school require in order to cater for the pupils' needs?** It is likely to be helpful to begin by analysing the needs, and then decide whether each need can be most appropriately met by clerical time; ancillary or welfare assistance; the class teacher with or without adjustment of other demands on time; a part-time or full-time support teacher with or without a specialist qualification; a visiting peripatetic teacher.

- **What hardware is required?** Some items will be necessary to the resource base as a whole; others may be required for individual children placed in the school. An initial capital sum will be required to establish a resource base, but provision should be made for some expenditure in later years in order to take account of individual needs and developments in available technology. (See section 9 and appendix C for further details.)

- **What allowance is to be made for expendable items and running expenses?** There will be a need for special writing materials, extra telephone calls, services carrying a charge (such as braille transcription or the making of raised diagrams), batteries for equipment, tapes and typewriter ribbons. Administrative time is also required, and additional secretarial hours may well be considered. A great deal of daily irritation and inadequate classroom provision can be avoided if such minor matters are budgetted for from the start, and if the implications under LMS are fully examined.

Attitudes

The success of a resource base in a mainstream school will be influenced by all these considerations, but above all it will be dependent on the attitudes of all involved. The following questions should be asked.

- **Does the scheme have the full understanding and support of the head teacher?** The children placed in the resource base will only benefit from integration if the head teacher regards them as full members of the school and is able to carry the staff along with this philosophy. It is important that all newly appointed members of staff accept the situation.

- **Is the Governing Body in sympathy with this development?** Governors are in a position to play a significant role in supporting special educational provision in a school. Their interest and understanding of the issues involved can be a valuable asset. Governing bodies of secondary schools are likely to find RNIB's video 'With Support' particularly useful. (See Appendix E for details).

- **What awareness training is required before the scheme begins?** Everybody concerned should be appropriately prepared by training, the provision of reading material and outside visits as appropriate. This should apply not only to teachers in the school, but to pupils, clerical and domestic staff, dinner ladies, governors, parents.

- **How will the scheme be monitored?** A settling-down time will be required, and the people concerned are likely to be more tolerant if they know that an opportunity for airing their concerns is to be provided. If a school is being asked to innovate or accept a challenge, senior LEA staff should try to continue to show an interest in how they respond, and to give moral support and encouragement.

d) Special school for learning difficulties

Many pupils in schools for moderate or severe learning difficulties have some visual impairment. It is only too easy for the significance of this impairment to be disguised by a more dominant handicapping condition.

- **Does the Statement on every pupil in such schools contain information on visual functioning?** In the case of severely handicapped children, reliable assessment may be difficult, but medical and educational personnel should be working in partnership to assess and monitor response to visual stimuli.

- **Do all teachers know where to obtain information and advice concerning visual impairment?** They may need up-to-date advice on available resources, and help in devising relevant teaching programmes, although they may be expected to be competent to implement such programmes with only occasional oversight from a specialist teacher.

- **What is the approach to behaviour problems associated with visual impairment?** It is sometimes found useful for at least one educational psychologist in an LEA to develop special experience in this field.

- **Is training in mobility and orientation provided for such pupils?** The provision of transport to special schools, and a protective atmosphere at home and at school may leave little scope for children to learn to circulate confidently in the community, unless specific training is provided. This will not apply to the most severely multi-handicapped children, but mobility training can be beneficial to a wider range of blind and partially sighted children than is sometimes realised.

e) Special school for visually impaired children

Since there are now few such schools in existence, placements will frequently be residential and outside the pupil's home authority.

- **Is a special school placement the most appropriate one?** For some children this undoubtedly will be the best solution, but it should not be automatically assumed that, if visually impaired children in a particular LEA have always been placed in special schools, this practice should necessarily continue for all of them. There have been changes in parental expectations, in the attitudes of mainstream teachers, in technological equipment and in levels of support staffing, all of which factors should be assessed in determining the most appropriate placement.

- **Is the LEA well informed about integration schemes in neighbouring authorities?** In some cases, even though an authority may not be able to provide the necessary resources to cater for a pupil's needs, it may be possible to place the child in a mainstream school in a neighbouring authority which has a more developed service. This is the established arrangement in Martin's LEA (page 113).

- **Does the LEA have recent information about the type of visually handicapped child for which the various available special schools cater?** Visual handicap is a swiftly changing field of special education, with some schools closing and others extending the range of pupil for whom they cater. Where a residential placement is required, there may be suitable schools which are as yet unknown to the LEA.

- **Does the school provide an appropriate curriculum for the pupil in question?** Generally the curriculum should be comparable with that found in the mainstream, and the only difference should be in the way it is taught. There should be a clearly articulated policy about any disapplication of the National Curriculum. At secondary level in particular the school should be providing a range of areas of study comparable to that found in a medium sized comprehensive school. The ability of the special school to achieve this may of course be influenced by the size of the school and the nature of its intake.

- **How is a reasonable level of contact between parents and the school ensured?** If parents do not have their own transport, visiting the school may be very difficult, and the LEA needs to have a policy on the provision of financial support for this purpose.

- **Should consideration be given to the week-end and holiday needs of children attending residential schools?** Families often have great difficulty in finding opportunities for social integration when these children are at home. There may also be a need for mobility training in the home and community environment, and advice to parents on how they can best help their child, since they may not be receiving regular advice from the school.

In the sections above, it will be clear that there is some overlap of issues which need to be considered. Similarly, the sections which follow all have relevance to requirements in the various types of placement, but the emphasis will vary according to the particular local situation.

214

5. Further education/tertiary provision

The extent to which special education support services include further education in their brief varies considerably from one LEA to another. There is an increasing trend for advisers, inspectors, support services and peripatetic teachers to extend their role in this way, particularly where the existence of tertiary systems has blurred the edges between "school" and "college."

It has already been mentioned that an RNIB survey of further education provision, conducted in 1987, has revealed that many colleges are receiving visually impaired students, particularly in the mature students range, a high proportion of whom will be following part-time rather than full- time courses. Despite the increase in numbers, only two LEAs were found to have an articulated policy for further education provison for the visually impaired.

Whether LEAs decide to develop such a policy must, of course, depend on the authority's overall tertiary policy, on the nature of further education provision in the LEA, and on the level of individual need. The following notes may, however, serve to guide officers who wish to examine this aspect of their service. This section is again presented as a series of questions which may need to be addressed.

- **Do colleges have appropriate information about existing visually impaired students?** It may now reasonably be expected that students with special educational needs who move direct from school to college will have Statements and review papers transferred with them. However, this may not be the case for older students, and a referral system may be required so that appropriate assessments and advice may be obtained.

- **Do recruitment policies encourage people with visual impairments to embark on studies?** Provision in schools has not always been as satisfactory as it should be, and there are undoubtedly many under-qualified visually impaired adults who are capable of better educational attainments than they achieved at school.

- **Is there a policy for integrating more severely impaired students than in the past?** Many colleges are now more alert to the issues of special needs and may show a great deal of goodwill in taking on new challenges. This is good in itself, but it must be supported by effective planning and resourcing for a specific disability such as visual impairment.

- **What alternatives to integrated provison are there?** A number of specialist colleges exist at national level, and details are given in appendix D. This may be more appropriate for some students if they are to achieve certain vocational skills, and others may need the social and independence training which are offered. In certain cases a young person who has been successfully integrated at school level may benefit from a period away from home at the further education stage. It was seen that Ashraf (pages 159-160) and Khalid (page 155) both had some difficulty in adjusting to a specialist residential college after the more open experience of integration but this can nevertheless be a very worthwhile phase of education for many young people. In this area, too, there is a need for a continuum of available provision on which LEAs can call according to need.

- **How should provision be made for students with additional disabilities?** In fact, many visually impaired mature students entering colleges also have hearing impairments, physical handicaps or learning difficulties. The approach will depend on the college's global special needs policy, but it is important that specific visual difficulties should be catered for.

- **Should the LEA designate one further education/ tertiary college to make provision for visually impaired students?** This will inevitably depend on local circumstances and in particular on whether colleges are generic or specialised. There are undoubtedly advantages to be gained from concentrating the human and material resources in one place and the problems of travelling distance and separation from the home community will be of less significance than in the school years.

- **Is a further education college able to offer a course in independence skills/daily living skills?** This is likely to be a significant area of need for visually impaired young people, and the absence of suitable local provision is sometimes the reason why such students need to attend residential colleges. A student may well be able to benefit from an academic or vocational college course, but still need support and training in various aspects of lifeskills if he is to become an independent member of the adult community.

Once a policy on further education has been agreed, the details of its implementation fall broadly into the same areas as provision in schools, including curriculum, resources, staffing and training. The following sections of this booklet should therefore be seen as being relevant to the full span of education, despite certain obvious differences in application.

6. Meeting communication needs

For some children with special educational needs it is necessary to provide an alternative curriculum or one that is significantly modified in terms of its aims/objectives, content, teaching methods and processes of evaluation. For visually impaired children, however, the issue is generally one of access to the normal or mainstream curriculum rather than one of substitution. Since most school learning in the mainstream environment is dependent on visual media, any impairment of vision constitutes a communication handicap and thus a barrier to education. In this context, therefore, communication is being defined in terms of the media and means of transmitting, storing and receiving information.

In making provision to meet communication needs consideration must be given to visual, auditory and tactile media. Most children will benefit from supplementing a primarily visual or tactile approach with some audio work based on cassette tape recorders while others may use all three media depending on the task at hand. A multi-media approach is certainly likely to be worthwhile in tackling the complex range of activities involved in a school curriculum.

In planning to meet individual communication needs it is necessary to consider the following issues:

- **Assessing individual needs**. Factors affecting individual needs include educational stage, learning environment, curriculum area, level of difficulty and the child's potential to master particular skills and aids. Measurement of potential must take account of medical and functional examination of the visual, auditory and tactile senses and their associated skills. Motor development, verbal and non-verbal ability and motivation will also influence a pupil's capacity to master skills. Trained support teachers and peripatetic staff may be able to assess individual communication needs and potential but it is difficult to keep abreast of developments in the communication aids field and it may be worth seeking advice on current possibilities.

- **Providing resources.** Children should be provided with the resources which enable them to function most efficiently and thus gain maximum benefit from the curriculum on offer. This may or may not involve investment in sophisticated technological devices, but a notable instance of the full exploitation of technology is seen in the case of Kathleen (page 138). Where children are placed in mainstream schools, it is desirable to find communication systems compatible with microcomputers already in use in the school, but this is not always possible. It is also important to reassess needs since needs will change over time and new possibilities will emerge.

- **Teaching communication skills.** It is easy to assume that communication needs have been met when the communication aids have been supplied, but this trap must be avoided. A child's ability to use effectively even the apparently simple tape recorder or closed circuit television reading aid should not be taken for granted. Educational progress is dependent on effective communication and all systems in use should therefore be taught effectively and monitored closely.

- **The role of technology.** We must avoid the danger of assuming that technology can provide the only or best solution, but it would be equally wrong to ignore its potential. The outstanding benefit of computer technology is that it facilitates a multi-media approach. From one input, be it qwerty, braille or other electronic keyboard, it is possible to access the stored material in visual media via VDU displays and hardcopy print, in tactile media via hard copy and soft braille and in auditory media via synthetic speech. Hence there is the potential for teachers to prepare materials for all pupils simultaneously and for visually impaired pupils to complete work in one medium for their own use and in another for their teacher.

The four areas outlined above hold resource implications not only for equipment but also for staffing, since communication systems must not simply be provided but also taught and maintained. Hence there will be a need for technical and educational support. An outline of the range of communication aids currently available and the various sources of information and support is given in Appendix C.

7. Curricular considerations

The starting point for considering the curricular needs of a visually impaired child is that the visual impairment should in itself in no way affect the range of curricular provision which should be made available. If the child has any other handicapping conditions, a modified or developmental curriculum may be appropriate, but in cases where the visual impairment is the only or principal difficulty, serious consideration should be given to making the full span of the national curriculum available. After acknowledging this basic principle, four issues need to be considered.

- Close attention must be paid to the **visual content of the curriculum.** Much teaching has an essential visual appeal, the more so since the general trend in education is away from abstract, academic thinking. A child who does not see the world about him as clearly as others may have incorrect or confused visual concepts which can seriously impede learning. A striking example of this is Helen's difficulty in understanding the word "shadow" (page 99).

Teachers may need the guidance of a specialist colleague in taking account of this difficulty, but it need not constitute a daunting problem, and can indeed bring a new dimension to the teacher's understanding of other children's difficulties. Some subjects are visually dependent and teachers will need to employ sensory channels in abnormal ways. Others, particularly in the humanities, are less visually dependent, needing mainly aids to recording language.

A clearer presentation of visual concepts and visual materials can be beneficial to all. Where there is considerable dependence on pictorial materials, diagrams and maps, arrangements must be made to transpose these into a suitable medium, using tactile diagrams, cassette recordings or written texts. The class teacher will need to plan in advance for this to be possible, but a classroom or technical assistant should be available to prepare the materials. It is inexcusable for a visually handicapped pupil to sit wasting time in a lesson because he does not have access to the learning materials.

- **How should practical difficulties arising in certain subject areas be tackled?** The child may need individual help or supervision in art, CDT, science and home economics lessons. Indeed, it ought not to be necessary for children to be excluded from CDT because of visual impairment, as has happened for Imram (page 133). It may not be possible for certain pupils to participate with sighted peers in team games, but with the broader approach now adopted to physical education, it should be possible to provide access to activities which fulfil the main objectives of a PE curriculum.

If the approach to teaching mathematics is practical, appropriate tactile materials and aids are available. Advance planning and thought will be required, but insuperable difficulties should not be encountered if the starting point is not how the child can do everything in the same way as his peers, but how the stated objectives of the curriculum in each subject area can be fulfilled in each child's case. How this may be done at secondary level is well illustrated in the case of Tracey (pages 121-122).

Much ingenuity is shown by teachers, and RNIB seeks to make more widely known initiatives which have proved successful. RNIB's Education and Leisure Division is able to provide a range of leaflets and to offer advice related to curriculum issues.

- **What difficulties may the children have in acquiring basic skills?** Depending on the nature of the visual impairment, children may be delayed in developing basic skills because of the reduced experience of the immediate environment, problems in gross or fine motor development or even lack of confidence. The skills of a teacher qualified in visual impairment may be needed to tackle these problems, but the appropriate support can often be given while the children continues to learn alongside their peers. This is illustrated in the case of Emma (page 91).

- **What extra skills does the child need to acquire because of the visual impairment?** Skills which enable the child to benefit from education may appear to be the first essential, but consideration must also be given to

220

social and vocational needs. At any stage in school life, according to the child's individual needs, specific teaching may be required in reading, handwriting, braille, word-processing and the use of technological aids, mobility, self-care skills, body awareness and inter-personal skills. It is likely to be necessary for a specialist teacher to devise and oversee programmes of work in these areas and to undertake some direct teaching, but with this support much of the actual teaching may be undertaken by the class teacher.

- **The time factor** is a consideration which may need particular attention. If extra skills need to be acquired, these have somehow to be fitted into a school day, and in certain cases will need to be specifically time-tabled. Furthermore, a visually handicapped child will need more time to accomplish many tasks. It is important to be realistic about the volume of demands which are made on such pupils, if they are not to experience failure merely because they are being asked to do too much. If this means that the child has to undertake a reduced range of subjects, a well-balanced individual curriculum should nevertheless be preserved.

  It may also sometimes be desirable for a child to work one year below the normal age-group. A child with a severe handicap may not be ready for reception class teaching at the age of five; another may achieve far greater success in GCSE if an additional year is spent on the syllabus; a child who becomes suddenly blind may need a year's rehabilitation before taking up normal studies again. This will not be the right solution in all cases, but age groups are not sacrosanct, and surely children who are contending with special difficulties deserve an extended education at any stage when they can benefit from it. This approach was used effectively for William (page 149) and Khalid (page 152). If a change of age group is considered, the balance of social and educational implications needs to be carefully weighed.

Curricular issues are by definition central to the educational process, and they cannot be examined in full detail here. The issues raised above are pointers to general areas of concern which should be taken on board in designing any integration programme. More detailed advice will be obtained from specialist teachers and from various publications listed in appendix E.

8. Staffing and training

The staff involved are undoubtedly the determining factor in the extent to which an integration scheme is successful. It is also the most expensive element in provision. A bland allocation on a child's Statement of x hours of additional staffing is not the answer. So many different approaches to teaching and non-teaching support are available that it is desirable to analyse the exact areas of support which are needed, to allocate the type of staffing appropriate to each, and to build into the scheme a facility for modifying the provision as the child's educational needs evolve. Such an approach is likely to lead to provision which is educationally relevant and also as economic as possible.

The following notes are designed to provide a framework for discussions on the need for various types of staffing support and on the provision which may be required for staff training.

- **The class teacher or subject teacher** has main responsibility for every pupil's education. Whatever extra support is given, this role should not be undermined. Awareness training is essential and advice specific to the pupil should be provided, but the class teacher does not need to undertake an award-bearing course in visual impairment. Extra demands will be made on the teacher, and it is worth considering how this can be acknowledged. In some cases a reduced class size can be arranged; some time may be allocated for consultation, outside visits or contacts with colleagues; there should be periodic opportunities for concerns to be aired in review meetings. It is well worth trying to remember that, whatever other staff are involved, they are all there ultimately to support the work of the class teacher, and not to replace it.

- **An advisory or peripatetic teacher** should be available within the authority to provide oversight of the pupil's progress, to devise special programmes of work where required, to advise on special equipment and its use, to provide support and guidance to the class teacher. An advisory teacher will often have a very heavy caseload, and a great deal of skill is required in allocating this valuable resource as effectively as possible. The need for managing the peripatetic service effectively has been stressed already. If the teacher tries to share time equally between all visually impaired children in the LEA, little of real value may be achieved. There may be a week or two when the teacher needs to be almost full-time in one school when a severely handicapped child is admitted as happened for Kathleen (page 138) or when there is a change of class, as in the case of Helen (page 97). On the other hand, if intense help is needed over a long period, another teacher is required, since the needs of less severely impaired children must be protected. It is also important that visits from an advisory teacher should be structured so that the school can benefit from the visit. If the class teacher is only in a position to listen to advice offered with half an ear whilst continuing to work with the rest of the class, the visit is unlikely to be very fruitful.

Advisory and peripatetic teachers should have a qualification in visual handicap, in addition to substantial previous experience in mainstream teaching. This is not, however, the end of their training needs. They may need advice in counselling skills, opportunities to update their knowledge of trends in mainstream education, contacts with colleagues in other areas, and release for further training in their specialist field. They have a major role in helping to train others, and they need to be properly equipped to undertake this.

- **Individual teaching in special skills** may be required by some pupils. This applies particularly to braille, mobility, typing and the use of technological aids. This may entail employing a part-time teacher with the appropriate skills, and it is an aspect of provision which is often neglected in initial planning.

- **A classroom/welfare assistant** is likely to be required to support a child with a significant level of difficulty. Appropriate areas of activity are help with self-care, preparation of materials, recording work for or on behalf of the pupil, helping in practical lessons and generally trying to ensure that the child has full access to lessons. This is a very difficult role into which willing people are sometimes cast without any training or detailed guidance. Ironically, the greatest danger is that, through feeling the need to justify their presence, they actually do too much for the pupil and hinder the growth to independence.

The number of hours of help required should be assessed according to need, full-time help rarely being desirable for one child. A broader, secondary role should be assigned, to include working with a group of children, preparing some materials for the class as a whole, or helping on out-of-school visits. The level of help needed should be reviewed periodically and adjusted if required, as has happened in the case of Tracey (page 120). Above all, the assistant's work with the visually impaired pupil should be clearly defined, help given in establishing an appropriate relationship with class or subject teachers, and training should be given.

The provision of training for classroom assistants is currently a difficult area. Funds are often not available, the assistants may not be able to travel far for training, and appropriate ready-made courses do not exist. It should be borne in mind that welfare/classroom assistants are often the key element in the success or failure of an integration scheme, and efforts should be made to give these people apropriate preparation for their work.

- **A support teacher within the school** may be required for certain pupils. The role of such a person is not the same as that of a welfare assistant, and if the two types of person are used interchangeably, then no real analysis of the child's needs has been made.

A teacher may be required to train a young child in gross and fine motor skills; to interpret the curriculum where there is a substantial visual element; to perceive situations in which the pupil is failing to learn effectively; perhaps to counsel the child; to help and support class and subject teachers in the preparation of course content. The same person may provide teaching in skills such as braille, mobility or typing if able to do so. A clear example of this role is shown in the case of Stephen (page 104).

In schools which have a resource base for visual handicap, it is desirable to employ support teachers with a specialist qualification. It is highly unlikely that such people can be employed for a single pupil in a school. Arrangements should therefore be made for local training, for release for attendance at outside courses, and for regular consultation with a specialist teacher within the LEA. In particular, it is very helpful if such a support teacher can obtain a substantial level of relevant in-service training, for instance by undertaking a 30 hour module within an advanced diploma course. This level of specialism is now being offered in some areas. There is a valuable role for support teachers, but if they are not prepared for the work and guided effectively, they may in fact only carry out a function which could equally well be undertaken by an unqualified classroom assistant.

- **Clerical and technical support** should not be forgotten. The production of large print and tactile materials, the management of technological aids, correspondence with supporting agencies and similar activities do not need to be undertaken by a teacher. This is a waste of expertise, and in fact may be less than efficient because the teacher may not have the time or relevant skills required. An allocation of clerical/technical time should be considered when the pupil's Statement is drawn up, thus avoiding the situation at Imram's school where teachers have to undertake all the reprographic work (page 132).

It will be apparent from the comments above that the staffing issue is not one of "How many?" and "What will it cost?" but rather "Who is required to do what?" and "What training is needed?"[1]

9. Equipment and materials

LEAs sometimes seek advice about the range of equipment and materials necessary to meet the needs of all visually impaired pupils who may come along. Unfortunately, it is not possible to provide such a list since appropriate provision can only be made when detailed consideration is given to the needs of particular children. This has become increasingly true as advances in technology present numerous alternative approaches to solving the same problem. Factors affecting the equipment and materials required include:

- **Organisation/location of resources.** As a general rule it is advisable to locate resources as close as possible to the working situation. Nevertheless, where a service has a base in one school it may be possible to achieve some economy in provision by using the base for the production and duplication of learning materials for other schools. In

---

[1] A particularly useful resource for training all involved with integration at secondary level is RNIB's video: *With Support*. Further details are given in appendix E.

225

practice, however, this can only work where such bases are staffed to meet this need and not where one school merely has the freedom to use resources based in another.

- **Media through which children work.** Each individual pupil may work in visual, auditory or tactile media or through some combination of the three. The chosen medium/media will affect expenditure in most of the areas detailed below.

- **Degree of visual impairment.** Even for those working entirely or primarily through visual media, the resource implications in meeting the needs of a severely partially sighted pupil are far greater than for a pupil with good residual vision.

- **Number of children involved.** Economies can be achieved where several pupils can make use of the same materials.

The points below help to outline areas where expenditure may be necessary:

- **Classroom furniture.** It is likely that a visually impaired pupil in a permanent classroom base will require greater working and storage area. It is possible to buy units which combine both, but as children grow such furniture can become redundant. Special furniture can create a physical barrier with attendant social implications. Special storage arrangements can also exclude the visually impaired child from normal classroom routines and thus reduce the scope for independence. Generally, therefore, it is advisable to allow additional space but to avoid tailor-made furniture and special organisational arrangements.

- **Resource area provision.** It is likely that a resource area will be needed where equipment and materials, not currently in use, can be stored and easily accessed. Such an area should be furnished to house visual, auditory and tactile materials. Tailor-made furniture will be appropriate in this area, and it is advisable to find an area which can be made secure when the school is closed.

- **Preparation and reproduction of learning materials:**

(a)   *Large print* - the simplest method is by means of photo-enlarging but this can often result in A3 size materials that are very difficult to manage. An alternative approach is to wordprocess the required text and either photo-enlarge from a small master or print text using large print software. RNIB Outreach offers a computerised large print service using high quality laser printers, but satisfactory results can be achieved using school microcomputers with Epson compatible dot matrix printers and appropriate software.

(b)   *Braille* - traditionally braille has been transcribed by skilled braillists using mechanical braillers. An alternative approach is to wordprocess the required text and transcribe it into braille using translation software. There is now a wide choice of embossers on which to print the hard copy. This system has a number of advantages: a braillist is not required for text entry, braille can be edited on screen to achieve the level of contraction appropriate to the particular needs of a child in the process of learning braille, and multiple copies can be produced without the need for separate duplication equipment. Mechanically produced braille masters would require a vacuum-forming duplicator for reproduction.

(c)   *Tactile diagrams* - there are two main methods of producing tactile diagrams. The first is to prepare a master by laying a variety of materials on an adhesive sheet to create different levels and textures of relief. The master is then reproduced on plastic paper using a vacuum-forming process. The alternative is to produce an ink print master for reproduction on a Minolta 3D copier or similar swell-paper processor. The thermoform system offers greater scope and durability but the preparation of masters requires skill and is very time consuming. Swell paper diagrams are less satisfactory in quality but more flexible in shape and, most importantly, they can be prepared quickly and by any staff member. There is probably a place for both systems, but a choice needs to be made as to which system should be located on site and which might be seen as a central resource either within the LEA or beyond.

(d)   *Audio tapes* - the auditory medium can provide valuable support for those working primarily in either visual or tactile media. It is therefore worth investing in cassette recorders offering a full range of facilities including 4-track record/playback, tone indexing, and variable speed pitch-compensated playback. Master tapes should not be used by pupils and some fast-copying facility should therefore be considered.

(e)   *Binding equipment* - it is essential that materials which have been painstakingly produced should be bound for ease of use and storage.

● **Communication aids:** Individual communication needs vary so widely that generalisation is difficult, but the following items may need to be considered:

(a)   Task lighting
(b)   Raised desk-top.
(c)   Large print or talking calculator.
(d)   Special drawing aids.
(e)   Multiple-facility tape recorder.
(f)   *Reading aids* - for the partially sighted pupil this may range from simple magnifiers to a closed circuit television system. It is possible, though much less likely, that a blind pupil may require sophisticated aids such as the Optacon or Delta aids.
(g)   *Writing aids* - it is highly likely, especially at secondary level, that both blind and partially sighted children will benefit from suitable word processing systems. These may be based on school microcomputer systems or much more sophisticated specialist devices such as the VersaBraille or Viewscan Text System.
(h)   *Homework provision* - when homework becomes an impor-tant part of the complete educational experience it is essential to ensure that pupils have access to appropriate equipment and materials at home, even if it involves duplication of expensive items.

● **Curriculum support equipment and materials** - each curriculum area is likely to give rise to specific needs for equipment and/or materials. Most subjects will involve the purchase of schemes of work in large print, braille or on tape, where they are available. In addition, areas such as Science, Maths, PE, Home Economics and CDT are likely to involve the acquisition of special aids. At the lower primary level it will be necessary to provide modified games and activities which can be played by groups of children including blind or partially sighted members.

- **Consumable materials** - these will include:

(a) Stationery for use by pupils.
(b) Stationery for duplication purposes.
(c) Computer stationery including paper, ribbons and discs.
(d) Cassette tapes.

In addition to the provision of necessary equipment and materials it will be important to give careful consideration to the management of resources and the maintenance of machinery. Adequate time must be allowed for staff to maintain and develop resource bases. LEA computer centres might usefully be encouraged to become involved where pupils are using hi-tech communication aids. Above all it will be necessary to adopt a flexible policy which allows for the provision of resources as needs become apparent.

10. Finances

The cost of any highly specialised provision is inevitably substantial. Estimates depend on a wide range of circumstances, and it would not be useful to attempt to offer reliable estimates of expenditure for various types of provision. RNIB's LEA Development Officer is happy to participate in discussions with LEA officers who are preparing to develop visual impairment services and to offer advice on likely expenditure in the particular local situation. The following is a checklist of the items on which expenditure may arise, and which may need to be costed in the preparation of committee papers. It may be reassuring to note that high initial costs incurred in setting up a new service scale down over a few years, and costs are less prohibitive when they are seen as being shared over several pupils.

Salaries	Advisory/peripatetic teachers
	Support teachers within school
	Part-time skill teaching
	Welfare/classroom assistance
	Clerical support for visual impairment service
	Technical support for visual impairment service

	Clerical support in schools
	Technical support in schools
Equipment & Materials	Office-type equipment
	Hardware for pupil use
	Computer software
	Braille paper
	Cassette players
	Cassettes and discs
	Small items of classroom equipment
	Books in large print or braille books
	for staffroom libraries
	Staff training materials
	Equipment for home use
Other Expenditure	Transport
	Building modifications
	Agency services (for example, brailling
	of texts)
	Servicing and insurance of equipment
	Pupil's out-of-school activities.

LEAs will obviously wish to assess the expenditure involved in integration in the light of the cost of alternative, special school provision. Several points should be borne in mind:

- **Both types of provision are expensive.** Local circumstances are likely to determine which scheme produces the higher cost, but the difference between the two may well not be great enough for cost to be regarded as the deciding factor in determining council policies.

- It should not be assumed that, if an integration policy is introduced, **all children currently in special schools** can be returned to the mainstream. Such a move was requested by Kathleen's parents but unless parents positively wish for the move, it is unlikely to be successful (page 136). It is therefore unwise to assume that all the money for integration can be clawed back from the current special placement budget, although some of it may be.

- In establishing a new service, **there may be high initial costs**, but the implications for per capita expenditure will scale down over a few years.

- Many visually handicapped children have additional handicaps, social/emotional problems, or other special needs. **It is likely that there will always be the occasional child for whom special school placement will need to be financed**.

A final point is that the integrated pupil's needs will evolve and may give rise to additional or reduced expenditure. It is often not possible to make a firm prediction of expenditure required. This may be unpalatable to finance committees, but some element of **flexibility**, or certainly regular review, does need to be built into plans.

11. Inter-disciplinary responsibilities

Certain inter-disciplinary responsibilities are now clearly defined in law and in official DES guidelines. In particular, medical officers are required to inform parents of under fives of voluntary organisations if they are of the opinion that these organisations can give advice or assistance in connection with any special educational needs (Section 10,2, 1981 Act). Medical officers are expected to co-ordinate information from all doctors who have a contribution to make to the assessment of a child's special educational needs (Circular 1/83, paragraph 29). LEAs are required to seek any advice they consider desirable for making a satisfactory assessment of a pupil's special educational need (Statutory Instrument 1983, Regulation 4(I)d) and set out in a Statement non-educational provision to be made by health authorities, social service departments or other bodies (Statutory Instrument 1983, Regulation 10 (c) (i)). Further to this the LEA may suggest the name of a voluntary body to parents if it is felt this body can help (Circular 1/83, paragraph 20).

A framework for inter-disciplinary links is usually well established in LEA Special Education sections. The following points may, however, be worthy of note.

- Contacts with **medical services** are through the local health authority, but the Community Medical Officers are not generally specialists in visual disorders. It is very helpful if local ophthalmologists can be drawn into discussions on educational provision. This is not always possible, but it is a matter worth exploring with health authority colleagues. In particular, the provision of low vision aids is a medical responsibility, but it clearly needs to be handled in the light of educational needs. The ophthalmologists do not have educational expertise, and it is therefore essential that representatives of the two professions should work in partnership.

- **Social services** departments normally have mobility officers who may be available to help in training children in mobility. However, they do not always have the resources to provide this service adequately, and may not have the specific training or experience required to meet the needs of children, since most of their work is with elderly people. Education departments may employ their own mobility officers, but it is a matter which may require interdisciplinary agreement.

- **Pre-school children** are of course often supported by a variety of agencies. Co-ordination is required to ensure that resources are not wasted by an overlap of services, but that all necessary support is given.

- It is helpful if **voluntary bodies** are known to parents and all professionals involved in provision. In addition to RNIB, mention may be made of SENSE, the Partially Sighted Society, various organisations of the blind, and MENCAP. Local societies for blind people offer services to families, as do various other national bodies.

- **As a pupil approaches school-leaving age,** it is important that the child and parents should be fully informed of services and opportunities available to visually handicapped adults. Such information is readily available in special schools and it is an area where integrated children can find themselves at a disadvantage.

12. Conclusion

It is hoped that this section may serve as a working tool for those who are concerned in developing visual handicap services. It does not provide definitive answers, but merely seeks to set a framework for discussions, based partly on the material presented in the earlier sections of the book. RNIB is happy to participate in such discussions if that is the wish of LEAs, or to seek to provide more specific guidance on any of the issues raised.

Appendix A

Selective glossary

The first part of this glossary deals with medical terms related to visual impairment, and the second part contains terms used in relation to educational provision.

1. *Medical terms*

Acuity:
Clarity or sharpness of vision.

Albinism:
Congenital absence or deficiency of pigment in the skin, hair and iris of the eye, frequently accompanied by lowered visual acuity, nystagmus, photophobia and refractive errors.

Aniridia:
Absence of the iris of the eye, either congenital or acquired.

Astigmatism:
Refractive error that prevents light rays from a single point coming to a single focus on the retina of the eye, due to unequal refraction or bending of light by the eye's refractive media.

Binocular vision:
Ability to use both eyes simultaneously to focus on the same object, fusing the two images into one perception.

Cataract:
Condition in which the crystalline lens of the eye loses transparency, either partially or totally, resulting in the loss of visual acuity.

Central visual acuity:	Ability of the macula of the eye to separate details of images brought to focus upon it.
Coloboma:	Congenital cleft (fissure, crack) due to the failure of the eye to complete growth in the part affected. It usually exists as a blind spot or scotoma corresponding to the location of the defective part.
Colour deficiency:	Inability, partial or complete, to discriminate among different hues.
Contact lens:	Lens made to fit directly on eyeball, used for correction of vision in patients with cone-shaped cornea (Keratoconus), to provide an improved retina image and for cosmetic reasons. A corneal lens may be used after cataract extraction to replace the lens that has been removed. The contact lens may provide less distortion and image size difference than conventional eyeglasses.
Cornea:	Clear, transparent portion of the outer coat of the eyeball, forming the front of the aqueous chamber and serving as the eye's major refracting medium.
Cortical visual impairment:	Usually profound visual loss, following brain damage after an acute cardiac or respiratory arrest.

Count fingers (CF):	Method of recording vision among people who cannot see well enough to read the Snellen chart. The examiner records the number of inches at which the person being examined can count his fingers.
Dark adaptation:	Ability of the pupil and retina of the eye to adjust to dim light.
Depth perception:	Ability of the eye to perceive the solidity of objects and their relative position in space.
Diffused light:	Light spread out to cover a large area of space, to prevent glare.
Dislocation of the lens:	The lens is not in its normal position. The condition is caused by a defect in the suspensory ligament and results in difficulties with accommodation which in turn affects the ability of the lens to focus properly.
Enucleation:	Complete surgical removal of the eyeball.
Field of vision:	The space within which an object can be seen while the eye remains fixed upon one (central) point, including the limits of peripheral or indirect vision.
Fixation ability:	Ability of the eyes to direct gaze on an object and hold it steadily in view.

Glaucoma:	Disease of the eye marked by an increase in intraocular pressure causing organic changes in the optic nerve and defects in the visual field.
Hand movements (HM):	Method of recording vision among people who cannot see well enough to read the Snellen chart or to count fingers. The examiner moves his hand at a relatively close distance from the eyes and records this distance if movement is discernible.
Light perception (LP):	Ability to distinguish light from dark.
Low vision:	Partial sight or subnormal vision which nevertheless allows vision to be used as a primary channel for learning or receiving information.
Low vision assessment:	Comprehensive assessment of a visually impaired person's visual impairment, visual potential and capabilities.
Low vision clinic:	Facility that gives eye examinations, provides low vision assessments, prescribes low vision aids and offers instructions on how to use the aids.
Macula:	Small area of the retina that surrounds the fovea and which, with the fovea, comprises the area of most distinct vision.

236

Macular degeneration:	Disease affecting cone cells in the macula, usually resulting in gradual loss of central vision, but never total blindness. It is often associated with the aging process.
Monocular:	Pertaining to one eye.
Myopia:	Nearsightedness, a refractive error in which the point of focus for rays of light from distant objects falls in front of the retina.
Near vision:	Ability to see objects distinctly at the required reading distance.
Night blindness:	Condition in which rod function is diminished to cause deficient acuity at night and in dim light.
Nystagmus:	Involuntary, rapid movement of the eyeball; it may be lateral, vertical, rotary or mixed.
Ophthalmologist:	Doctor of medicine or MD who specializes in diagnosis and treatment of defects and diseases of the eye, performing surgery when necessary or prescribing other types of treatment, including spectacles or other optical devices.
Optic atrophy:	Degeneration of the nerve tissue that carries messages from the retina to the brain.

Optician:	One who grinds lenses, fits them into frames, dispenses and adjusts glasses or other optical devices on the written prescription of an optometrist or physician.
Optometrist:	A person qualified to carry out sight testing, including checking the motor co-ordination of the eyes and, where indicated, to prescribe spectacles or contact lenses to correct refractive errors and those anomalies of binocular function which are amenable to optical correction.
Orthoptist:	Non-medical technical person who provides scientifically planned exercises for developing or restoring the normal teamwork of the eye system.
Peripheral vision:	Perception of objects, motion or colour by any part of the retina, excluding the macula.
Photophobia:	Abnormal sensitivity to or discomfort from light.
Prosthesis:	Visually speaking, an artificial eye.
Retinitis:	Inflammation of the retina.
Retinitis pigmentosa:	Hereditary degeneration and atrophy of the light-sensitive cells of the retina.
Retinoblastoma:	Most common malignant intraocular tumour of childhood, usually occuring under the age of five.

Retinopathy of prematurity (ROP):	Previously known as Retrolental Fibroplasia. A disease of the retina occuring most frequently in prematurely born infants of low birth weight who receive excessive oxygen.
Snellen chart:	A chart for testing distance central visual acuity. Letters or symbols are drawn to a measured scale in such a way that a normal eye sees the largest at 60 metres and the smallest at 4 metres. The measure of a person's visual acuity is given by the fraction indicating the smallest row he is able to read at a given distance.
Tunnel vision:	Gun-barrel vision, tubular vision - a contraction of the visual field to such an extent that only a small area of central visual acuity remains.
Visual acuity:	A measurement of the ability of the ocular system to distinguish detail.

2. *Educational terms*

Braille contractions:	In Grade II braille, standard abbreviations are used for certain common words and letter combinations. These have to be learnt and in the early stages a child will use Grade I which has no contractions and obviously takes longer to use.

Closed circuit television (CCTV)	Special device that electronically enlarges print material on a television screen. The user usually is able to choose black print on a white background, or white print on a black background, as well as to alter the degree of illumination and the amount of magnification.
Educationally blind:	A person who, though not necessarily without any sight, needs to be educated by non-sighted methods, using tactile and auditory means of communication.
Fine motor skills:	The effective, precise use and co-ordination of hands and fingers for practical and everyday activities and in educational pursuits such as writing and drawing.
Functional vision:	Presence of enough usable vision so that the person has the ability to use sight as a primary channel for learning or living. Relates to the total act of seeing and how the person uses sight to function.
Functionally blind:	Person whose primary channels for learning and receiving information are tactual and auditory.
Gross motor skills:	The effective use and co-ordination of limbs for general movement purposes and physical activity, including socially accepted behaviour patterns.

Large print or type:	Print that is larger than type commonly found in magazines, newspapers and books. Ordinary print is 6 to 10 points in height, about 1/16 to 1/8 of an inch. Large type is 14 to 18 points, 3/16 to 1/4 of an inch, or larger.
Long cane:	Blind people, including some children, use a long cane which is not just a symbol of blindness, but a practical aid to mobility. It is moved from side to side to give warning of obstructions in the blind person's path.
Low vision aids:	Optical devices of various types such as magnifiers, monoculars, lenses, hand-held telescopes or prism lenses, which are useful to people with visual impairments.
Mobility:	Term used to denote the ability to navigate from one's present fixed position to one's desired position in another part of the environment (also see Orientation).
Orientation:	Process in which a blind or visually impaired person uses remaining senses to establish his position and relationship to all other significant objects in the environment (also see Mobility).
Partially sighted:	Visual acuity that may range from 20/70 to 20/200 in the better eye with correction.

Reading stand: Device that supports regular or large print books and allows the reader to change the position.

Soft braille: An electronic device on which braille dots are raised in sequence on a metal pad as the reader progresses along the text.

Appendix B

Print sizes

Reading Test Types approved by the Faculty of Ophthalmologists, London, and reproduced with the kind permission of Keeler Ltd, Clewer Hill Road, Windsor, Berkshire SL4 4AA, England.

READING TEST TYPES

as approved by

THE FACULTY OF OPHTHALMOLOGISTS,

LONDON, ENGLAND

N. 5

He moved forward a few steps: the house was so dark behind him, the world so dim and uncertain in front of him, that for a moment his heart failed him. He might have to search the whole garden for the dog. Then he heard a sniff, felt something wet against his leg — he had almost stepped upon the animal. He bent down and stroked its wet coat. The dog stood quite still, then moved forward towards the house, sniffed at the steps, at last walked calmly through the open door as though the house belonged to him. Jeremy followed, closed the door behind them; then there they were in the little dark passage with the boy's heart beating like a drum, his teeth chattering, and a terrible temptation to sneeze hovering around him. Let him reach the nursery and establish the animal there and all might be well, but let them be discovered, cold and shivering, in the passage, and out the dog would be flung. He knew so exactly what would happen.

(From "Jeremy" by Hugh Walpole).

wire sons vain error unwise cream remove

N. 6

The camp stood where, until quite lately, has been pasture and ploughland; the farm house still stood in a fold of the hill and had served us for battalion offices; ivy still supported part of what had once been the walls of a fruit garden; half an acre of mutilated old trees behind the wash-houses survived of an orchard. The place had been marked for destruction before the army came to it. Had there been another year of peace, there would have been no farmhouse, no wall, no apple trees. Already half a mile of concrete road lay between bare clay banks, and on either side a chequer of open ditches showed where the municipal contractors had designed a system of drainage. Another year of peace would have made the place part of the neighbouring suburb. Now the huts where we had wintered waited their turn for destruction.

(From "Brideshead Revisited" by Evelyn Waugh)

nervous manner immune over unanimous wear

N. 8

And another image came to me, of an arctic hut and a trapper alone with his furs and oil lamp and log fire; the remains of supper on the table, a few books, skis in the corner; everything dry and neat and warm inside and outside the last blizzard of winter raging and the snow piling up against the door. Quite silently a great weight forming against the timber; the bolt straining in its socket; minute by minute in the darkness outside the white heap sealing the door, until quite soon when the wind dropped and the sun came out on the ice slopes and the thaw set in a block would move, slide and tumble high above, gather way, gather weight, till the whole hillside seemed to be falling, and the little lighted place would crash open and splinter and disappear, rolling with the avalanche into the ravine. *(From "Brideshead Revisited" by Evelyn Waugh)*

immense snow came near arrow use.

243

Presently we drove on and in another hour were hungry. We stopped at an inn, which was half farm also, and ate eggs and bacon, pickled walnuts and cheese, and drank our beer in a sunless parlour where an old clock ticked in the shadows and a cat slept by the empty grate.

We drove on and in the early afternoon came to our destination : wrought-iron gates and twin, classical lodges on a village green, an avenue, more gates, open park-land, a turn in the drive; and suddenly a new and secret landscape opened before us.

(From "Brideshead Revisited" by Evelyn Waugh)

scan access river oarsmen view

We were instructed by a man of about my age, who treated us with defensive hostility; he wore very dark blue shirts, a lemon-yellow tie and horn-rimmed glasses, and it was largely by reason of this warning that I modified my own style of dress until it approximated to what my cousin Jasper would have thought suitable for country house visiting.

(From "Brideshead Revisited" by Evelyn Waugh)

excess ransom case minor answer vain exercise

The office was furnished in sombre good taste that was relieved by a pair of bronze puppies on the chimney-piece. A low trolley of steel and white enamel alone distinguished the place from a hundred thousand modern American reception-rooms ; that and the clinical smell. A bowl of roses stood beside the telephone ; their scent contended with the carbolic, but did not prevail.

(From "The Loved One" by Evelyn Waugh)

muse waxes over iron sawn ream vows

The two weak points in our age are its want of principle and its want of profile. Chin a little higher dear. Style largely depends on the way the chin is worn. They are worn very high just at present.

nice women rave cocoa essence

It is always right that a man should be able to render a reason for the faith that is within him.

sincere omen sour voice over

I am glad to say that I have never seen a spade.

vows mice immune

A poet can survive everything but a misprint.

verse ransom

Appendix C

Educational technology

1. Input, storage and output

A wide range of input, storage and output facilities is now available and these can be combined in a variety of ways. This is a quickly evolving field and equipment soon becomes obsolete, but it is hoped that information on items currently available may be of some use, at least in the short term. The list is not exhaustive and not all devices listed are microelectronic.

It is only possible to give here a brief overview of the field. For further information, please contact the Educational Technology Officer, RNIB National Education Centre, 190 Kensal Road, North Kensington, London, W10 5BT. Tel: 081-968 8600.

Input systems

Where keyboards are concerned, there is now a range of input options to choose from, according to user skills. Optical character recognition is a method whereby printed text can be read by a computer for subsequent output as speech or translation into braille. Examples include:

> Qwerty keyboards under software control
> Electronic braille keyboards
> Alternative keyboards such as microwriter, concept, adventure
> Optical character recognition
> Touch screens

Storage systems

Developments in data storage methods are permitting increased storage capacity at low cost. Examples include:

> Cheap non-volatile memory
> Cassette and microcassette
> Databases
> Disk
> Information retrieval systems

Output systems

The current variety of visual, tactile and auditory computer output systems makes it possible for a user to work in the preferred medium.

247

LED and LCD displays
Large character screen displays
Hardcopy braille
Soft/paperless braille
Tactile graphics
Synthetic speech

2. Systems and devices

Some of the items below appear more than once. The designs or modifications which enable visually impaired people to use these systems can be achieved through hardware, firmware or software. The trend in recent years specially designed towards software has greatly reduced costs and has at the same time increased flexibility and compatibility with mainstream technology.

Portable word processing systems:

The following systems comprise different combinations of input, storage and output media but all can be moved easily from place to place and in most instances can be used without connection to mains electricity. Examples include:

Microwriter
Dolphin Window
Dolphin Mimic
Viewscan Text System
VersaBraille
Braillewriter
Eureka
Keynote
Braille'n'Speak

Desk-top word processing systems

It is often appropriate to use a portable word processing device in conjunction with a desk-top system since the latter generally offers increased processing power and opportunities for transferring data between visual, tactile and auditory media.

Examples include:

Vincent Work Station
Vista
Vert
Frank
Audiodata Soft Window
HAL40

Reading aids

The following devices represent four different approaches to accessing printed material: enlargement, synthetic speech, a tactile image of the printed character and the braille code equivalent of printed text.

CCTV systems (enlargement)
Kurzweil Reading Machine (synthetic speech)
Optacon (tactile image of the printed character)
Viewscan
Delta

Braille/print translation systems

Each of the following devices/systems permits the simultaneous production of hardcopy print and braille:

Braille'n'print
M'Print
Vincent Work Station

Peripheral devices

A more flexible approach is now being adopted whereby a range of peripheral devices can be attached to the same basic computer system thus enabling it to be used for different applications.

Examples include:

Concept keyboard
Touch screen
Speech synthesiser
Printer (including colour)
Braille embosser
Soft braille display
Window display

Reprographic equipment

The following range of equipment can contribute to the production of learning materials in visual, auditory and tactile media according to individual needs:

Copier/enlarger
Swell paper copier
Braille embosser
Graph plotter
Tape copier
OCR system

Communications software

The following areas are examples of where software solutions have been developed to overcome difficulties in accessing information held on a computer system:

> Large character screen displays
> Hardcopy large print
> Braille/print translation
> Screen readers (speech)

Cassette recorders

A wide range of facilities which can greatly enhance the use of cassette recorders is now available:

record/playback	tape counter
cue/review	variable speed playback
variable speed recording	pitch compensation
four-track record/playback	tone indexing
voice indexing	remote control
tactile markings on controls	tape motion sensor
switchable microphone	rechargable nickel-cadmium batteries

3. Sources of information and support

Access Centres - there are seven access centres attached to colleges throughout the country in Coventry, Oldham, Letchworth, Grantham, Wakefield, Bridgend and London. Although DES funded they are not controlled by the Microelectronics Education Support Unit. While primarily concerned with the assessment of physically handicapped students, some also offer assistance to visually impaired students. For further information contact the national co-ordinator, Janis Firminger on 0203 461231.

Microelectronics Education Support Unit (contact the MESU Information Officer on 0203 416994). Activities include:

1. Special Education Microelectronic Resource Centres (SEMERCs). There are four regionally based centres which are especially geared to software development and the use of peripherals but with each tending to have its own particular emphasis:

    Bristol: 0272 733141
    Manchester: 061-225 9054 x289
    Newcastle: 091-266 5057
    Redbridge: 081-478 6363

2.   *Aids for Communication in Education* (ACE Centre). The Centre was established in May 1984 and is based at Ormerod School, Oxford (0865 63508).

3.   *Special Needs Software Centre* (Manchester, 061-225 9054 ext 284). The emphasis is on the production of 'framework' software usually disseminated through the Blue File system.

4.   *Briefing Sheets* (available from SEMERCs). A series of leaflets deal with different aspects and No. 16 considers "Visual Handicap."

5.   *National Information Base* for Support for Teachers of the Visually Handicapped (contact Richard Pountney, Project Director, 0203 362420). This [two-year] project focused on three main areas: collection and dissemination of information, good classroom practice and INSET.

RCEVH: Research Centre for the Education of the Visually Handicapped, University of Birmingham, School of Education, PO Box 363, Birmingham B15 2TT tel. 021-414 6733. There is a well established CAL project geared to the production and modification of software for the visually impaired. In addition to software, a regular newsletter is published along with a range of useful papers.

RNIB Education and Leisure Division

1.   RNIB Educational Supplies Catalogue, 3rd edition 1989. Contact RNIB Education and Leisure Division's Information Officer, see below). Particularly useful as a reference to suppliers of specialist equipment.

2.   Loan Service for blind and partially sighted children in mainstream schools. Contact, RNIB National Education Centre, Garrow House, 190 Kensal Road, North Kensington, London W10 5BT, Tel. 081-968 8600.

3.   Support scheme for educationally blind pupils in mainstream schools. Contact RNIB, LEA Development Officer, Tel. 071-388 1266.

4.   Visability contains regular articles on technology and communication.

5. A series of leaflets, many of which deal with technology are available from RNIB, Education and Leisure Division. For a complete list contact Information Officer, RNIB, 224 Great Portland Street, London W1N 6AA.

RNIB Employment Development and Technology Unit produce a series of "Fact Sheets" that may be of interest to those wishing to become more familiar with current technology: including information on braille embossers, BBC microcomputer/talking word processors, calculators, electronic reading aids, large character displays, large print typewriters, paperless braille devices, recorders, speech devices and note-taking. Contact EDTU at RNIB, 224 Great Portland Street, London W1N 6AA Tel: 071 388 1266.

RNIB Technical Research Section

RNIB has a number of different services and sources of information relating to technology. A series of 'International Guides' is being compiled, aimed at the research community and covers non-medical research, available equipment, research and development needs, agencies, grants etc. It is intended to make the information available in several media including floppy disk.

The following directories are currently available in print:

'Agencies for Visually Disabled People: An International Guide'
'Research for Visually Disabled People: An International Guide'
'Equipment for Visually Disabled People: An International Guide'
Contact RNIB TRS, RNIB 224 Great Portland Street, London W1N 6AA, Tel: 071 388 1266.

RNIB Outreach located at RNIB New College Worcester, Whittington Road, Worcester, WR5 2JX. Outreach activities include evaluation and demonstration of specialist equipment. A large print and braille transcription service is available to schools. For further details contact Outreach Service, Tel: 0905-357635.

Royal National College for the Blind: Advisory and Resource Centre. This centre has been nominated by the DES as a consultant on Microelectronic equipment for visually handicapped students in colleges of further education. Contact ARC Tel: 0204 265725.

Appendix D

Special schools and colleges in the UK for visually impaired pupils

Many blind and partially sighted children are educated with specialist support in mainstream schools. The schools and colleges listed below cater specifically for visually impaired pupils and students.

(a) *England*

Greater London

John Aird School, Cobbold Road, London W12 9LB.
Tel: 081-743 1472.
Acting Headteacher: Mrs T Van Ryssen.
Hammersmith and Fulham LEA; partially sighted; day; 2-18 years. Some pupils with additional learning difficulties.

RNIB Sunshine House School, Dene Road, Northwood, Middlesex HA6 2DD. Tel: 09274-22538.
Headteacher: Mrs M Walker.
RNIB; day/boarding; some pupils with additional learning difficulties; 2-8 years.

Clapham Park School, 127 Park Hill, Clapham, London, SW4 9PA.
Tel: 081-674 5639.
Headteacher: Mr J Dibble.
Lambeth LEA; Some pupils with additional learning difficulties; day; 3-16 years.

Joseph Clarke School, Vincent Road, Highams Park, London, E4. Tel: 081-527 8818.
Headteacher: Mr F J Smith.
Waltham Forest LEA; Some pupils with additional learning difficulties; day; 2-19 years.

Linden Lodge School, 61 Princes Way, Wimbledon, London, SW19 6JB. Tel: 081-788 0107.
Headteacher: Miss M J Grubb.
Wandsworth LEA; boarding/day; Some pupils with additional learning difficulties. 5-16+ years.

Whitefield School & Centre, MacDondald Road, Walthamstow, London, E17 4AZ. Tel: 081-531 3426.
Headteacher: Mr P R Turner.
Waltham Forest LEA: pupils with both vision and hearing loss: 2-19 years. Boarding/day.

South East

Dorton House School, Seal, Sevenoaks, Kent TN15 OED.
Tel: 0732-61477
Headteacher: Mr P J Talbot.
The Royal London Society for the Blind; boarding/day 4-16 years.
Some pupils with additional learning difficulties.

RNIB Sunshine House School, Dunnings Road, East Grinstead, West Sussex, RH19 4ND. Tel: 0342-323141
Headteacher: Mr M Shaw.
RNIB; boarding/day; some children with additional learning difficulties, 2-8 years.

South West

West of England School for Children with Little or No Sight, Topsham Road, Countess Wear, Exeter, Devon EX2 6HA.
Tel: 0392-413333.
Headteacher: Mr T K Slade.
Independent non-maintained; day/weekly boarding; 3-19 years. Some pupils with additional learning difficulties.

Midlands

George Auden School, Bell Hill, Northfield, Birmingham B31 1LD. Tel: 021-475 3826.
Headteacher: Mr B Jackson.
City of Birmingham LEA; day; 2-12 years. Some pupils with additional learning difficulties.

RNIB Condover Hall School, Condover, Shrewsbury, Shropshire SY5 7AH. Tel Bayston Hill 074372-2320.
Headteacher: Mr A Jarvis.
RNIB: day/boarding; school for pupils with additional learning difficulties; 5-19 years.

Pathways, (address as above)
Head of Deaf-Blind Education: Mr Graham Evans
Deaf Blind Unit; 4-18 years.

Exhall Grange School, Wheelwright Lane, Exhall, Coventry CV7 9HP. Tel: 0203-364200
Headmaster: Mr R G Bignell.
Warwickshire LEA; Some pupils with additional learning difficulties; boarding/day 3-19 years.

RNIB Rushton Hall School, Rushton, Kettering, Northampton NN14 1RR. Tel: 0536-710506
Headteacher: Mr D Hussey.
RNIB; day/boarding; 7-12 years.
School for impaired children with additional learning difficulties.

Priestley Smith School, Perry Common Road, Birmingham B23 7AT Tel: 021-373 5493
Headteacher: Mr C G Lewis.
City of Birmingham LEA; Some pupils with additional learning difficulties. day; 2-17 years.

RNIB New College Worcester, Whittington Road, Worcester WR5 2JU Tel: 0905 354627
Headteacher: The Revd. B R Manthorp.
RNIB: day/boarding; 11-18 years of good academic ability.

North East

Henshaw's College, Bogs Lane, Starbeck, Harrowgate, North Yorkshire HG1 4ED. Tel: 0423 886451.
Headteacher: Mrs S C Jones
Independent/non-maintained; boarding/day; 11-19 years. Some pupils with additional learning difficulties.
Also **Independence Centre, Deaf-Blind Unit** for adolescents, and **Intermediate Housing Scheme** providing temporary accommodation for pupils.

Tapton Mount School, 20 Manchester Road, Sheffield S10 5DG. Tel: 0742 667151.
Headteacher: Mr K Doney.
Sheffield LEA; boarding/day; Some pupils with additonal learning difficulties; 4-12 years. Pupils of secondary age may be considered for an Open Education Integrated Scheme within Tapton Secondary School.

Temple Bank School for the Visually Impaired, Daisy Hill Lane, Bradford, West Yorkshire, BD9 6BN. Tel: 0274 541714.
Headteacher: Mr R C Neal.
Bradford LEA; 2-19 years. Some pupils with additional learning difficulties.

North West

Shawgrove School, Cavendish Road, West Didsbury, Manchester M20 8JR. Tel: 061-445 9435
Head of Service: Mr H S Taylor.
City of Manchester LEA; day; 3-16 years.
Some pupils with additional learning difficulties.

St Vincent's School for the Blind and Partially Sighted, Yew Tree Lane, West Derby, Liverpool L12 9HN.
Tel: 051-228 9968.
Headteacher: Sister Josephine Hawes.
Independent; day/boarding 4-17 years.
Some pupils with additional learning difficulties.

RNIB Sunshine House School, 2 Oxford Road, Birkdale, Southport, Merseyside PR8 2JT. Tel: 0704-67174
Headteacher: Miss Helen M Townend.
RNIB; day/boarding 2 8+ years. Some pupils with additional learning difficulties.

Royal School for the Blind, Church Road North, Liverpool L15 6TQ. Tel: 051-733 1012.
Headteacher: Mr H S D Marks.
Registered charity administered by a committee of Management, day/boarding; 5-19 years. Some pupils with additional learning difficulties.

(b) *Northern Ireland*

Jordanstown Schools, 85 Jordanstown Road, Newtownabbey,
Co Antrim BT37 OQE. Tel 0232-863541.
Headteacher: Mr J G McClelland.
Voluntary maintained; boarding/day; also some pupils with hearing impairment; 3-17+ years.

(c) *Scotland*

Royal Blind School, Craigmillar Park, Edinburgh EH16 5NA.
Tel: 031-667 1100
Headteacher: Mrs Mary L S Meek.
Royal Blind Asylum; Boarding; opportunity unit for multi-handicapped students; public examinations and professional training; 4-19 years

Kaimes School, 140 Lasswade Road, Edinburgh, EH16 6RT.
Tel: 031-664 8241.
Headteacher: Miss Jennifer Ruddick.
Lothian LEA; day; partially sighted, also some pupils with additional learning difficulties; 5-17 years.

Kelvin School, 69 Nairn Street, Glasgow, G3 8SE.
Tel: 031-339 5835.
Headteacher: Mrs Patricia Potter.
Strathclyde LEA; day; nursery unit for blind and partially sighted, also some pupils with additional learning difficulties.
5-16+ years.

St Vincent's School for the Blind, Deaf and Partially Sighted,
30 Fullarton Avenue, Tollcross, Glasgow, G32 8NT.
Tel: 041-778 2254
Headteacher: Mrs Alicia A. Crilly.
Strathclyde LEA; boarding/day; 5-18 years.

(d) *Wales*

Ysgol Penybont for Visually Handicapped Children, Ewenny
Road, Bridgend, Mid-Glamorgan, S. Wales, CF31 3HT.
Tel: 0656-653974
Headteacher: Mr G B Morgan.
Mid Glamorgan LEA; boarding/day; 5-16 years. Some pupils with additional learning difficulties.

Further/Higher Education

More details are given about the colleges because each offers a somewhat different mix.

Dorton College of Further Education, Seal Drive, Seal, Sevenoaks, Kent TN15 OAH. Tel: 0732-61477.
Principal: Mr P J Talbot.
The Royal London Society for the Blind; Some pupils with additional learning difficulties. Boarding/day; 16+ years.

RNIB Hethersett College, Gatton Road, Wray Common, Reigate Surrey RH2 OHD. Tel: 07372 45555.
Principal: Dr Michael Rowe.
RNIB, 16+; day/residential college offering pre-vocational and vocational education, and training in living skills.

RNIB North London School of Physiotherapy for the Visually Handicapped., 10 Highgate Hill, London N19 5ND.
Tel: 071-272 1659.
Principal: Mr D P G Teager.
RNIB; 18+; the three-year course of post A level study leads to membership of the Chartered Society of Physiotherapy and eligibility for State Registration.

Queen Alexandra College, 49 Court Oak Road, Harborne, Birmingham B17 9TG. Tel: 021-427 4577
Principal: Mr T S Gould.
BRIB: day/residential; 16-55 years; also students with additional learning difficulties; vocational courses in engineering; cycle mechanics; telephone/reception; information processing; light assembly; links with other Further Education colleges for other courses; rehabilitation; counselling; national certification.

RNIB Vocational College, Radmoor Road, Loughborough, Leicester LE11 3BS. Tel: 0509-611077.
Principal: Mr K Connell.
RNIB; a residential college in partnership with Loughborough College; 19+ offers shorthand; typing; audio-typing; telephony; information processing; computer programming; use of special aids to Employment and access with support courses at the mainstream Loughborough College.

258

Royal National College and Academy of Music for the Blind,
College Road, Hereford HR1 1EB. Tel: 0432-265725.
Principal: Dr M Semple.
Independent residential; 16+ Foundation course; GCSE; A Levels; business studies; computer programming; piano tuning. The college also acts as an assessment centre for visually impaired students going into further education.

Appendix E

Publications on Education and Leisure

RNIB Education and Leisure Division produce and distribute a range of information leaflets, booklets and magazines. Topics include:

- pre-school and early education
- mobility
- availability of tape, braille and large print
- learning and teaching braille
- diagrams
- medical conditions
- leisure (including sports and the arts)
- school curriculum
- RNIB reference library
- student information pack
- RNIB school brochures
- equipment
- magazines

For a complete list of publications and further information please contact the Information Officer, Education and Leisure Division, RNIB, 224 Great Portland Street, London, W1N 6AA.

Tel: 071-388 1266.

Appendix F

RNIB Education and Leisure Division

RNIB's Education and Leisure Division helps visually handicapped children and adults to obtain access to the education and leisure facilities they need.

Services available include:

- information, advice and support for parents, teachers, local authorities and others involved in providing education and leisure services.

- our own schools and colleges for pupils who need education in a special school setting

- support and advice for staff and parents of visually impaired pupils in mainstream (ordinary) and other special schools

- addresses of parent support groups

- vacation schemes for visually impaired pupils attending mainstream schools

- advice about adaptation of examination papers

- integration support scheme for educationally blind children in mainstream schools

- advice about the use of technology with visually impaired children and loan of specialist equipment for use in mainstream schools

- a range of books and information pamphlets

- information on teaching materials

- in-service training courses for teachers, social workers, health professionals, leisure providers and others in the field

- training for care staff working with visually impaired children

- practical support for visually handicapped students in further and higher education, including advice, grants and loan of equipment

- advice on careers and help in job seeking

- support for organisations setting up new education or leisure projects

- information about braille and tape books and library services

- specially adapted equipment and games

Often the best way of providing services to visually handicapped people is through integration into local schools, colleges, clubs and cultural activities and RNIB is keen to support this, wherever it is appropriate.

RNIB also campaigns to ensure that central and local government, and private and commercial organisations, are aware of what is needed and how they can best help.

For further information on any of the above please contact:

Information Officer, Education & Leisure Division
Royal National Institute for the Blind
224 Great Portland Street
London
W1N 6AA
Tel: 071-388 1266

Printed in the United Kingdom for HMSO
Dd294068 8/91 C20 G3390 10170